BEYOND THE STRAIT:
PLA MISSIONS OTHER THAN TAIWAN

Roy Kamphausen
David Lai
Andrew Scobell

Editors

April 2009

*****

Published by Books Express Publishing
Books Express, 2011
ISBN 978-1-780395-25-8

Books Express publications are available from all good retail and online booksellers. For
publishing proposals and direct ordering please contact us at: info@books-express.com

CONTENTS

FOREWORD

As the John M. Shalikashvili (Shali) Chair in National Security Studies at The National Bureau of Asian Research (NBR), a role in which I have served since 2007, I participated in the 2008 Carlisle Chinese People's Liberation Army (PLA) conference entitled "PLA Missions beyond Taiwan." Throughout my career and most recently as the Shali Chair, I have spent a great deal of time in China meeting with senior defense officials and discussing the security environment in the region. While U.S. - Sino relations are arguably the best in at least a decade, continued examination of China's security policy is essential in order to anticipate and understand future Chinese military missions within China and on its borders, across the Taiwan Strait, and around the region.

On September 26, 2008, over 70 leading experts from academia, government, the military, and policy think tanks assembled at Carlisle Barracks, Pennsylvania, for that very purpose, to look beyond the PLA's primary focus on Taiwan and to the evolving new roles of the PLA. The conference could not have been timelier, given the PLA's active involvement in events during 2008, including earthquake relief, counterterrorism, humanitarian assistance, space activities, and blue water naval operations.

While preventing de jure independence likely remains the central aim of the PLA vis - à - vis Taiwan, Chinese foreign policy objectives worldwide are rapidly growing and diversifying. *Beyond the Strait: PLA Missions Other Than Taiwan* analyzes the PLA's involvement in disaster and humanitarian relief, United Nations peacekeeping operations (UNPKO), counterterrorism and border defense, security in outer space and cyberspace, and the level of activity in regional "joint" operational contingencies. On the whole, the volume provides a discerning analysis of these varied PLA developments and how they affect policy towards both Taiwan and the entire Asia - Pacific region.

Just prior to the PLA conference, the world watched China debut on the international stage as it hosted the 2008 Summer Olympic Games. While the significance of China has long been understood, the nation's rise to prominence on the world scene is becoming more acutely felt. I believe an understanding of the PLA's growing roles, both within China and internationally, is of critical importance to the United States.

I commend the Strategic Studies Institute of the U.S. Army War College, NBR, and the Bush School of Government and Public Service at Texas A&M University for the conference and publication of this book in such a timely manner. *Beyond the Strait: PLA Missions Other Than Taiwan* is an essential read for those seeking to understand the evolving roles of the PLA in carrying out China's foreign policy.

DENNIS C. BLAIR
Admiral, U.S. Navy (Ret.)

CHAPTER 1

INTRODUCTION

David Lai and Marc Miller

The volatile year just past will no doubt go down as a milestone for the People's Republic of China (PRC), and no less so for its People's Liberation Army (PLA). Two major developments in particular have buffeted the PLA's ongoing modernization and in the process created an especially fruitful environment for PLA studies. The first development has been the recent warming of relations between Taiwan and mainland China to a degree unimaginable only a few years ago. The second development has been the marked growth and diversification in active PLA missions in 2008, including those resulting from a series of natural disasters, the Beijing Olympics, unrest in China's western provinces, and the fallout from the global financial crisis. This remarkable series of events challenged the PLA to fulfill a greater variety of missions than ever before and makes this volume's theme all the more timely.

The title of this year's volume, *Beyond the Strait: PLA Missions Other Than Taiwan,* does not suggest that the Taiwan issue has been resolved as a potential flashpoint or is no longer at the center of the PLA's strategic planning, but rather that recent trends make the consideration of the PLA's growing number and variety of missions *other* than its traditional focus on Taiwan of particular relevance. In 2008 The National Bureau of Asian Research (NBR) and the Strategic Studies Institute (SSI) of the U.S. Army War College were pleased to welcome the Bush School of Government and Public Service at Texas A&M University as a co-sponsor of the PLA conference, which brought together more than 70 scholars and other close observers of the PLA. This volume represents the papers presented in Carlisle, PA, in September 2008, revised to incorporate discussion and feedback from conference participants.

Defining the Concept of "Mission."

Any discussion of "mission," particularly in the Chinese context, is fraught with potential misunderstanding. This stems from confusion as to whether the PLA makes the same definitional distinctions as the U.S. military does between such concepts as "mission," "role," and "strategy." For example, in the American context, the Department of Defense (DoD) defines "mission" as the task, *together with the purpose*, that clearly indicates the action to be taken and the reason therefore. A "mission statement" specifies the "who," "what," "where," "when," and "why" of an interrelated set of military tasks, but it rarely discusses the "how," which is seen as the prerogative of the commander assigned the mission. During active military operations, for military commanders, missions are tasks that are undertaken and completed as part of campaigns. At higher levels of command and during peacetime, military missions are wider-scale tasks that are repeated for an extended period or prepared for and partially but never fully completed.

As such, in the American military context, a "mission" is distinguished from a "role." Roles typically describe enduring functions or duties, usually aligned with individual Services (Army, Navy, Air Force). Roles are associated with responsibilities for maintaining capabilities. Any discussion of missions and roles will

2

lead into a discussion of strategy. Strategy in military doctrine is relating ends to means. Missions are the ends, and roles provide the means.

Whether the PLA makes the same distinctions among strategy, roles, and missions is unclear. In fact, evidence indicates to the contrary. For example, the six key points defining China's national defense policy as outlined in its 2006 *National Defense White Paper* are a commingling of strategy, roles, and missions.[1] Taking all of these into consideration leads to a number of challenging questions. For example, does China have a military "strategy" in the Western understanding of the term? Does it specify political-military objectives, the responsibility for achieving them, capacity needed to achieve them, and assign the duty to develop the capacity? How do the Chinese conceive of these concepts? Do they functionally align missions by services or with roles? China's military, while subject to the Constitution, the National Defense Law, and other laws, is also directly controlled by and responsible to the Chinese Communist Party (CCP). How does this dual command chain drive the development of the concept and the implementation of "mission"? What role does bureaucratic behavior play in mission—for example is the PLA Navy's aspirational mission of protecting China's oil sea lines of communication (SLOC) derived from a *strategy*, or is it a justification of additional resources?

Our purpose in this volume is not to seek definitive answers to these challenging questions, or to expound on the meaning of mission in a Chinese context. Rather, it is to ensure that we carefully distinguish roles from missions in the PLA and then concentrate our analysis in the following chapters on a selection of existing or potential *missions*, defined here as those military contingencies that seek to bring about a political-military end state.

Drivers of PLA Modernization.

When Deng Xiaoping launched China's economic reform and embarked China on its "Four Modernizations" mission 30 years ago, he put the modernization of China's national defense forces on the back burner. He pointedly told senior leaders of the Chinese PLA the following:

> The four modernizations include the modernization of defense. Without that modernization there would be only three [agriculture, industry, and science and technology]. But the four modernizations should be achieved in an order of priority. Only when we have a good economic foundation will it be possible for us to modernize the army's equipment. So we must wait patiently for a few years. I am certain that by the end of the century we can surpass the goal of quadrupling the GNP [gross national product]. At that time, when we are strong economically, we shall be able to spend more money on updating equipment. . . . If the economy develops, we can accomplish anything. What we have to do now is to put all our efforts into developing the economy. That is the most important thing, and everything else must be subordinated to it.[2]

But the PLA did not have to wait long to acquire the resources to improve its fighting power. Several triggers set China's defense modernization in motion earlier than Deng had expected; one of the most significant was the 1995-96 Taiwan Strait crisis.

From an historical perspective, the Taiwan issue is a product of the Chinese Civil War (1946-49). After the Chinese Communists defeated the Nationalists and founded the PRC on the mainland, the Nationalists retreated to Taiwan and restored the Republic of China (ROC) government on the island. For much of the Cold War, the PRC and the ROC governments remained bitter enemies, but both stood for eventual unification of China, though on very different terms. PRC leaders have made the unification of mainland China with Taiwan part of their efforts to redress China's "century of humiliation from the West" and one of their three historic missions—modernization of China, unification of the motherland, and maintaining world peace.[3] Over time, the CCP came to count on the success of these missions to legitimize its rule of China. However, by the early 1990s, the pro-independence movement in Taiwan emerged to challenge China's resolve in its unification mission. In 1996, Taiwan held its first-ever direct presidential election and Taiwanese independence became a rallying call in the election campaigns. Furious, Chinese leaders ordered the PLA to fire missiles toward Taiwan (landing in waters close to the northern and southern tips of the island). In response, the United States dispatched two aircraft carrier battle groups to demonstrate its commitment to maintain peace and stability in the Western Pacific (or more bluntly, to show its commitment to the defense of Taiwan).[4]

The crisis passed, yet hostility and tension across the Taiwan Strait continued: Taiwan's pro-independence movement challenged the PRC government's core interest and the PRC vowed to prevent Taiwanese independence at all costs.[5] Although the PRC states that it will pursue peaceful unification with Taiwan, it has not foresworn the use of force should peaceful means fail. Building up a credible military deterrence is China's ultimate measure to keep Taiwan in the fold. This determination is clearly translated into an increase in defense spending beginning in the early 1990s, but accelerating in the years following 1996 (see Figure 1).[6]

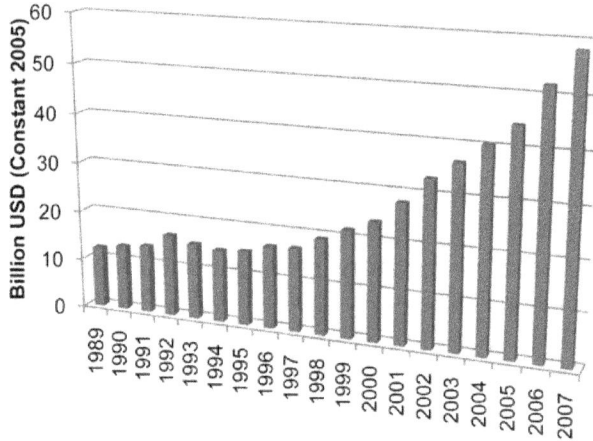

Data Source: SIPRI Military Expenditure Database, <http://milexdata.sipri.org/>

Figure 1. China Military Expenditure, 1989-2007.

The PLA putatively spent a significant portion of its increased budget to purchase advanced weapon systems from Russia, as documented by the Stockholm International Peace Research Institute (SIPRI). According to the records, from the mid-1990s to the present, China spent an average of $2.5 billion a year on acquiring advanced conventional weapons (mostly advanced Russian fighter aircraft and warships). This heavy spending puts China at the top of the SIPRI's list of recipients of major conventional weapons during these years.[7]

Acquiring advanced weapons from Russia was only a small portion of China's accelerated military buildup. The PLA also spent much of its increased resources internally to improve its overall fighting capability (see the Pentagon's annual reports to the Congress on the military power of the PRC since 2000 for detailed accounts of PLA capabilities). However, the accelerated increase in China's defense spending since 1996 as shown in Figure 1 suggests something else in addition to Taiwan is driving China's efforts. Two factors seem to be at work in this context. One, Chinese leaders know well that in their efforts to deter Taiwanese independence, they must develop forces to deter potential U.S. intervention as well—the U.S. show of force during the 1996 Taiwan Strait crisis is a constant reminder to the Chinese leaders that the PLA must develop a fighting power larger than that necessary to take on Taiwan alone.[8]

Second, China's accelerated military buildup against Taiwan may have jump-started China's overall defense modernization. Indeed, while the PLA was upgrading its deterrence vis-à-vis Taiwan, the Chinese economy was registering phenomenal growth. Much as Deng prescribed, when the economy advanced, China could afford to put more money into its defense modernization. Over the last 15 years, the PLA has not only improved its hardware, but also its "software" as well, including placement of increased emphasis on improving the PLA's human resources.[9] Moreover, the PLA has benefited from the information revolution. Discussion of the "revolution in military affairs" and impressive U.S. fighting power in the Gulf War of 1991, the Kosovo air campaign, and the initial wars against the Taliban and Saddam Hussein gave the PLA further impetus to accelerate its modernization efforts.[10]

As a result of these improvements, the PLA is emerging as a more capable and more professional military power. In retrospect, Chinese leaders could not have wished for better timing for the acceleration of their defense modernization, corresponding as it has with the demands on the PLA to serve China's expanding national interests at home and abroad.

The Evolution of PLA Missions.

The PLA's recent period of rapid modernization follows a series of evolutions in the PLA's fundamental mission over the course of its 80-plus year history. From 1927 to 1949, as the Red Army, its primary missions were political revolution and nation-making. Indeed, as Mao Zedong famously put it, political power grows out of the barrel of a gun, and the PLA was one of the three key "Magic Instruments" (三大法宝 *san da fa-bao*) Chinese leaders used to establish the PRC: the Communist Party, the Red Army, and the Chinese people.

Upon the founding of the PRC, the PLA's mission shifted to China's national defense and nation-building. In the early decades of the PRC, the PLA bore heavy responsibility for defending China's vast and disputed borders. It also had to confront the ROC's attempts to reclaim China by force. In pursuing this mission, the PLA fought directly against the United States in the Korean War and indirectly in the Vietnam War. It also participated in the Indo-China War of 1962, the Sino-Russo border skirmishes of 1969, the 1974 naval battles with Vietnam in the South China Sea, the Sino-Vietnamese War of 1979, and the 1988 naval clash with Vietnam, among others.

Since the early 1990s, China's rise has sparked a debate in the West about the "China threat" to the outside world, especially the United States. Before long, some observers in the United States and China predicted a coming "power transition" between the two great powers, worried that Taiwan could be the flashpoint that would bring them to an unwanted war.[11] Neither the United States nor China took this issue lightly. While working on diplomatic and economic fronts to find common interests, the United States and China nevertheless tried to develop strategies to hedge against each other. The United States strengthened relations with its Cold War allies, as well as its forces in the Asia-Pacific. China made great efforts to mend fences with its neighbors—settling border disputes in particular—so that the PLA could be freed from concerns of China's "backyards" and focus on the Taiwan issue and a potential confrontation with the United States, if necessary, efforts which have kept the PLA busy over the last 15 years.

While undertaking heavy duties in China's national defense, the PLA was also actively involved in Chinese nation-building and maintaining internal order and stability. During the "Cultural Revolution," Chairman Mao even sent the PLA to take over Chinese government at all levels for an extended period of time, perhaps the largest-scale PLA involvement in the PRC's internal affairs. Then came the Tiananmen Square student movement in 1989. The PLA was called in to maintain order, resulting in a bloody confrontation with protesters.[12]

After Tiananmen, Chinese leaders carefully removed the PLA from the frontline of maintaining China's internal order. In its place, China developed the People's Armed Police (PAP) force, with the PLA to be the instrument of last resort. In the following years, the Taiwan issue and China's confrontation with the United States over the 1996 Taiwan Strait crisis, the bombing of the Chinese embassy in Belgrade in 1999, and the 2001 collision of a PLA F-8 fighter with a U.S.

Navy EP-3 reconnaissance aircraft led the Chinese to develop new expectations for PLA missions.

Even more importantly, China's economic development was going global. As a result, China saw the need to protect its expanding interests and resource supply lines. In this changing strategic environment, Chinese leaders started to prepare a new mission for the PLA. In December 2004, Chinese President Hu Jintao carefully articulated the new mission for the PLA in the 21st century. Hu's call was later codified in China's 2006 *National Defense White Paper* (NDWP), reaffirmed in the Chinese Communist Party's constitution in November 2007, and reissued in the 2008 NDWP. Thus in addition to the traditional duties, i.e., upholding national security and unity, the PLA is now tasked with the following:

> Providing an important source of strength for consolidating the ruling position of the CCP, providing a solid security guarantee for sustaining the important period of strategic opportunity for national development, providing a strong strategic support for safeguarding national interests, and playing a major role in maintaining world peace and promoting common development.[13]

This new mission reflects several developments in Beijing's conception of its national interests and the principles upon which China expects to advance its interests. First, China defines its national interests in the order of survival, security, and development. While China still has work to do to lift a large portion of its 1.4 billion people out of poverty, its pursuit of development has gained greater significance.

Second, China's national interests have already expanded beyond its geographic borders — in the words of an important *PLA Daily* editorial, China's national interests are spreading everywhere in the world, into the open seas, outer space, and even into cyber space. In China's national security vocabulary, one can now find new terms such as "high frontier," "space power," and the "fifth-dimension battleground."[14]

Third, China claims that the 20th century was one characterized by war and confrontation whereas the 21st century will be one of competition and marginalization. All nations, especially great powers, must therefore seize strategic opportunities and make development their top national priority or face marginalization. China tasks its military to ensure that China's pursuit of such opportunities will not be compromised by internal or external interference.

Finally, China accepts that its expanding global interests will eventually come into conflict with those of other nations, and that its military must be prepared to come to the defense of these expanding national interests. For that matter, many of China's new global interests require a powerful military foundation. So long as China believes it must have a military force commensurate with its rising international status, the missions of the PLA will follow the development of China's national interests wherever they go.[15] This new mission set is truly revolutionary. However, as we will see, China may not have fully thought through the challenges and complexities the PLA will encounter in the process of carrying out these new missions.

Taiwan and the Future Direction of the PLA.

The year 2008 witnessed changes in national leadership in many Asian-Pacific nations. New faces appeared in Japan, mainland China, Taiwan, South Korea, Russia, Thailand, and the United States, among others. These changes brought new dynamics to the region, two of which are especially significant. The first is the changing of the guard in Japan and the warming of relations between Japan and China. Japanese Prime Ministers Shinzo Abe and Yasuo Fukuda initiated what the Chinese called an "ice-breaking" journey to Beijing designed to move beyond the cold and contentious relations between the two nations under Prime Minister Junichiro Koizumi (2001-06). China responded with an "ice-melting" visit to Tokyo by Premier Wen Jiabao and President Hu Jintao. These high-level efforts began to improve relations between two nations often characterized as "hot in economic relations but cold in political aspects,"[16] and to allow the leaders of these two Asian giants to address, on more cordial terms, bilateral issues stemming from the "burden of history" to territorial disputes in the East China Sea, among many others.

The other significant change came from Taiwan in March 2008, when the Taiwanese people voted the pro-Taiwan independence party, the Democratic Progressive Party (DPP), out of office. The previous ruling party, the Kuomintang (KMT), regained control of the ROC government. The ROC Legislative Yuan is also under KMT control, thanks to its landslide victory in December 2007. Riding this momentum, President Ma Ying-jeou set his agenda for a change in cross-Strait relations, characterized by three components: a peace agreement with the PRC, a revitalization of Taiwan's economy, and an expansion of Taiwan's international space.

As a start, Ma answered PRC President Hu Jintao's call on October 15, 2007 that the two sides negotiate an end to hostility and establish a peace agreement. Specifically, Ma agreed that the two sides return to the so-called "1992 consensus" in which the two sides agreed on a "one China" policy, but disagreed on its definition and political content, and start the process

12

of reconciliation.[17] Upon taking office on May 20, 2008, Ma immediately pushed for the opening of direct commercial flights between Taiwan and mainland China, easing restrictions on Taiwan-China economic exchanges, allowing Taiwan to take advantage of China's booming economy, and allowing mainland Chinese tourists to visit Taiwan, a multibillion (USD) business and a service market for more than 40,000 jobs.

In June and November 2008, the ROC Straits Exchange Foundation (SEF) and the PRC Association for Relations across the Taiwan Straits (ARATS) convened historic meetings in Beijing and Taipei, respectively. The SEF and ARATS are two "unofficial agencies" created in the early 1990s, designed to handle rapidly increasing cross-Strait people-to-people issues, and intended to function until the PRC and ROC governments can open direct dialogue and negotiations. However, their contact was suspended after the Taiwan Strait crisis and under the Chen Shui-bian administration for the last 8 years. Now that they are active again, the heads of these agencies signed pacts to implement Ma's initiatives.

With these positive turns in cross-Strait relations, tensions have been greatly reduced. In the coming years, Ma Ying-jeou promises to maintain the "Three No's" (no unification, no Taiwan independence, and no mainland China use of force), and continue to promote Taiwan's international space. Beijing appears to have acquiesced to these principles for the time being. For their part, PRC leaders are confident that the growth in direct links will bring about a virtual unification between the two sides that future ROC administrations will not be able to undo. China also feels more comfortable that its military deterrent developed over the last 15 years can effectively prevent Taiwan from challenging the status quo. With Taiwan dropping lower on the list of international flashpoints, the PLA may be able to refocus its attention on missions other than Taiwan.

In his chapter to this volume, "How China Manages Taiwan and Its Impact on PLA Missions," Andrew Scobell considers this critical relationship between the future trajectory of the Taiwan issue and the continuing evolution of the missions of the PLA, arguing that the two critical variables are whether or not Taiwan is "resolved" and whether a future resolution was achieved with or without conflict. He thus suggests a basic framework of analysis for the following chapters to consider. As we will see, the authors of papers presented at the 2008 PLA Conference took China's new missions to task, with each taking on an issue related to the prospects or difficulties the PLA will encounter in pursuing its expanding missions.

New Missions, New Battlefields.

Events over the past year, including severe winter snowstorms, the Sichuan earthquake, unrest in Tibet and Xinjiang, the Beijing Olympics, and continued conflict in Sudan, have seen the Chinese armed forces involved in a wide variety of missions. While not all of these missions are new, the depth of PLA involvement in so many different kinds of activities, including frontier security, peacekeeping, and humanitarian relief efforts, as well as traditional internal security roles, has brought into stark relief the gaps between PLA missions, current capabilities, and existing operational doctrines.

In the realm of peacekeeping operations (PKO), authors Bates Gill and Chin-hao Huang argue that

China has made a conscious effort to participate much more deeply in United Nations (UN) peacekeeping operations around the world, increasing its contribution of peacekeepers 20-fold since the 1990s. In their chapter, "China's Expanding Presence in UN Peacekeeping Operations and Implications for the United States," they show that the PRC is now the 12th largest contributor of peacekeeping personnel overall and the second largest contributor of civilian police. Although Chinese peacekeepers serve in UN PKO around the world, three-quarters of them are concentrated in Africa, and the majority of those in Liberia and Sudan. The four main drivers of China's increased PKO efforts include, first, the desire to gain international stature and reassure uneasy neighbors about its peaceful rise; second, to contribute to the stabilization of areas of conflict, especially those affecting Chinese national interests; third, to use its PKO efforts to balance what it sees as overly strong U.S. and Western influence in international security organizations; and finally, to gain benefits for its own modernization efforts through increased operational and cultural experience. In some cases, China also seeks specific diplomatic gains vis-à-vis international recognition of Taiwan, and economic benefits, especially access to energy resources and raw materials.

However, China remains constrained in its PKO efforts philosophically by its principle of nonintervention in other states' sovereign affairs, and geographically by its wariness of becoming involved in PKO operations close to home or outside a UN mandate. Moreover, PKO operations can become dangerous and messy, and the question remains how China would react to a major fatality incident involving Chinese peacekeepers. To date China has been less involved in humanitarian relief missions than in peacekeeping ones, in part because of a lack of necessary capabilities such as heavy lift; however China has taken note of the goodwill accumulating to the United States in the wake of its tsunami relief efforts in the region and is currently pursuing relevant capabilities such as a hospital ship.

In addition to new *functional* missions, the PLA is also putting increasing resources into new *fields* of battle such as outer space and cyberspace. As Dean Cheng shows in his chapter, "Prospects for China's Military Space Efforts," China is already an important space power with the ability to design and produce its own satellites and launch systems. Several recent firsts, such as its downing of a defunct satellite and first manned space walk, have emphasized this, as well as raised questions about China's strategic goals in space and willingness to follow existing international norms. As early as 2002, outer space was already being described in Chinese sources as becoming part of the global battlefield, and in 2004 Chinese President Hu Jintao underlined the importance of outer space to the future of the PLA. In Chinese thinking, the concept of outer space dominance is closely tied to information dominance, which it sees as key to operational success against more conventionally powerful foes. Outer space is potentially unique from more traditional battlefields in other ways as well, including that whoever moves first would seem to have the advantage, and that there are both "hard kill" (i.e., destroying hardware) and "soft kill" (i.e., electronic jamming) options available. In this as in other PLA missions beyond Taiwan, it is less clear whether China has a specific military space doctrine to go along with its rapidly developing capabilities, though there is some evidence that there may be greater willingness to use space deterrence capabilities compared to traditional deterrence because of the perceived lower risks.

Computer network operations (CNO) is another expanding mission for the PLA that has received a lot of attention in recent years with the rise in reports of Chinese hacking incidents. However, one thing that has become clear is that from the perspective of the Chinese government, "patriotic hacking" by Chinese civilians is not entirely good, as the "noise" from large scale cyber attacks can actually undermine military objectives such as signaling and strategic pausing. In recent years the Chinese government has sought to guide such "patriotic hackers" through opinion pieces in government news outlets. Nonetheless, as James Mulvenon reminds us in his chapter, "PLA Computer Network Operations: Scenarios, Doctrine, Organizations, and Capability," it remains unclear to what degree the PLA operates its own hacking capability and where within the PLA the cyber attack "actor" is located. Also opaque is whether CNO has been fully integrated into the PLA operationally and doctrinally.

Portable Capabilities, Stationary Doctrine.

As the PLA retools for these new missions and battlefields, one constraint is the continuing lag between the development of new capabilities and the attendant military doctrines to guide their use and integration. Thus, some suggest the PLA might be investing in cyber or space assets before they have necessarily thought through how to use or integrate these capabilities into the larger force or PLA strategy. As Brad Roberts reminds us in his chapter, "Strategic Deterrence beyond Taiwan," it is clear from the arrival of previous PLA capabilities, such as short-range ballistic missiles (SRBMs), that operational doctrine often substantially lags (and certainly does not inhibit) the development and deployment of a new military capability.

The lack of clear doctrinal guidance is exacerbated by the concern that many of the capabilities under development are potentially "portable," meaning that while created for use under one scenario or mission they might easily be used in service of another. For example, amphibious landing craft originally acquired for a Taiwan contingency might be used in any number of other maritime scenarios; similarly, space and cyberspace assets developed for civilian needs could be used to disrupt an enemy's command and control capabilities during the opening phases of a military conflict. The lack of clear strategic guidelines for when and how such "portable" PLA capabilities would be employed, especially in the type of complex "joint contingencies" outlined in Larry Wortzel's chapter, "PLA 'Joint' Operational Contingencies in South Asia, Central Asia, and Korea," leads to increased concern over PLA modernization efforts more generally. This is particularly true in China's development of technologies potentially useful in sea control and access denial, subjects Mark Cozad discusses at length in his chapter, "China's Regional Power Projection: Prospects for Future Missions in the South and East China Seas."

A final critical piece of the nexus between PLA capabilities and doctrine in considering missions other than Taiwan is the poorly understood relationship between China's civilian and military leadership, and how the PLA itself views new missions. Does the PLA primarily view missions such as UN peacekeeping operations as an opportunity to gain access, assets, and operational experience, or as a distraction from its core national security mission? This question is complicated by the fact that different services within the PLA might benefit from the inclusion of different missions and capabilities; likewise it remains unclear to what degree PLA elites are shaping PLA modernization priorities and strategic thinking vis-à-vis their civilian counterparts.

Frontier Dilemmas.

Many of the PLA's missions and fields of battle other than Taiwan involve China's frontiers, broadly defined. This is important because the areas of instability of greatest concern to China are often found along its own borders, from weak Central Asian states, to rogue regimes in Myanmar (Burma) and North Korea, to contentious areas in the East and South China Seas. In his chapter, "PLA Missions in Frontier Security and Counterterrorism," Robert Modarelli argues that the challenges of maintaining security and stability in its frontier regions pose several uniquely difficult issues for the Chinese government and the PLA. Not least of these is that China seeks ways to encourage stability and economic development on its doorstep while still adhering to its central doctrine of nonintervention in the affairs of other sovereign states. The PLA is particularly challenged by states that exercise less than full sovereignty over their own territory and people, as well as by nontraditional spaces in which the concept of sovereignty is less fully developed (air, space, cyber). Another frontier dilemma confronting the PLA is that the very same activities in which it engages in pursuit of stability and security, such as infrastructure development and a heavy security presence, are also those that can contribute to increasing problems on its borders such as illicit trade and public discontent among minority populations.

Finally, there remains a great reticence to use the PLA in matters of border or internal security, despite its many and increasingly relevant capabilities. This is partly as a result of the scars of Tiananmen, as well as China's desire to develop a more professional force able to focus on power projection and war fighting contingencies. As Murray Scot Tanner shows in his chapter, "How China Manages Internal Security Challenges and Its Impact on PLA Missions," this doctrinal shift over the last decade was illustrated by the relatively minor and surreptitious role played by the PLA during the unrest in Tibet. For example, the shortages of manpower and leadership during the crisis were partly a result of this change in mindset and the continued strategic ambiguity about the use of the PLA in cases of domestic unrest. The resolution of this dilemma surrounding the minimal use of the PLA in support of what is supposedly its most central mission, and its differing employment in the Southeast and Western frontier of China, remains critical to any understanding of potential PLA missions beyond the Strait.

China and the Future of the PLA.

It is often said that one's intentions are proportional to one's capabilities. Great powers by nature place greater demand on the international system and play a greater role in world politics. The PLA's expanding missions show that 21st century China is no exception to this rule.

China has developed. Its economy and comprehensive national power have expanded. Its economic, political, cultural, and military interests now reach every corner of the world, and in so doing constitute new frontiers for China's national interests. China is proud of its accomplishments and does not hesitate to tell the world that it will protect and defend its national interests at home and abroad with a strong military power.[18] But while few would dispute a nation's right to develop and defend its national interests, the world is anxious to see how China carries out this defense. There are two broad questions confronting China and the PLA: one is philosophical, the other more practical.

At a philosophical level, Chinese leaders have long held that China is a peace-loving nation, that it values harmony over conflict, and that China has always been on the defensive side in its use of force.[19] China has also criticized the West and the United States for their "hegemonic" approach to international politics and claimed that China would never pursue a similar path. These claims, however, beg many questions. Why do Chinese assert that China is inherently peaceful? China has no less warfare in its history than that of the West, so why is harmony the most dominant theme in China's approach to international affairs?[20] China is not a superpower today, but who is to guarantee that if China were to become one, it would act differently from how the United States has conducted itself in international affairs? Or put differently, is there really a "Chinese way" of international affairs?

At a practical level, Chinese leaders claim that "history has proven time and again that using force to advance national interest has come to a dead end; and China will not go down this path again."[21] They may be right about this claim. However, how does China expect the PLA to carry out its new missions in the new century without the use of force? Some PLA thinkers propose that China develop a "strategic deterrence force (战略威慑力量)" to provide a security guarantee for the development and defense of China's national interests,[22] such as the nuclear deterrence, space capabilities, and info-cyber capabilities discussed in this book. Others suggest that China work within the UN framework and use force only under UN mandate.[23] These might be steps in the right direction, but China will soon find many operational problems as they develop the doctrine that would guide how they execute these missions.

A more practical issue confronting China and the PLA is how they come to terms with the global military and security arrangements of the United States. China's desire and efforts to develop sea, air, and space power have all run into this obstacle. At the present, many Chinese analysts argue that China's efforts in these areas are in the service of China's sovereign interests and security, and not attempts to challenge U.S. global (and hegemonic) positions.[24] In addition, Chinese also argue that the force capabilities of the PLA will be limited for a long time to come and that China does not pose any serious threat to the United States. Indeed, PLA capabilities in most dimensions are assessed to be well behind those of the United States. Finally, Chinese leaders argue that in their effort to pursue a "peaceful rise," they can develop appropriate policies to avoid the collision of vital interests between the two nations.[25] While these arguments may be reassuring at the moment, there is no guarantee that China's rapidly growing national interests and capabilities will not change China's intentions in the future.

For the United States, the PLA's pursuit of missions other than Taiwan could be a positive development. For instance, the PLA's participation in international security affairs (at this point largely limited to UN peacekeeping missions, but soon to expand with the deployment of a PLA Navy task group to assist in anti-piracy efforts off the African coast of Somalia) can serve as a means of burden-sharing with the United States. With its global military presence, the United States has been in essence providing security to the international community; China could share the cost of this global good by providing manpower and financial support, as well as bearing some of the international resentment about great-power intervention in regional affairs. Welcoming the PLA into international security affairs also provides the international community the opportunity to encourage the PLA to adapt global norms of behavior and play by generally accepted international rules. Through direct engagement with the PLA on issues of international security, the United States has the opportunity to prod China to become more transparent and cooperative, especially as regards the PLA's growing roster of missions beyond the Strait.

However, at another level, the development of PLA missions beyond Taiwan can have the opposite effect, particularly if the PLA undertakes missions deleterious to U.S. interests. Here the peacetime development of space and cyber capabilities might prove most troublesome. Additionally, the potential for the use of PLA forces to shore up bad actors on the international scene remains a potential outcome that concerns U.S. analysts. This volume looks at all of these dimensions as we seek to better understand *Beyond the Strait: PLA Missions Other Than Taiwan.*

CHAPTER 1 - ENDNOTES

1. For full text, please see the report at *www.china.org.cn/english/features/book/194485.htm*.

2. Deng Xiaoping, "Speech at an Enlarged Meeting of the Military Commission of the Central Committee of the Communist Party, June 4, 1985," *Selected Works of Deng Xiaoping*, Vol. III (1982-1992), Beijing, China: *People's Daily Online*.

3. Modernization of China has been an aspiration for generations of Chinese leaders since China suffered from Western invasion in the 1840s and especially since the fall of China's last dynasty, the Qing, in 1911. Unification with Taiwan is an added mission since the division of China between the mainland and Taiwan in 1949. But it was Deng Xiaoping who articulated these three missions in the early 1980s. See Deng's opening remarks to the CCP 12th National Convention, September 1, 1982, in *Selected Works of Deng Xiaoping*, Vol. 3, Article 1, Beijing, China: Ren-min Chu-ban She, 1993. Deng Xiaoping initially calls it "Three Major Tasks (三大任务)," but Chinese leaders use the words "tasks (任务)" and "missions (使命)" interchangeably. We use the term "mission" in this book.

4. When the United States recognized the PRC government in 1979, Congress passed the Taiwan Relations Act (TRA) to define U.S. relations with Taiwan. The TRA declares that peace and stability in the Western Pacific is a vital interest of the United States; any use of force to change the status of Taiwan will be of grave concern to the United States; and the United States maintains the capacity to resist any resort to force or other forms of coercion that would jeopardize the security, or the social or economic system, of the people on Taiwan.

5. The Chinese president, premier, and other senior officials repeatedly conveyed this view to the international community, especially the United States. Yan Xuetong is probably the most outspoken Chinese policy analyst in advocating unification with Taiwan at all costs. Yan believes that this is the only way to convince the pro-Taiwan independence folks and the United States that China means business. See Yan, "A Cost-Benefit

Analysis of Using Force to Prevent Taiwan Pro-Independence Advocates from Seeking Taiwan de jure Independence," *Zhan-lue Yu Guan-li (Strategy and Management)*, Beijing, China, No. 3, 2004.

6. There are numerous writings about the Taiwan issue. For a good read, see Martin L. Lasater, *The Taiwan Conundrum*, Boulder, CO: Westview Press, 1999; and Richard C. Bush, *Untying the Knot: Making Peace in the Taiwan Strait*, Washington DC: Brookings Institution Press, 2006.

7. SIPRI Yearbooks, 1992 to 2008.

8. See Roy Kamphausen and Andrew Scobell, eds., *Right-Sizing the People's Liberation Army: Exploring the Contours of China's Military*, Carlisle, PA: Strategic Studies Institute, U.S. Army War College, 2007, for more analysis.

9. See Roy Kamphausen, Andrew Scobell, and Travis Tanner eds., *The "People" in the PLA: Recruitment, Training, and Education in China's Military*, Carlisle, PA: Strategic Studies Institute, U.S. Army War College, 2008, for the PLA's investment in this area.

10. See David L. Shambaugh, *Modernizing China's Military: Progress, Problems, and Prospects*, Berkeley: University of California Press, 2004.

11. The original writings about power transition and hegemonic war come from A. F. K. Organski's work, *World Politics*, New York: Alfred a. Knopf, 1958; and Robert Gilpin's *War and Change in World Politics*, Cambridge, United Kingdom: Cambridge University Press, 1981. Numerous writings have emerged since the mid-1990s to analyze certain aspects of power transition between China and the United States. Steve Chan's recent work is perhaps the only lone voice to cast some doubts on this issue. See Chan, *China, the U.S. and the Power-Transition Theory: a Critique*, London, United Kingdom: Routledge, 2008.

12. See, for example, Andrew Scobell, *China's Use of Military Force: Beyond the Great Wall and the Long March*, Cambridge, United Kingdom: Cambridge University Press, 2003, chapters 5 and 7.

13. From China's 2006 *National Defense White Paper*.

14. Editorial, "On the PLA's Historical Mission in the New Stage of the New Century," *Jiefangjun Bao* (PLA Newspaper) January 9, 2006.

15. Numerous publications by PLA writers celebrate this new mission. The afore-mentioned editorial by the PLA mouthpiece newspaper, *Jiefangjun Bao*, provides perhaps the most authoritative expansion of the thoughts behind the new mission.

16. See Wu Jinan, "The Importance of Sino-Japanese Relations in China's National Security Strategy," *Guoji Wenti Luntan (International Issues Forum)*, Shanghai, Issue 1, 2003.

17. The idea of a peace agreement between China and Taiwan first came from Kenneth Lieberthal, a noted China observer and one-time Senior Director for Asia on President Clinton's National Security Council staff. Lieberthal proposes that the two sides sign a 20-to-30-year "agreed framework" in which China would pledge not to use force to threaten Taiwan, and Taiwan, for its part, would pledge not to seek formal independence; and it was thought that the passage of time would minimize differences between the two sides. Kenneth Lieberthal, "Preventing a War over Taiwan," *Foreign Affairs*, March/April 2005. Since his inauguration, Ma Ying-jeou and Hu Jintao have exchanged goodwill across the Taiwan Strait in line with such an agreed framework. If they can reach this agreement, Hu and Ma might be considered for the Nobel Peace Prize. Indeed, a peace agreement may not even be necessary to win a Nobel. For instance, Kim Dae-jung of South Korea won one in 2000 for going to Pyongyang and holding a historic summit with North Korea's Kim Jong-il.

18. See China's 2006 *National Defense White Paper*; the *PLA Daily* editorial cited earlier; and Li Huaixin, PLA Senior Colonel and Professor of the PLA Logistics and Command College, "China's Peaceful Development and the PLA's Historical Mission," *Junshi Jingji Yanjiu (Military Economics Studies)*, No. 8, 2006.

19. See Lieutenant General Li Jijun, *Traditional Military Thinking and the Defensive Strategy of China*, Carlisle, PA: Strategic Studies Institute, U.S. Army War College, 1997. For a critical analysis of this set of beliefs, see Scobell, *China's Use of Military Force*, chap. 2.

20. According to a PLA research task force, China has witnessed 3,766 wars from the Xia Dynasty of about 2200 B.C. to the fall of the last dynasty, Qing, in the early 1900s, averaging more than one war per year. See Chinese Military History Task Group, *Zhongguo li dai zhan zheng nian biao* (*Chronology of Warfare in Chinese History*), Beijing, China: PLA Publishing House, 2003.

21. Author's note from speech by senior PLA officials at the Second PLA Xiangshan Forum, International Security Cooperation and Asia-Pacific Security, Beijing, China, October 23-26, 2008.

22. *PLA Daily* editorial, "On the Military's New Mission in the New Century," January 9, 2006. Also see Luo Yabo, "A Scientific Interpretation of the PLA's New Mission in the New Century," 军队政工理论研究 (*Theoretical Studies on PLA Political Work*), Vol. 6, No. 3, June 2005.

23. Author's note from discussion points by senior PLA officers at the Second PLA Xiangshan Forum, International Security Cooperation and Asia-Pacific Security, Beijing, China, October 23-26, 2008.

24. See Zhang Wenmu, "On China's Sea Power," *Journal of Ocean University of China*, No. 6, 2004; Ye Zicheng and Mu Xinhai, "Several Thoughts about China's Sea Power Development Strategy," *Studies of International Politics*, Issue 3, August 2005. Perhaps the most noted views are from Liu Zhongmin. See his writings, "Thoughts on Sea Power and the Rise and Fall of Great Powers," *World Economy and Politics*, Issue 12, 2007; "Sea Power in the Theory of Geopolitics, I, II, and III," *Ocean World*; "Sea Power and US-China Relations," *Ocean World*; and Wang Jisi, "US Hegemony and China's Rise," *Foreign Affairs Review*, Issue 10, October 2005.

25. See particularly Liu Zhongmin, "Some Thoughts on Sea Power and the Rise and Fall of Great Powers," *World Economy and Politics*, Issue 12, 2007; Zheng Bijian, "China's New Path of Development and Peaceful Rise," Speech at the 30th Annual World Forum, Lake Como, Italy; *Xuexi Shibao*, Beijing, China, November 22, 2004.

CHAPTER 2

HOW CHINA MANAGES TAIWAN
AND ITS IMPACT ON PLA MISSIONS

Andrew Scobell

Introduction.

This volume examines possible People's Liberation Army (PLA) missions "beyond Taiwan." The use of the term *"beyond Taiwan"* is not meant to imply that Taiwan's status has been resolved in Beijing's eyes—let alone resolved to its satisfaction. Rather, the intent is to explore future PLA missions other than Taiwan.[1] Nevertheless, as one explores possible military missions "beyond Taiwan," an important factor determining the future trajectory of the PLA is how China deals with the island. Rather than directly influencing the kinds of missions identified, or the weapon systems and training China's military adopts, how Beijing manages Taipei will most directly impact the political environment in which fundamental decisions about Chinese defense policy are made. Indeed, how China handles the Taiwan issue will inevitably affect not just the kind of national defense policy China adopts but also how China deals with almost every other issue— foreign and domestic. Therefore, it seems only prudent to take some time to consider this topic.

Two critical dimensions in how China manages Taiwan are (1) whether or not the issue is resolved, and (2) whether or not military force is used to attempt a resolution. The word "resolution" is preferred over "unification" because the former term is broader and could encompass a wide range of alternatives that in the future might be acceptable outcomes to Beijing. It may be useful to examine how China manages Taiwan by constructing a 2 x 2 matrix depicting the four possible combinations of the two variables (see Figure One). Each cell represents a distinct future scenario. Cell A represents a scenario in which there is no military conflict and no political resolution. Cell B represents a scenario in which there is no conflict but the Taiwan issue is resolved. Cell C represents a scenario in which there is a military conflict but the Taiwan issue is not resolved. Cell D represents a scenario in which there is conflict with resolution of the Taiwan issue.

	No Resolution	Resolution
No Conflict	No conflict/No resolution **Status quo persists** A	Resolution w/o conflict **Positive trends continue** B
Conflict	Conflict w/o resolution **Major shock** C	Conflict with resolution **Minor shock** D

Figure 1. How China Manages Taiwan.

Because of the centrality of the Taiwan issue to both Chinese domestic politics and foreign policy — including China's relations with the United States — and the enormous sensitivity of the matter to Chinese elites and common people, there is a considerable literature on the subject. Most relevant to this chapter are previous works that explore various Taiwan scenarios and their larger implications.[2]

Cell A: No Conflict, No Resolution.

In this scenario, the status quo in the Taiwan Strait persists. In other words, while positive economic trends would continue, mutual distrust and suspicion would also persist. Thus no real progress would be made on the political resolution of the Taiwan issue in Beijing's eyes. While no military conflict would erupt, both China and Taiwan would feel it necessary to build up defense capabilities to counter or deter those of the other. Economic and social interaction across the Taiwan Strait would continue, but this interaction would probably fluctuate according to cyclical economic trends and the ebb and flow of political strains. Although the PLA would be expected to manage other responsibilities and to take on other missions, its primary warfighting scenario would be centered on the Taiwan Strait.

Cell B: Resolution without Conflict.

In this scenario, the positive trends in the Taiwan Strait would continue. Cross-Strait economic ties would continue and deepen—trade, investment, and transportation links would expand and become increasingly direct, relying less and less on transshipment and transportation hubs such as Hong Kong. Contacts between political leaders on both sides of the Strait would continue and become routine—evident in particular since the election of Ma Ying-jeou to Taiwan's highest office in March 2008. In this scenario, resolution is not so much thought of as an outcome as it is a process. A formal or informal agreement between Beijing and Taipei on political unification would not necessarily be the defining condition. Rather, improved and closer ties between individual political leaders and institutions would naturally and inexorably draw the two sides together in webs of cooperation and collaboration. If both sides found these incremental steps acceptable and mutually beneficial then unification would happen almost imperceptibly — by stealth.

In this scenario, PLA forces would probably not be stationed on Taiwan, although increasing cooperation and coordination might eventually mean that PLA liaison officers would be posted to various commands on the island and vice versa. This cooperation and coordination would likely include combined exercises in search and rescue, counterterrorism, and anti-piracy operations. A significant volume of exchanges would occur, and officers might attend institutions of professional military education on the other side of the Strait.

The PLA would truly begin to move beyond thinking and planning for a Taiwan scenario. Moreover, the PLA would also begin to think of Taiwan's military as a partner in various roles and missions — especially those involving naval forces.

Cell C: Conflict without Resolution.

In this scenario, no resolution refers to any outcome that would NOT be acceptable to China. Any conflict outcome that resulted in *de jure* Taiwan independence would certainly be deemed unacceptable.

A key assumption here is that in a conflict in which China failed to achieve an acceptable outcome over

Taiwan, the United States would be involved and U.S. military intervention would have been a decisive factor—probably the decisive factor—in thwarting a successful Chinese military operation. Implicit in the assumption is direct combat operations between the PLA and the armed forces of the United States—likely between the air and naval arms of each military. Losses to Chinese forces would likely be considerable both in terms of casualties and weapon systems destroyed or disabled. Losses to U.S. forces would likely be more limited but significant nevertheless.

It is likely—but by no means certain—that in a conflict between Chinese and U.S. forces over Taiwan both sides would strive to exert escalation control over the conflict both horizontally and vertically. From China's perspective, the stakes in a military conflict over Taiwan would be quite high, and Beijing might be willing—or feel itself forced—to gamble that controlled escalation would be possible. In other words, China's leaders might convince themselves that if they upped the ante, the United States might back down.[3] At the very least, Beijing might gamble that Washington would simply respond with controlled escalation of its own.

Whatever the level of escalation on each side, at some point both sides would probably either voluntarily or out of necessity reach a juncture in the conflict where they would suspend combat operations. This would either be though some kind of ceasefire or informal understanding. Of course, the degree of destruction or devastation wrought by each side on the other would determine the level of impact on each country (e.g., how much of the PLA was destroyed and how much of China's infrastructure or economic assets were destroyed).

In any case, the outcome would be a "major shock" in both terms of China's position in the Asia-Pacific region and in its relations with the United States. Beijing's standing in other capitals around the region and around the world would likely be seriously damaged. Moreover, hostilities would probably lead to a new cold war between Washington and Beijing. It is likely that the United States would station at least token military forces on the island and perhaps even formalize a security agreement or defense treaty with Taiwan. As a result, China would harbor significant animosity and resentment toward the United States that would not soon dissipate. The United States would likely begin a serious and accelerated defense modernization program. China would likely lick its wounds and immediately begin to rebuild its military in a rapid and sustained manner at a rate much higher that the double digit annual increases in the defense budget during the last 2 decades.

At the same time, the economies of both countries would suffer major shocks. Traditional trade patterns and investment flows would be disrupted, and it would take time for these to find new equilibria. Regional and even global economic activity would also be jolted, and the geopolitical map of the Asia-Pacific would also be altered as countries were forced to align with China or the United States.

In the event of a conflict without resolution scenario, a primary assumption is that China would NEVER accept the outcome. Moreover, the Chinese people might express dissatisfaction with their government's handling of the Taiwan issue. The result would be an angry and disaffected country that would harbor a serious grudge against the United States and other countries deemed to have assisted the United States during the hostilities and/or sided with Washington against Beijing afterwards.

Cell D: Conflict with Resolution.

In this scenario, resolution refers only to a solution that is agreeable to China. The logic behind the assumption is that for the Taiwan issue to be resolved once and for all, the outcome must be satisfactory to Beijing. If China does not consider a situation satisfactory, then it is not going to be truly resolved because China will never accept this as the "final" outcome.

Another assumption in this scenario is that there would be no U.S. military involvement or at least only minor involvement. The logic behind this assumption is that China could only be successful in a military conflict over Taiwan if the United States did not intervene. Under what circumstances would there not be any U.S. involvement? There seem to be two possibilities. First, Taiwan does something that the United States deemed excessively provocative and irresponsible. As a result, Washington informs Taipei that it can expect no U.S. help. Second, China launches a lightning military operation that swiftly subdues Taiwan before the United States had time to react.

In this scenario, China and the PLA could truly move beyond Taiwan in terms of thinking, planning, and preparing for future military roles and missions. Of course, the outcome would likely reverberate around the Asia Pacific as governments came to terms with it. The seizure of Taiwan would create a "minor shock" that would require adjustments by China as well as other countries. There would likely be some fallout in terms of at least some condemnation. However, it is possible that this might be minimal especially if the military campaign was limited to the area of the Taiwan Strait and resulted in very little loss of life and destruction of infrastructure.

Economic sanctions might be token and for a limited period of time. Especially, if Beijing moved promptly and conciliatorily, economic damage might be limited. There might be some adverse effect on China's economy from skittish foreign investors and trading partners. However, this would probably be temporary and would very possibly be offset by the patriotic euphoria among Chinese citizens over the sudden and dramatic realization of a long cherished dream. International trade and investment would at least take a modest hit because there would be fallout felt in Taiwan's stock market and foreign trade. There would also be some capital flight from the island. The extent of the shock would depend whether or not there was continued resistance to China's rule either in the form of guerilla warfare and/or civil disobedience. It is an open question as to whether or not the Taiwanese people might be fatalistic and receptive to their new political masters (if grudgingly and gradually).

In this scenario, it is likely that China would station at least modest numbers of military personnel on the island indefinitely. If China used the Hong Kong model, the PLA garrison would probably be virtually invisible to the island's populace, especially if the people did not engage in widespread or prolonged resistance to the new occupiers. If China used the Tibet model, sizeable concentrations of security forces would remain visible for extended periods of time. Moreover, if Taiwanese engaged in widespread or prolonged resistance, then this would require a far more substantial troop presence on the island.

Back on the mainland, the Chinese Communist Party would enjoy at least a temporary boost in popularity for having realized unification. And the PLA would enjoy a significant boost in its status as well as in troop morale.

Conclusion.

How China manages Taiwan will affect the future trajectories of China and the PLA. Taiwan is perhaps the most critical issue in determining whether or not China's rise will continue to be peaceful. If the issue is resolved, then China and the PLA can truly move "beyond Taiwan" in preparing for future roles and missions. If the issue remains unresolved, although the PLA can prepare other roles and missions, it must also remain prepared for a Taiwan scenario. If military force is used, the PLA will react and learn relatively quickly on the basis of whether the conflict was successful and to what degree it was successful or not. If military force is not used, the PLA's trajectory is likely to evolve in a more gradual manner.

CHAPTER 2 - ENDNOTES

1. Use of term "beyond Taiwan" is therefore consistent with this term's usage in the Office of the Secretary of Defense, *Military Power of the People's Republic of China 2008* Annual Report to Congress, Washington, DC: Department of Defense, 2008, pp. 29-30.

2. See, for example, Roger Cliff and David A. Shlapak, *U.S.-China Relations After Resolution of Taiwan's Status*, Santa Monica, CA: RAND, 2007; Steve Tsang, ed., *If China Attacks Taiwan: Military Strategy, Politics, and Economics*, New York: Routledge, 2006; Andrew Scobell, ed., *The Costs of Conflict: The Impact on China of a Future War*, Carlisle, PA: Strategic Studies Institute, U.S. Army War College, 2001.

3. Chinese elites, especially soldiers, tend to believe that where Taiwan is concerned, their country possesses an "asymmetry of motivation" which can be leveraged against the United States. In other words, China's "will to fight" is deeper than that of the United States and the "threshold of pain" that China is prepared to endure is far higher than that of the United States. See, for example, Andrew Scobell, *China's Use of Military Force: Beyond the Great Wall and the Long March*, New York: Cambridge University Press, 2003, pp. 186-187.

CHAPTER 3

HOW CHINA MANAGES INTERNAL SECURITY CHALLENGES AND ITS IMPACT ON PLA MISSIONS

Murray Scot Tanner[*]

This chapter examines the understudied topic of the Chinese People's Liberation Army's (PLA) internal security missions, and the relationship between the PLA's missions and those of the other organs that make up the Chinese Communist Party (CCP) state coercive apparatus.[1]   Although most of the chapters in this volume examine the PLA's missions beyond Taiwan, beyond China's borders, or even beyond the confines of earth, this chapter reminds us that so long as the CCP remains in power, the mission which is still perhaps most fundamental to the PLA will remain firmly fixed in China's domestic society.

RELATING INTERNAL SECURITY TO THE PLA'S OTHER MISSIONS

How does the PLA's internal security mission relate to the army's fundamentally important Taiwan mission, as discussed by Dr. Andrew Scobell in the introduction, and its other tasks? The internal security mission entrusted to China's civilian and military

* For their excellent critical comments on earlier drafts of this article and for their generous assistance with finding source materials, the author wishes to thank the conference commentator Lonnie Henley, as well as James Bellacqua, Tom Bickford, Dennis Blasko, John Corbett, June Teufel Dreyer, Lin Chong-pin, Daniel Hartnett, Roy Kamphausen, Susan Puska, Andrew Scobell, Travis Tanner, and Fred Vellucci. All remaining errors of fact and interpretation are my sole responsibility, but they would certainly have been more numerous without these colleagues' help.

security organs is probably the only mission analyzed in this volume whose significance for the CCP's rule, and whose pervasive impact on other PLA missions, exceeds even the Taiwan mission. Analysts of the post-Tiananmen PLA have noted the PLA's enduring role as ultimate guarantor of the Party's hold on power. Most have also pointed to the decline of internal security as an active mission relative to the PLA's external mission during the 1990s and into the 2000s, emphasizing the assumption of that mission by the People's Armed Police's (PAP).[2] Hu Jintao, however, has officially reasserted the status of the PLA's internal security mission in his 2004-05 expositions on the PLA's "Historic Missions" (see discussion below) by listing first the PLA's role of *providing a powerful guarantee to stabilize the Party's grip on governance*. Only in his second package of missions does Hu allude to the fight against Taiwan independence—actually setting forth a combined, tripartite mission of "protecting national sovereignty, unity and stability" (维护国家主权、统一和稳定的神圣职责) that also references domestic security.

The success of the internal security mission and the Taiwan mission, moreover, are intertwined in potentially important ways. The Party-state's capacity to successfully carry out its internal security mission by relying overwhelmingly upon its civilian and paramilitary security organs—with only limited support from the PLA—is critical to freeing the PLA to reform its overwhelming historical orientation toward ground forces, and allow it to modernize and concentrate its resources and capacity on mastering its Taiwan mission as well as its other largely externally-oriented missions. Thus, as this chapter will argue below, any sign that the Beijing leadership believes its civilian and paramilitary forces are unable to carry out their internal security missions without significant support from the regular PLA—as may have occurred in Lhasa in March 2008—has important ramifications for the army's other missions.

Conversely, the CCP has invested the Taiwan issue and mission with such fundamental importance for its popular legitimacy that the PLA's capacity to carry out that mission successfully—or at least its perceived capacity—could very easily have a major impact on Chinese domestic stability. It could even determine the CCP's need to rely on the PLA to maintain its hold on power. Simply put, many Chinese security intellectuals appear to believe (as Dr. Scobell has hinted earlier) that if the CCP leadership were to launch a precipitous attack to reunify Taiwan with the mainland, and that operation failed (Dr. Scobell's "Cell C: *Conflict without Resolution*"), the resulting popular fury could result in the CCP's overthrow. Moreover, it would very likely be an open question whether or not the Party leadership could again rely upon the PLA to use force to save it in such circumstances. Concerns about internal stability could also complicate the conduct of any Taiwan operation. The prospect of massive social unrest in the event of failure would, I strongly suspect, make it much trickier for China's leaders to engage in "escalation control" with the United States. Any resultant post-war social chaos might also undermine—at least in the short term—Chinese state efforts to mobilize resources and pursue an accelerated military build-up aimed at redeeming a failed Taiwan operation. Thus, the pervasive importance of the internal security mission—for China's civilian and paramilitary security organs as well as the PLA and all of its missions—is important to bear in mind.

OVERVIEW OF THIS CHAPTER

June 3-4, 2009, will mark 20 years since the CCP ordered the PLA to suppress student and worker demonstrators in Beijing. That operation not only traumatized Chinese society; it also left the PLA as an institution scarred to such a degree that one of the Party's major motivations for reforming and reconstituting China's civilian and paramilitary police systems over the next 2 decades has been to minimize the likelihood that the PLA would ever again have to be ordered to carry out this domestic security mission.[3]

As the other chapters in this volume make clear, however, the PLA is being asked to undertake and prepare for an increasingly broad and complex array of new international and domestic security missions consistent with China's rising international power and its rapid and challenging domestic social and economic development. This trend raises a serious dilemma for the PLA—how can it cope with the challenges and burdens of trying to prepare for these new professional and high-tech missions at the same time that the CCP expects it to be available—if only as a last resort—to fulfill its internal security missions?

This chapter examines three major questions concerning China's response to internal security challenges and the impact of that response on the PLA's missions: *First, what are the formal internal security missions that the CCP has assigned to the PLA with regard to defending the Party's control of the state and its dominance over society?* What do the key authoritative documents on this topic issued by the Party and state (e.g. Party Documents, laws, regulations, etc.) tell us about what the Party expects of the PLA? What do PLA training regimens tell us about the nature of this mission and how the PLA prepares for it?

Second, what is the Party and state's overall strategy for dealing with social unrest, and how does it relate to the internal security mission of the PLA? How does the internal security strategy developed for the civilian and paramilitary security organs that form the front and second lines of social control in China relate to the PLA and its role as the "third line" in domestic stability operations? China's chronic rising levels of social unrest over the past decade raise serious concerns for the PLA. Since about 1998-99, the Party's other internal security organs have struggled not merely to keep a lid on social protest, but also to forge a new, more sophisticated, sustainable, and lower-violence strategy for containing and managing chronic unrest. This chapter will examine how this evolving social order strategy affects what is probably the PLA's central concern—the Army's strong preference that these other internal security organs effectively contain unrest by themselves, and thereby continue to allow the PLA to keep its distance from domestic security missions while it focuses on a complex and growing list of other national security missions it is being asked to undertake.

Third, what do recent events in Lhasa tell us about potential problems in China's response to social unrest and its implications for the PLA? This chapter will examine the March 2008 loss of social control in Lhasa as a critical case study of some of the potential shortcomings in China's social control management and the implications this could have for the PLA and its missions. Following the outbreak of rioting and a short loss of control over portions of Lhasa by the Public Security and PAP forces, the media were full of reports suggesting that the PLA had been forced to undertake its greatest involvement in internal security operations in years—perhaps its greatest since the 1989 Lhasa and Tiananmen protests. This chapter will examine how and why civilian and paramilitary forces lost control, and based on the available evidence, will attempt to clarify how and in what ways the PLA became involved in internal security missions. From this critical case study, the chapter will try to draw some general lessons about the circumstances under which the PLA might be forced to actually carry out its internal security mission, and what tasks that may involve.

The Mission That Dare Not Speak Its Name.

As Scobell and Brad Hammet pointed out a decade ago in their analysis of "paramilitary" functions, the CCP system is still far from comfortable in its efforts to clarify the boundaries between military and police missions.[4] A review of post-Tiananmen authoritative Party and state documents on the PLA's mission (see below) demonstrates clearly that the CCP's official conception of the PLA's mission has always included a strong internal security element. But this domestic repression mission for the most part continues to be a "mission that dare not speak its name" in terms of conveying the precise political, legal, and social circumstance under which the Party reserves the right to order the PLA to use force against its own people, as well as the levels and forms of violence and coercion it may order the Army to use. With rare exceptions (the Law on Martial Law, for example), the details of the PLA's roles and responsibilities in these missions are usually referred to in a very understated fashion. Thus, while authoritative documents are sometimes explicit in stipulating *portions* of the PLA's domestic security mission, much more commonly the Party and state leadership only convey to the army a very clear presumption—that if the Party's other security organs should ever prove incapable of defending the Party against domestic and foreign political threats, social unrest, or ethnic and religious separatism, the PLA must understand that it might once again be called upon to defend the Party's control over society. Since Tiananmen, however, the Party has spelled out the PLA's mission with legal conditions and institutional commitments intended to demonstrate that the Party strongly prefers that the Public Security, State Security, judicial and procuratorial organs, and PAP forces should form the first and second lines for maintaining social control, and the PLA very much in the third line.[5] Still, the Party never has never issued—and probably never will issue—an authoritative document that even implies it would ever let the PLA "off the hook" entirely on its domestic security mission.

Moreover, for a little more than a decade, domestic socio-economic and global military trends have, in a sense, pulled in opposite directions, posing a growing institutional dilemma for the Party and its efforts to define, narrow, and professionalize the PLA's domestic and international missions. China's explosive economic growth and persistently rising social unrest have placed increasing burdens on the state's domestic social order, crisis response, and disaster relief systems at precisely the time that the Party demands that the PLA prepare to undertake a broadening array of modern, high-tech, highly professional externally-oriented security missions. The Party has made powerful institutional efforts to free the PLA to focus on its transformation into a modern military with mostly externally-oriented missions (save for counterterrorism, border security, intelligence, and a few other tasks). But the Party cannot even implicitly excuse the PLA from its formal internal security missions unless if feels confident that the Public Security, State Security, PAP, and various other state organs have developed appropriate strategies and institutional capacity to maintain domestic security and social stability by themselves. But long before the snow storms, ethnic unrest, and earthquakes of 2008 raised serious questions about the competency of these civilian and paramilitary security organs to handle truly major crises on their own, the Party and the PLA were apparently aware that the expansion of the army's international missions could not yet be accompanied by a contraction of its domestic missions. Consequently, even while the modern PLA prepares for complex futuristic high-tech missions such as "integrated air and space combat" (*kongtian yiti zuozhan*), it has also very recently been issuing new training materials on its role in maintaining social stability and a variety of other traditional and nontraditional domestic "noncombat military operations."[6]

Realistically evaluating the PLA's internal security missions requires, therefore, not only examining its formal duties as expressed in authoritative documents such as leadership speeches, state laws, Party and state documents (including white papers), training systems, etc. It also requires looking beyond these formally defined duties for which the Party has ordered it to be prepared—just in case. We need to evaluate the PLA's relationship to China's first and second line internal security organs, their evolving anti-unrest strategies, command structures, and institutional capacities. A key question is: do the strategies, structures, and capacities of these other internal security organs provide the PLA with the assurance that it will not be called upon again to perform the tasks it found so distasteful in 1989?

For the most part, the record appears to be clear, and from the PLA's perspective, cautiously promising. Despite high and rising levels of unrest in China since 1989, the PLA has been spared from taking part in the actual operations of suppressing protests or riots. But the recent loss of control in Lhasa and other parts of Tibet and China's west, coupled with widespread but imprecise reports of PLA involvement in at least some parts of that internal security mission, raise serious questions. Does China's civilian and paramilitary internal security infrastructure have an appropriate strategy, a sufficiently responsive political control system, and the institutional resources to carry out its mission? More importantly for purposes of this chapter, do the Lhasa riots provide an insight into broader weaknesses in the security system that might gradually draw the PLA back into greater involvement in the domestic security mission from which the PLA has been able to distance itself for the past 20 years?

On balance, this chapter finds that there was something of a low probability "perfect storm" quality about the loss of control in Lhasa that might be unique, and that—at least given *present* social trends—appears unlikely to be repeated in many other locations. Lhasa saw the coincidence of several factors that caused the civilian authorities to fail in what they see as their missions and tasks of social intelligence and early warning, security force deployments, and in particular the politics of ordering a quick, forceful, repressive response. In the end, though, available evidence suggests the public security and PAP forces were able to regain control through their own repressive power, relying upon the PLA primarily for logistical, public safety, and perhaps some intelligence/information operations support services. At the same time, this low probability failure offers several insights concerning the factors and conditions that can cause a protest to slip out of control and, as in this case, apparently compel the Party to call upon the PLA to provide support to other security forces during a crisis.

This chapter notes several problems in Lhasa authorities' response to the outbreak of rioting on March 14 that undermined their capacity to contain the protests quickly; some of these reflect the special demands of China's efforts to find a strategy for dealing with unrest that minimizes violence and popular backlash and maximizes Party control. There is still a shortage of solid information about several key aspects of the March 14, 2008, Lhasa riots, and any conclusions about how authorities coped with the crisis must remain tentative. For example, the strategy places an especially high premium on intelligence about protestor plans and advance warning to forecast and contain these incidents, both of which clearly failed in Lhasa. Large numbers of security forces were also badly deployed and slow to respond to the first outbreak of violence. Lhasa security officials also delayed several hours before attempting to retake control of the riot areas, which may in part reflect regulations requiring relatively high level political authorization before anti-protest forces can employ coercive tactics and lethal and nonlethal weapons.

PLA Internal Security Missions: The Official Version.

With few exceptions, the available laws, regulations, leadership speeches, white papers and other authoritative documents that have defined the PLA's domestic security and safety-related missions have done so in fairly general, hortatory terms. In the past decade, the Party has issued many documents that reminded the PLA of its mission to defend the Party's hold on power against its enemies. But these documents make little effort to define the objects or adversaries against whom these missions would be carried out—most of whom would be Chinese citizens. Nor do these documents carefully distinguish the specific operational tasks that might be assigned to the PLA, as distinct from those that would be entrusted to civilian and paramilitary units. These documents also do not define the specific circumstances of social instability under which the PLA would be used. Frequently, the PLA's specific responsibility is obscured by use of the term "armed forces" (*wuzhuang liliang*)—an official term that also includes the PAP and the militia.

Probably no available authoritative legal or policy document issued in recent years is more complete or more explicit in its conception of a domestic suppression and social control role for the PLA than the 1996 Martial Law Law (MLL) of the PRC.[7] The law explicitly identifies many of the circumstances in which martial law might be declared, including "turmoil" [*dongluan*], "riots" [*baoluan*], or "disturbance" [*saoluan*]), and summarizes the overall mission as helping to "preserve social order and protect the people's lives and property." The law stipulates that martial law enforcement institutions must secure keypoint institutions, including leadership

49

and military institutions, foreign embassies, mass media units, public enterprises, airports and railway stations, prisons, and other priority institutions.

While the MLL does not distinguish between the missions of the PLA and either the public security forces or the PAP, it does clearly presume that the PLA should be deployed only as a last resort, in a supporting role, and under the direct command of PLA officers. Article 8 stipulates that:

> Martial law will be executed by the People's Police or the People's Armed Police; if necessary, the State Council can refer to the Central Military Commission[CMC] for a decision on sending PLA units to assist in martial law enforcement.

Article 10, in turn, stipulates that PLA forces shall be commanded by a distinctive leadership organ and leaves the relationship of that organ to the martial law enforcement institutions and the martial law command organs.[8]

> Article 10: Martial law enforcement institutions shall establish martial law command organs, which shall coordinate and enforce operations related to martial law enforcement, and implement martial law measures under a unified plan. PLA units enforcing martial law are commanded by a military institution designated by the CMC under a unified plan of the martial law command organs.

The MLL is also as clear as any authoritative document available in spelling out the support, social control, and repressive actions the martial law enforcement forces, including the PLA, are authorized to undertake in support of their mission. These chapters authorize the martial law enforcement organs to ban demonstrations or group activities or strikes, impose censorship, restrict individuals' movements, and many other coercive actions. It also clearly authorizes the use of police weapons and instruments, and even deadly force, to protect the lives and safety of citizens or martial law personnel (including fire and rescue workers), or to prevent violent attack on key establishments. Finally, the closing Chapter V admits the possibility of Armed Police and even PLA forces being brought in to restore order, disperse crowds, and detain protest leaders even though national officials have not officially declared martial law.

The PRC's *National Defense White Papers* since 1998 have gradually elaborated the domestic security-related missions of China's "armed forces" generally and, at times, the PLA in particular. The *1998* and *2000 White Papers* include among the "basic objectives" of China's defense policy entrusted to China's armed forces ". . . curbing armed subversion, and defending state sovereignty, unity, territorial integrity, and security." The *2002 White Paper* noticeably elaborated the list of internal security missions for the armed forces, adding an entire section devoted to the suppression of specifically domestic threats.[9] The *2002 White Paper* a devotes great space to elaborating the PLA and the broader armed forces' commitment to supporting Hu and Wen's development of China's restive Western regions. It notes that to support this development project, "the CMC has established a special leading group and a dedicated office, and made unified arrangements. The PLA and the Armed Police Force have contributed more than 1.5 million troops and 450,000 motor vehicles and machines to actively participate in and support the western region development efforts." These development support

51

tasks included environmental work such as reforest-
ation, aid to the poor (including installing power lines
and transport projects), capital construction projects,
and encouraging retired or demobilized PLA veterans
to relocate to these regions.

The *2004* and *2006 White Papers*, by contrast,
place less emphasis on the domestic security goals of
the armed forces than the 2002 paper, with the 2004
paper noting only the need to "safeguard the political,
economic, and cultural rights and interests of the
Chinese people; crack down on criminal activities
of all sorts; and maintain public order and social
stability." The paper also devoted somewhat more
attention to domestic security threats in its analysis of
the international security situation, which noted that
"nontraditional security issues . . . [were] . . . posing
a growing threat" among which it noted terrorism,
information, energy, financial and environmental
security, transnational crime, epidemics, and natural
disasters. The security analysis closed by musing that
the difficulty of alleviating the root causes of terrorism
meant that this global struggle would remain "a
long and demanding task before the international
community." The *2006 White Paper* adds repeated
references endorsing Hu Jintao's domestic stability-
related strategy of developing a "socialist harmonious
society" and includes such internal security goals as
"Upholding national security and unity, and ensure
the interests of national development. This includes .
. . taking precautions against and cracking down on
terrorism, separatism and extremism in all forms."

Hu Jintao placed his personal stamp on a current
version of these internal security missions in his
December 2004 "Historic Missions for Our Military
in the New Period and the New Century."[10] Hu

attempted a more comprehensive review of missions, and not surprisingly began by calling on the military to "provide an important guarantee of power for the Party to stabilize its hold on governance." In writings and speeches delivered amid the wave of "colour revolutions" (颜色革命) of late 2004-early 2005, Hu pointedly and almost poetically calls on the Army to "guarantee that the socialist red rivers and mountains will forever not change their colour (保证社会主义红色江山永不变色)." Hu argues that so long as the Party relies on the people and keeps a grip on the people's army, the country can never become seriously chaotic. In the second of his missions, Hu calls upon the military to "place the sovereignty and security of the country in the first position," and do a good job preserving the country's "sovereignty, unity, and stability." The available excerpts of Hu's speech, however, say virtually nothing about the circumstances under which the PLA might be asked to perform these domestic security missions, or these missions' targets and adversaries.

FROM THEORY TO PRACTICE: PLA TRAINING FOR INTERNAL SECURITY MISSIONS

By going beyond publicly proclaiming a "mission" for the PLA and ordering the military to organize training for that mission, the Party and PLA leadership sends the message that it means for the military to take the mission with more seriousness and devote a measure of time and resources to preparing for it. Internal security-related training also, of course, has an additional impact on several aspects of the PLA's capacity to take part in these missions. In terms of the psychology and morale needed to carry out a mission that may be against its own citizens, requiring PLA forces to engage in regular training that is explicitly geared toward domestic internal security missions (and not just labeled "peacekeeping preparations" for example) can send an important signal to troops that they may, in fact, someday be called upon to perform this potentially distasteful task. Training regimens are also a valuable indicator of whether or not high-ranking PLA officers take seriously the possibility that civilian Party leaders might order them to deploy their forces in suppressing protests. Whether or not the strategy, techniques, and methods of internal security work taught to PLA forces mirror those taught to Public Security, PAP and other forces will have an important effect on their capacity to cooperate effectively with these forces and with local Party and government leaders, should the PLA be brought in. Finally, of course, the legacy of Tiananmen raises the issue of whether PLA forces that might be deployed for internal security operations would receive the kind of modern protest policing training that is necessary for them to carry out their operations with minimal violence. On these last two points, Dennis Blasko documents that counterterrorism training in Tibet and China's Muslim regions has provided PLA, PAP, and Public Security forces (and perhaps State Security forces) with an opportunity to train together. Blasko stresses, however, that the numbers of forces, scenarios, techniques, equipment, and levels of violence used for anti-terror special operations "are quite different from anti-riot and domestic stability operations used to control unarmed civilians." Recent authoritative sources on PLA ground forces military training indicate clearly that since at least the early 2000s, the PLA has indeed expected at least some of its ground force units to train for what are referred to as "noncombat operations" (*feizhanzheng xingdong*) and "counterterror/preservation of social stability" (*fankong weiwen*) missions. These sources, however, do not provide a great deal of detail on the nature of this training.[11] "The proliferating responsibilities born by the ground forces determine that the content of training must also become more multifaceted."[12] Training materials remind the ground forces that as a key component of the state's armed forces, their responsibilities and missions include protecting the security of the state and China's territorial integrity, and preserving its social stability (*weihu shehui wending*).[13]

While "counterterrorism" is considered a training category unto itself, "preserving social order" is considered part of the broader category of "training for noncombat operations" (*feizhanzheng xingdong xunlian*) that also includes "disaster rescue and relief," support for crime fighting operations, and "participation in international peacekeeping" (this last point makes it nearly explicit that the Chinese leadership expects that PLA participation in international peacekeeping will have spin-off training benefits for domestic social order control).[14] The stated goal of this training is to introduce trainees to the theory and methods (*lilun, fangfa*) of such noncombat operations, and make them familiar with the "special characteristics" and "regular patterns" (*tedian, guilu*) of these types of operations. These materials also note that these sorts of noncombat training can be divided into subunit noncombat training (*fendui*), leadership organ (*shouzhang jiguan*) and unit noncombat training. Training materials hint that internal security training is politically complex and involves learning to work with a wide array of other units, characterizing it as involving "broad theoretical knowledge, specialized content and methods, and complex command and coordination relationships."[15]

Somewhat more concretely, noncombat operations training involves "general knowledge of all sources of natural disasters and disasters of an accidental nature; and laws and policies related to preserving social stability and participating in international peacekeeping operations," also training in techniques and skills of these noncombat operations, also the guiding principles, employment of military forces (*bingli shiyong*), and operational methods (*xingdong fangfa*) of emergency rescue and "handling all types of suddenly occurring incidents" (*chuzhi gezhong tufa shijian*). Training also includes organization and command of noncombat operations, coordinated actions (*xietong dongzuo*), logistical and other supports (*gezhong baozhang*), political work, and work following the completion of the mission. To systematize this work, the PLA has also developed training materials on noncombat operations.[16]

These training materials issued since Hu Jintao's ascent also state rather plainly that this category of missions should by no means be considered a rare or esoteric part of the PLA's work. "During periods when the nation is relatively at peace, shouldering the responsibility of these non-combat operations should be seen as a regular duty and responsibility (*yi xiang jingchangxing de shiming renwu*)."[17] Another recent manual is even more blunt and criticizes "some comrades" in the PLA who believe that social order challenges are not their job or beneath them, and that if these duties are left to the public security forces, that will be just fine. As constituent parts of the Party and state's armed forces, both the PAP and the PLA are also expected to help carry the burden of maintaining social stability inside China's borders.[18]

While this training material indicates an explicit intent to train PLA troops to be prepared to undertake or support internal security operations, it leaves many crucial questions unanswered. Available materials, for example, provide little information about the strategies, tactics, methods, arms, and equipment the PLA would train to employ in the event it had to intervene against protestors. Unclear, for example, is whether the specific missions and roles, and crowd control, protest policing, and anti-riot techniques the PLA is being taught are intended to support the more sophisticated lower-violence official strategies the Ministry of Public Security has been developing since about 1999. Or is it implicitly understood that if the PLA should have to be deployed to suppress a protest, the Party and PLA anticipate that the circumstances would have to be so dire it would once again, as in 1989, be a highly bloody affair? Likewise, it is unclear whether the techniques Chinese PLA peacekeepers employ to maintain social order overseas are the same as those it would use domestically.

CHINA'S EVOLVING INTERNAL SECURITY STRATEGY

Ever since Tiananmen, the PLA's ability to refrain from, or limit, its entanglement in the potential internal security missions that are broadly defined by these state documents has always depended upon the state's ability to build and provide alternative internal security and public safety organs that were capable of successfully carrying out these sensitive missions without resort to PLA help. This placed an especially heavy burden on the state to develop paramilitary, civilian police, intelligence, and civil affairs/emergency rescue forces capable of responding to a wide range of contingencies and serving the needs of a wide range of leadership stakeholders.[19] This not only required the state to be able to stand up, train, and finance such capable non-PLA forces, the state also needed to develop strategies and plans for their deployment, and response mechanisms that would enable these civilian and paramilitary units to monitor social problems, forecast and prevent incidents of social unrest, and, when they occur, respond quickly, powerfully, and effectively to threats to internal order.

With regard to disaster relief missions, the post-Tiananmen Chinese state has never claimed or pretended that it had built public security, civil affairs, and PAP units which had the numbers, training, and particularly the institutional capacity and equipment necessary to permit the state to dispense with large-scale PLA assistance. The PLA has regularly taken part in major disaster relief efforts since 1990, including the 1998 floods, and the 2008 winter storm and Sichuan earthquake.

During the late 1990s-early 2000s, however, the Party and its security leadership began to revise its internal security strategies in ways that placed additional burdens on its non-PLA internal security forces. Available police materials on the handling of protest from the early-mid 1990s suggest little sophistication in their strategies, and a strong bias toward quickly and decisively putting down "emergency social order incidents" or "suddenly occurring incidents," as they were called.[20] But by about 1998-99, faced with a rapid increase in social protest among peasants, state industrial workers, and other social support pillars of the regime, and a recognition that violent mishandling of these protests risked causing backlash and further loss of control, security leaders began looking for more sophisticated strategies and tactics to contain unrest.

These strategies create new challenges on security forces, because they place a significantly higher burden of professionalism on the public security, state security, and PAP forces to forecast, prevent, and quickly contain unrest. Moreover, the Party feels so intensely the political imperative of handling unrest properly that it has imposed strong rules regarding local CCP leadership, especially over the use of coercive or deadly force in response to protest, in the interest of minimizing police resort to tactics that might risk sparking violent backlash among the crowds.

These institutional rules aimed at minimizing the risk of violence and backlash very likely come at a cost, however — because when a genuine riot suddenly breaks out, as occurred in Lhasa on the early afternoon of March 15, 2008 — these rules of Party control and engagement put a heavy premium on local Party officials' ability to make a quick judgment on whether or not the incident has an "antagonistic political nature" (e.g., whether it is anti-CCP) and to quickly mobilize and deploy both civilian public security and PAP with authorization to employ coercive tactics and possibly deadly force. Unless these actions are taken quickly, the likelihood for losing containment of the protest or riot increases greatly and, along with it, the likelihood that local officials may feel that they have no choice but to turn to the PLA for help.

The fact that the Party has rarely (indeed, perhaps only this one time) called upon the PLA for this type of support since 1989 suggests that Lhasa had something of a political "perfect storm" quality about it—the coming together of a number of relatively low probability problems and errors all at once. The security work surrounding the Lhasa incident also had several aspects that were, frankly, puzzlingly inept— most notable was the relative lack of preparation for protests during one of the most sensitive dates on the Tibetan calendar when security officials are explicitly instructed to be on guard. Nevertheless, they provide one window into some of the weaknesses in the civilian and paramilitary internal security system that has been developed since 1989 that had, as at least one of its aims, developing a set of capabilities that would permit the PLA to avoid having to carry out the formal internal security mission that many official Party and state documents have prescribed for it.

I have summarized the main points of this anti-protest strategy elsewhere.[21] But with respect to the goal of permitting the PLA to distance itself from social order missions, and what went wrong in Tibet, several points are particularly noteworthy.

Party and Public Security Anti-protest Materials.

Party and public security anti-protest materials stress that local Party leaders must learn to quickly and "accurately distinguish the political character" of protests, riots, and other mass incidents—in particular whether they should officially be judged "contradictions among the people" for which the appropriate methods are primarily education, the solving of real problems, and containment of protest, or are "contradictions between the people and the enemy" (antagonistic contradictions) for which dictatorial methods are appropriate. (It should be noted that available sources provide no evidence that the PLA is invited to assist in making this political judgment.)

Strengthening Social Intelligence and Advance Warning.

Anti-unrest strategies stress that to prevent protest, Public Security Departments—especially their Domestic Security Protection (*guonei anquan baowei*) units—and State Security Departments are expected to strengthen their monitoring and analysis of social contradictions and those social actors who are most likely to take advantage of these problems to foment dissent. Security experts writing about China's Western ethnic minority regions have for at least several years noted the need to strengthen monitoring, infiltration, and recruitment of sources within Buddhist temples, mosques, and other religious facilities.[22]

Forecasting and preventing social protest and controlling ethnic minority unrest have in recent years become an increasingly important focus of the Public Security system's Domestic Security Protection units. For example, in the training courses on domestic security work within its Investigation Department, China's People's Public Security University emphasizes intelligence work in handling "mass incidents" and "petition" cases, and offers an entire course on "Nationalities Security" work (*minzu baowei*).[23] There are also some hints that as part of their internal security mission, PLA intelligence units are expected to play a role in helping Public Security units gather electronic and other intelligence regarding protestors and protest organizers; one internal police manual on unrest, in its section on "perfecting an intelligence and information work responsibility system," calls on public security units to ". . . tighten coordination and cooperate with State Security and Military (*jundui*) and other political-legal departments, promptly exchange intelligence and information, and create cooperation on intelligence and information exchange work."[24]

Tight Party Committee Control over Police Use of Coercion, Weapons, and Deadly Force.

Official police directives and training materials for handling unrest lay special stress on the need for security departments to accept the "absolute, unified, unconditional" leadership of local Communist Party and government officials in handling protests. With regard to anti-protest and anti-riot work, this leadership is officially expected to be very detailed. Police forces are called upon to seek local Party and government permission before taking any crucial measures in responding to unrest, and they keep Party and government leaders closely apprised of their actions. Among the key aspects of their protest response activities for which local security departments are expected to obtain local Party and government approval or leadership are their unrest contingency plans, which spell out rules of engagement for deployment of security forces and the use of force. Local Party and/or government leaders are also expected to establish "command organs" at the scene to coordinate interagency anti-protest operations. Police are also supposed to obtain both local Party/government and superior-level police authorization for mobilizing police in riot gear. When police believe noncoercive control measures have failed and a protest risks serious threat to social stability or national security, they must seek permission from the "superior managing department" before employing such nonlethal weaponry as water cannons and batons, and may only employ violence, including deadly force, "under the unified leadership and unified command" of the local Party Committee and government.[26]

Concerning the use of deadly force, recent statements by some senior provincial police officials strongly suggest that official rules of engagement may have quietly moved toward a still more cautious standard or even an official ban on firing at crowds of protestors. No evidence is available that could tell us whether or not any such directive against firing at crowds also applied to public security and PAP in Tibet. But to date, setting rules on public security and PAP using guns in the line of duty has been the prerogative of Central-level political-legal leaders, not individual provincial police chiefs. Thus, references to tougher rules by one provincial police chief may well reflect changes in national-level regulations that have simply not yet been made public.[27]

Protests and riots in ethnic and religious minority regions, such as occurred in Lhasa, are explicitly seen by security officials as politically particularly sensitive incidents for which special bureaucratic procedures are advised to ensure that local Party, local government, superior level police, and CCP United Front Work departments are consulted and permission for response is sought. Indeed, the formal procedures suggested by some public security anti-protest manuals, if observed literally, would seem to risk becoming a recipe for delayed response and possibly even paralysis. Quoting from one manual, it advises police handling these cases:

> Regarding rioting incidents (*saoluan shijian*) that affect the unity of the motherland, as public security organs are handling (*chuzhi*) them, they should—at the same

time that they are seeking instructions (*qingshi*) from their Party Committee and government and upper level concerned departments—also strengthen their contacts with United Front Work departments, and jointly research the policy responses to use, and how to handle and pacify the incident of rioting.[28]

These aspects of official anti-protest strategy provide us a useful set of ideals or a yardstick for measuring how the public security and PAP forces were expected to perform. Thus, they can help us generate questions that we can use to spotlight and evaluate the missions/tasks that they failed to perform well, and the areas in which they did not perform as badly.

LOSING CONTROL IN LHASA AND THE QUESTION OF PLA INVOLVEMENT

Failures of Intelligence, Social Analysis, and Rapid Warning.

Any analysis of why Lhasa officials lost control on March 14 begins with the crucial failure of public security intelligence and early warning around the Ramoche Temple. In an April 9 interview, Tibet Autonomous Region (TAR) Government Chairman Qiangba Puncog essentially admitted that security forces were caught off-guard and unprepared for a variety of protests that sprung up in several different parts of Lhasa and its suburbs, sometimes simultaneously, during the week of March 10-15.[29]

The best available press sources indicate that public security and PAP forces, not PLA, handled the first several days of protests. These began on Monday, March 10—the 49th anniversary of the uprising against Chinese rule—with a large protest by 300-400 monks from the Drepung monastery and a much smaller protest by fewer than two dozen monks from the Sera monastery. Police detention of all or most of the Sera monks sparked a much larger protest on Tuesday by perhaps 500 to 600 monks who shouted for their fellow monks' release and later began chanting for independence.[30] Public Security and PAP forces reportedly dispersed these crowds by firing tear gas.[31] Wednesday, police had reportedly surrounded and sealed off the Drepung and Sera (and perhaps the Ganden) monasteries to prevent more marches, and had entered the monasteries, where they engaged in aggressive room searches and other activities, according to BBC and other reports.[32]

The lockdown and the passage of the anniversary may have misled authorities into believing that the worst of the protests was passed, and by Thursday government officials claimed Lhasa had been "stabilised."[33] In any event, by Friday morning police were so focused on preventing further marches and protests originating from the three monasteries outside Central Tibet that their forces were unprepared and out of position to respond quickly and effectively when protests, scuffles, and then rioting broke out near the Ramoche Temple shortly after noon.[34]

Some foreign press and academic sources report that the unrest began when a group of monks attempted to launch a protest and possibly threw stones at police outside the temple.[35] This version, if accurate, would indicate that despite security officials' efforts at surveillance and infiltration of the temples, they were unaware of the monks' plans and ill-prepared to respond quickly with adequate police personnel. Some Western journalists also cite Tibetan claims that the unrest began when local crowds attacked Chinese security officials for beating two monks on a side street near the temple, a version which, if true, indicates a failure of police discipline and restraint as well as early warning.[36] Columbia Tibetologist Robert Barnett, after careful efforts to document the Spring unrest through foreign and Tibetan sources, endorses the view that the monks did attempt to carry out a demonstration.

> At around midday on Friday, March 14, 4 days after the initial Lhasa protest, a small group of monks at Ramoche . . . set out from their compound to start a small protest march. They were soon stopped by police in a minor confrontation — which appears to have been exacerbated by Tibetans' anger at the presence of plainclothes police in the crowd. Unlike the great monasteries, Ramoche is in the heart of Lhasa, and opens onto a busy market street in one of the few areas of the city that remains a largely Tibetan quarter. Members of the public, apparently aroused by rumors that monks detained that Monday had been beaten in custody, began to attack the police and a small squad of PAP sent in to support them. The police and soldiers were pelted with stones, their cars were burned, and, pursued by a group of stone-throwing youths, they fled. No reinforcements were sent into the area for at least 3 hours (one Western journalist who witnessed the events saw no police for 24 hours), though they were waiting on the outskirts. [37]

Whatever the actual sparking event, police badly misjudged the Tibetan crowds' latent anger and the speed with which they would seize on a brief loss of control by police to turn violently against Han and Hui merchants. But, as journalist James Miles, who observed the protests, pointedly observed, "Ethnic Chinese shopkeepers in Lhasa's old Tibetan district knew better than the security forces that the city had become a tinder box. As word spread rapidly through the narrow alleyways on March 14th that a crowd was throwing stones at Chinese businesses, they shuttered up their shops and fled."[38]

James Miles' later reconstruction of events in the first 2 hours between the outbreak of the protest (around 11:30 a.m.) and 1:15-1:30 p.m. indicates that the protest burst forth from the immediate Ramoche neighborhood into a riot much more slowly than was originally reported. Police were especially slow to deploy reinforcements to the narrow alleyways near the Ramoche temple, where protests might have been bottled up more quickly. Miles has in recent months considered seriously the possibility that this delay and loss of control may have been a deliberate effort by local officials to justify a serious clampdown in advance of the Olympics and the Torch Relay.[39] My inclination is to attribute this slow response to the inadequate overall numbers of security forces per capita in the Lhasa area, and their serious misdeployment around the in-town monasteries on Friday morning, an interpretation supported by some foreign press and Chinese legal sources.[40] These deployments seem to have undercut these forces' ability to adequately reinforce their colleagues outside the Ramoche temple when rioting broke out. Unfortunately, official figures on the total number of public security and PAP deployed to Tibet are more closely guarded than most Chinese provinces, and also do not reflect the PLA troop presence in the region.[41] TAR budgetary data and police personnel data from surrounding ethnic minority provinces are at least consistent with the thesis that personnel numbers may have been an issue. The TAR reports the lowest total expenditure on law enforcement (2006: 882,340,000 yuan[42]) and the fourth-lowest provincial-level expenditures for PAP of any provincial-level unit in China (2006: 57,490,000 yuan; Qinghai, Guizhou, and Gansu are lower[43]), although it is unclear if these figures reflect any financial subsidies from Beijing, which many experts believe to be substantial. Western rural minority provinces other than Tibet also report some of the lowest police-per-citizen ratios in China, ranging from 6.8 officers per 10,000 in Sichuan (2004) down to just one officer per 10,000 in Ningxia (2006).[44] A Taiwan study of the PAP, whose data cannot be independently confirmed, reports Tibet has 9-10 PAP Internal Guards *zhidui*, which, assuming an average personnel of between 600 and 1,400 troops per *zhidui*, would yield a total internal guards force of between 5,400 and 14,000 internal guards forces for the entire TAR.[45]

Police reinforcements were soon overwhelmed and withdrew, and control of the area outside the Ramoche temple was quickly lost to the rioters. "Riot police . . ." reports the *New York Times*' Jim Yardley, "fled after an initial skirmish and then were nowhere to be found."[46] Rioters targeted Han and Muslim (Hui) businesses for stoning, looting, destruction, and arson, but marked shops known to be Tibetan-owned with white scarves.[47] For the next several hours, Miles reports government and police authorities seemed "paralyzed by indecision," and he "didn't see any attempt . . . to intervene." Instead, Miles reports they seemed to "let the rioting run its course, and it didn't really finish as far as I saw until the middle of the day on the following day."[48]

As to why police took so long to suppress the riots, the answer must for now be more speculative. In his earlier writing on the riot, Miles concluded that this was a conscious decision by authorities to "let the rioting run its course" for fear "that bloodshed would ensue" if they moved in immediately. This fear, Miles argued, was driven by worries of creating a violent bloody image in the run-up to the Olympics.[49] However, such a decision, if true, would be remarkable and would contradict all known official strategies for handling unrest that descends into "beating, smashing, burning, and looting," and in response to which Party, government, and security authorities are expected to authorize security forces to "decisively handle" the violence and quickly restore order.

Another contributing factor might be that the cautiously structured decisionmaking system for authorizing police to use weapons and violent tactics — designed to preserve local and superior-level Party control — failed in responding to a rapidly developing riot. Eyewitness and photographic evidence make clear that many police remained on the scene as the riot took off, but made no serious effort to put down the rioters until at least nightfall. One famous photo shows a police line in an alleyway crouching defensively behind their shields with a shower of bricks on the ground in front of them. Several Chinese security and military experts, interviewed shortly following the riots, noted pointedly that the briefings they received and the pictures they saw of public security and PAP forces during the riot, indicated "paralysis and passivity" to them, and they concluded the police had not received the necessary orders to respond more aggressively to the violence.[50]

TAR Party Secretary Zhang Qingli, Government Chairman Qiangba Puncog, and several other senior TAR officials whose authorization for police to use violence or even deadly force would have been, if not necessary, at least politically prudent, were all in Beijing for the National People's Congress and Chinese People's Political Consultative Congress session. One press report even noted Zhang was holding a press conference at or about the hour when the riot broke out.[51] Police may have been unable to get appropriate authorization or strong orders to respond more decisively from high-ranking Party and government authorities. Some Chinese interviewees who received official briefings on the riots have even speculated that because Tibet was, famously, General Secretary Hu's former province, the ranking Tibetan officials in Beijing may have felt wary about authorizing the use of force without first consulting Hu.[52]

PAP and public security established a perimeter around the Tibetan quarter, and not until late Friday night or early Saturday morning did they move in and begin retaking control of the city gradually.[53] Firefighters, escorted by a small number of armored personnel carriers (APCs) filled with armed security forces (no photographic evidence supports the widely reported assertion that tanks were used) moved cautiously into the Tibetan quarter to extinguish the fires. While the PAP possesses its own APCs, we can speculate that these escorts may have represented the earliest PLA involvement in the operation.[54] Witnesses report having seen the security forces who retook the city employ water cannons, tear gas, batons, and beatings, etc., according to witnesses cited by Western journalists. TAR Government Chairman Qiangba Puncog, speaking at a March 17 press conference in Beijing, admitted that security forces had used high-pressure fire hoses, armored vehicles, and unspecified "other special equipment" in these operations.[55]

How much live fire was used and by what units remains a major sticking point. While numerous sources, including U.S. citizens cited by the Embassy, reported hearing sporadic single-shot gunfire, Chinese government sources (including Qiangba Puncog) disagreed strongly with Tibetan exile authorities over whether and how much security forces opened fire on protestors and rioters during this time. Tibetan exile authorities claimed Chinese officials shot and killed 80 Tibetans. Qiangba Puncog countered "with all responsibility that we did not use lethal weapons, including opening fire." Xinhua, in one of its first reports after the riots, similarly claimed "Sources told Xinhua that policemen were ordered not to use force against the attacker. But they were forced to use a limited amount of tear gas and fired warning shots to disperse the desperate crowds."[56] Some well-informed western analysts have also concluded the security forces were under orders not to open fire, while others stress the lack of reliable eyewitnesses to such fire.[57] Nevertheless, experienced sources including Miles and others report hearing periodic individual shots, though Miles does not report having witnessed any killings, and he has stated his belief that these were probably warning shots. No other Western visitors to Lhasa report witnessing these shootings, either. [58] The New York Times' Jim Yardley as part of his careful reconstruction of events, however, cites a Tibetan teen who reported by phone having seen armed police shoot "four or five" Tibetans.[59] Several days later public security officials in Sichuan admitted that they had shot and wounded four protestors as part of putting down protests there, but made no similar admission regarding Lhasa.[60]

Miles notes that by dawn the Tibetan area had been sealed off, and officers had secured the square in front of the Jokhang temple.[61]   Security forces advanced slowly into the quarter during the morning, periodically launching tear gas, in some cases against stone-throwing crowds, and Miles reported hearing "persistent rumors" of small-scale struggles between security forces and rioters. Miles noted that in contrast to Tiananmen in 1989 — an event he also witnessed — he did not hear any "repeated bursts of machine gun fire."[62]

Evaluating Reports of the PLA's Involvement.

Although witnesses have compared the situation in Lhasa to martial law, neither the State Council nor Tibetan regional officials chose to declare martial law in response to the protests and rioting, nor is there evidence to suggest that they activated the provisions in the MLL that can authorize the mobilization of the PLA without declaring martial law. Such legal authority would have provided both a formal process for activating PLA forces and possibly triggered the creation of a distinct PLA command structure within a martial law command structure. As it is, it is unclear how and by what structure PLA forces involved in the post-riot operations were commanded and their work coordinated with civilian and PAP security and civil affairs officials.

Chinese officials initially denied that PLA forces were being used to put down protests or to support the anti-riot police who carried out that mission. Qiangba Puncog on March 17 repeated this claim, and reported that the first PLA involvement was in clean-up work beginning on Sunday and Monday.[63]   According to

Edward Cody of the *Washington Post*, as late as April 13, neither the Ministry of National Defense nor China's civilian security ministries would respond to journalists questions about whether or how PLA forces were deployed in Lhasa or elsewhere in Tibet. A Ministry of Foreign Affairs (MFA) spokesman stated that no PLA soldiers were deployed in the city of Lhasa, but would not comment on PLA deployments elsewhere in the TAR. [64]

Western journalists continued to report the use of what they believed to be PLA forces in Lhasa with their identifying insignia removed or covered up. [65] By Monday, March 17, the *South China Morning Post* reported the spread of the riots and protests to Sichuan and Qinghai, and indicated that "thousands" of PLA were moving into these regions to help restore order and arrest protest leaders.[66] "Lhasa is now occupied by thousands of paramilitary police officers and troops of the People's Liberation Army," reported the New York Times a few days later, and it cited reports of both military convoys and PAP units streaming westward—apparently from Chengdu, Lanzhou, and other locations—to help confront unrest in other parts of Tibet, Gansu, Qinghai, and China's Muslim Regions.[67]

LOGISTICAL SUPPORT, TRAFFIC CONTROL, AND PUBLIC SAFETY

Probably the missions for which claims of PLA involvement are most credible and for which available information (including photos) provides the strongest support (or at least, cannot provide firm refutation) are logistical support tasks. These include assisting with clean up, providing transport, and ferrying PAP and PSB forces in armored vehicles through the more dangerous sections of Lhasa.[68]

Among the other tasks in which reports of PLA involvement seem more credible was "traffic control," including securing roads to the major monasteries outside of Lhasa and controlling access to the riot-torn areas. Miles notes that he personally encountered large numbers of "troops" along these roads, many armed with bayonets, and reports that many of these forces and others situated at checkpoints displayed no insignia of any kind.[69] When he inquired about their affiliation, rather than claiming to be PAP or Public Security forces or providing any other cover story, they were unwilling to identify whether they were police or military. From this he concludes that "the army is almost certainly playing a big part in the city's clampdown . . ."[70]

Finally, PLA medical units played an important role in treating civilian and noncivilian victims of the violence. Xinhua credited "police," not PLA soldiers, with rescuing 580 people from fires and other danger during the riots, although it noted that at least several of these victims were treated in the Tibet Military Command Hospital.[71]

THE QUESTION OF PLA INVOLVEMENT IN RIOT SUPPRESSION

A few widely-read sources have spotlighted PLA involvement in the "crackdown" in a manner that raises the question of whether PLA forces were directly involved in the actual suppression of rioters on the night of March 14 or on March 15. The Students for a Free Tibet blog, citing Kanwa, spotlights the "cover-up" and notes that "some of the ground forces deployed in Lhasa during the crackdown of the last few days were elite squads from the People's Liberation Army," refuting the Chinese government's strenuous denial that it was "sending the People's Liberation Army to deal with the Tibetan protests."[72] The Voice of America (VOA) reported on March 22 that unsourced "[r]eports from China say Beijing has sent elite units of the People's Liberation Army into Tibet to crack down on the protests" without further comment or explanation concerning what "crack down on the protests" meant.[73] A March 15 Australian Broadcasting Corporation report noted that "A Chinese resident of Lhasa, speaking to AFP by phone who declined to let his name be used, said there were tanks and armoured personnel carriers in the streets on Saturday morning. 'There are many armed police, special police, and People's Liberation Army soldiers everywhere,' he said."[74]

For the record, this attention to the PLA's role is not only a reflection of the army's role in Tiananmen, but also owes much to the government's own seemingly blanket statements that later required amendment or significant parsing.[75] TAR Government Chairman Qiangba Puncog flatly stated in his March 17 news conference that the PLA was not involved in the actual quelling of the protests.[76] Foreign Ministry Spokesman Liu Jianchao flatly stated that "The PLA is not involved in the handling of the incidents . . . Their entering Tibet now is mainly to handle losses from the incidents."[77] Immediately after the riots broke out, General Yang Deqing, Political Commissar of the Guangdong Military Region (MR), told Western reporters at the National People's Congress (NPC) that "We'll let the police and the military police handle the disturbance. . . . We (the PLA) won't be involved." [78]

The reports by Students for a Free Tibet (SFT) and International Campaign for Tibet (ICT) both cite only one source—a widely-cited March 21 report by Kanwa Defense Review Editor-in-Chief Andrei Chang.[79] Chang asserts that "Elite ground force units of the People's Liberation Army were involved in China's recent crackdown on Tibetan protesters in Lhasa" and that these forces' equipment "appeared on the streets of Lhasa the same day the crackdown began." He notes somewhat accusatorily that "China has denied the participation of the army in the crackdown, saying it was carried out by units of the armed police."[80]

While Chang's analysis contains no footnotes or source citations, it clearly seems to rest upon the author's deductive analysis of photographic and video images taken in Lhasa on the first days after the riot (widely available on the internet), as well as the author's assertions concerning the availability or nonavailability of certain types of vehicles and uniforms to various PLA and PAP units.[81] Chang notes "the new T-90 armored personnel carrier and T-92 wheeled armored vehicles belonging to the elite ground forces" are widely visible in photos from the Lhasa streets, and that "Only a very small number of the PLA's group armies are armed with T-90 APCs, while the T-92s are used by its rapid reaction force units. The T-92s deployed in Lhasa are equipped with 25-mm guns. The export variant of this vehicle is called the WMZ-551A." "Such equipment as mentioned above . . ." notes Chang, ". . . has never been deployed by China's armed police." In a July 2, analysis, Chang also notes as an indicator that these troops are the elite PLA units he believes, that "the People's Liberation Army soldiers on the T-90/89 vehicles on the streets of Lhasa were all wearing the 'leopard' camouflage uniforms specifically designed for mountain warfare operations. These uniforms have appeared in video footage of the 149th Division during exercises."[82] Chang also notes, as did many analysts, that identification numbers and license plates on many of these APCs and armored vehicles have been covered with newspaper or cloth, and that no insignia or PLA red stars are visible on the helmets and uniforms of the security forces he has observed. He states without qualification that this was done "to cover up the involvement of regular armed forces in the crackdown."[83] Based on this evidence, Chang concludes specifically that "the 149th Rapid Reaction Division of the No. 13 Group Army under Chengdu Military Region and the No. 52 Mountain Infantry Brigade under the Xizang Military Region may have been involved in the crackdown operations."[84]

Several points can be made about this analysis. First — and most important — nowhere in these analyses does Chang make any assertion that as part of their "crackdown operations" these alleged PLA units actually took part in the suppression. Indeed, aside from touting their involvement in the "crackdown," Chang says nothing about what the troops' mission and duties are.

A great deal of Chang's analysis turns on his strong empirical assertion that only a few PLA units — and no PAP units at all — have received the particular versions of the Type 90/89 APCs and Type 92/WMZ551A wheeled infantry fighting vehicles observed in Lhasa — a claim for which Chang provides no source. But the present author has seen recent photographic evidence that — while not conclusively refuting Chang's assertion — raises serious questions about it: Photos of a PAP compound in Qinghai—admittedly taken about six months *after* the Lhasa riot, not before—that clearly show at least one dozen PAP-marked six-wheeled Type 92/WMZ551 vehicles very similar to those used in the Lhasa operations. Photos proving that PAP in Lhasa have their own four-wheeled white and camouflage versions of the T92 and perhaps the T90 tracked vehicle have long been available on the web.[85]

Even so, while it may well be that these APCs belong to the PLA units Chang suggests, this does not necessarily mean that the forces being ferried about in them are of the same unit. In one of the more widely-published March 15 photos of these security forces (showing 3-4 APCs and about two dozen security force members at a large, multilane "T" intersection), at least some of the officers sitting in the APCs have insignia on their caps which, though not completely clear, are discernibly PAP insignia and not PLA. Some others are clearly wearing uniforms in the darker olive PAP green.[86]

Likewise, Chang treats the type of mountain operations camouflage as an additional piece of proof that these are specific PLA units and not PAP. But photographs showing clearly identifiable PAP personnel wearing this same style of camouflage have been published by official Chinese press sources.[87] Other internet sources, including Chinese military enthusiast bulletin boards, assert that PAP forces in the provinces of the Lanzhou and Chengdu Military Regions, especially those in Tibet, have received the same type of camouflage for mountainous, barren areas as the PLA forces in this region.[88]

While all PLA and police analysts at some level share Chang's suspicions regarding the covering of unit and license plate numbers on trucks and APCs, as well as the absence of either PLA red stars or PAP state seals or other insignia on helmets and uniforms, this is still insufficient evidence from which to conclude, with the certainty Chang does, which security forces may or may not be PLA and PAP. More importantly, this information still tells us little about the precise missions and roles PLA or PAP may have undertaken in Lhasa, and in particular does not support any implication that PLA forces were directly involved in the suppression operations.

The timing of exactly *when* many of these PLA forces were on the streets of Lhasa may be a more significant indicator of *how* they were involved in these operations than the types of vehicles and uniforms, etc. Both official Chinese and foreign press sources concur that within about 18 to 24 hours after the outbreak of the riot—that is, by about Saturday noon—the rioters had overwhelmingly already been suppressed, and Lhasa had returned to a tense calm, with some Han and Hui shopkeepers returning to survey the conditions of their stores. This timetable suggests that the later the PLA forces first appeared on the streets after that 18- to 24-hour window, the less likely it is that they actually took part in the violent suppression of the rioting. For now, we can conclude that some assertions of the Kanwa reports (and the many press and NGO reports that hinge on them) are plausible, but other appear to be based on faulty assumptions or simply cannot be confirmed to the high level of confidence conveyed in the Kanwa research, and overall they tell us little about the pivotal question of how the PLA was involved in the Lhasa operations.

There is also no evidence that PLA forces played any role in the subsequent mass arrests and interrogations of demonstrators beyond possibly helping to secure main streets in dangerous neighborhoods to deter any large-scale resistance against the detentions. To avoid exacerbating popular anger, Public Security units are now urged to avoid arresting protest leaders on the scene, but to collect evidence for subsequent prosecution and quietly detain the organizers later. On Saturday, March 15, TAR officials called on all rioters who had broken the law to turn themselves in to authorities by midnight on March 17, offering that those who did might get more lenient sentences, while those who resisted faced severe punishment.[89] By March 20, authorities reported that 170 persons had surrendered voluntarily, and 24 had been arrested for a variety of state security-related crimes.[90] By April 9, TAR Government Chairman Qiangba Puncog noted specifically that the Public Security organs had already detained 953 persons suspected of engaging in "beating, smashing, burning, and looting," of whom 403 had been formally placed under arrest by procurators.[91] Later official reports put the number of detainees at more than 1,000.[92] As we would expect, there is also no evidence that PLA forces were involved in the collection of "evidence" security officials used to investigate the origins of the protests and the alleged role of the Dalai Lama's supporters. Public security and PAP officers were themselves caught on tape extensively videotaping those who took part in the unrest.[93] Authorities also relied heavily on oral confessions by detainees in determining the causes of the demonstrations, according to comments by Qiangba Puncog.[94]

Post-Riot Information and Intelligence Operations.

A final possible aspect of China's security operations in Tibet that may have been either a PLA or a civilian mission concerned cyber attacks and intelligence collection from overseas human rights groups monitoring and reporting on Chinese suppression activities. In the week following the protests, a number of pro-Tibet and human rights organizations — including Human Rights in China, Students for a Free Tibet, and Tibet Support Network — reported being the targets of cyber attacks designed to disrupt their work and steal information about their contacts and supporters. Computer security experts familiar with the attacks were unable to definitively trace the attacks either to the PLA or other Chinese agencies such as the Ministry of State Security (MSS), so any PLA or MSS role in this also remains speculative.[95]

CONCLUSIONS AND IMPLICATIONS FOR THE UNITED STATES

Twenty years after the PLA cleared Tiananmen Square, being prepared to act as the last line of defense for the Party's hold on power, its social control, and its guarantee of China's ethnic and territorial unity remains one of the most important missions of the PLA. This point is regularly restated in national laws, white papers, major leadership speeches, and other authoritative policy documents. Authoritative training materials note that at least some of the ground forces are expected to train for this mission, though we do not know which forces, how they will train, and how often.

Still, to a great degree, defending the Party's hold on power against Chinese society remains the PLA's "mission that dare not speak its name." With just a few rare and still rather ill-defined exceptions, such as the Martial Law Law, the targets, specific objectives, and authorized tactics of a PLA mission to suppress social disorder are rarely discussed in authoritative public documents. These documents, moreover, often use vague language that fails to distinguish between the roles that are specific to the PLA and those that would be born by China's other "armed forces," or they include legal and institutional qualifiers that implicitly make it very clear that the Party, state, and the PLA would all strongly prefer that the PLA remain a distant third and final line of defense for the Party-state. Their sincere hope is that before the army is asked to fulfill this mission, the Party-state's other security forces will continue to successfully carry that mission out for them (although, PLA intelligence involvement may be an exception here).

For this reason, scholars of the PLA and its domestic security mission need to devote more attention to the details of the relationship between the PLA and the civilian and paramilitary security organs whose own mission is, in part, to permit the PLA not to perform part of its internal security mission. This chapter notes that over the past 20 years the evidence strongly suggests that the Public Security, State Security, and PAP forces have, for all their failures, apparently spared the PLA much direct involvement in this mission.

But this chapter also argues that there are aspects of the new internal security strategy that have been going into place for almost the past decade that may somewhat increase the risk that incidents of unrest could grow out of control. The burdens the new strategy places on excellent intelligence and early warning; disciplined, low violence police work; and decisive, quick political responses by local and provincial Party authorities are complex and heavy.

Using a cursory case study of critical loss of control during the Lhasa riot (and much more needs to be known about this case), this chapter has tried to demonstrate some ways in which this system might break down or lapse into a brief but crucial political paralysis. In Lhasa, this admittedly occurred under unusual circumstances that played straight into the system's weaknesses—most notably the absence of much of the local Party elite in Beijing—and may be unlikely to occur again in similar fashion. At the same time, the massive resonant upsurge in Tibetan and Muslim protests and violence that quickly followed the March 14 Lhasa riots demonstrates clearly that Chinese authorities once again badly underestimated the latent ethno-religious anger seething in China's western regions even after years of "develop the West" and other policy initiatives. Without question, similar uprisings and loss of control are by no means impossible, and indeed seem likely. Under these circumstances, local officials may once again find themselves needing to call for back-up units, including units of the PLA, to help play the many roles and missions involved in restoring order. It will probably come as some relief to the PLA that, so far as we can tell from the best available open source data, there appears to be no solid evidence that the PLA's role in the Lhasa operation included active involvement in the violent suppression of rioters and protestors and appears to have been limited primarily to support roles, probably including securing major thoroughfares into and through the city. But the PLA/PAP operational security actions of obscuring/

covering up identifiers on APCs and uniforms means that there is still much we do not know for sure about this important case. Western analysts of the PLA need to keep digging to try to clarify exactly how it interacted with front and second line security forces in responding to this unrest. In particular, as information becomes available, we need to focus on the "lessons" the PLA feels it learned about its own internal security role, its relationship to public security and PAP forces in incidents of this type, and why the front and second lines of internal security buckled, however briefly, in Lhasa, leading to a need to draw on PLA support.

The degree to which the PLA can confidently continue to keep its distance from Lhasa-style (or more severe) internal security operations will, of course, have at least a moderate impact on its capacity to redirect its attention, forces, and resources toward the long and expensive list of new missions discussed in the other chapters of this book. It is also certainly an important factor in the state of Party-PLA relations. From the U.S. perspective, these are two of the greatest implications of the question of how much attention the PLA must devote to its internal security role. Lhasa does not appear to have tied up large amounts of PLA resources for any length of time, and one would have to imagine a far greater increase in social unrest, with greater loss of control by front and second line security forces, for social unrest to have a major impact on, say, the Party's willingness to allow the PLA to refocus personnel and resources away from the ground forces where they are presently available as a backup force for social unrest toward more high-tech air and naval forces. At the same time, the recent issuance of new PLA training materials for handling unrest, counterterrorism, disaster relief, and other domestic stability and safety missions is hardly a vote of confidence by the Party-state or the PLA that front and second line civilian and paramilitary security forces will always be able to spare the PLA from having to engage in its least favorite "historic mission."

CHAPTER 3 - ENDNOTES

1. By this, I mean primarily the public security, state security, and the People's Armed Police forces, but also the entire criminal justice system including the courts, procuracy, and prison system.

2. Even the most detailed scholarly analyses of the PLA and Civil-Military and Party-Military relations have not uncovered many materials discussing the internal security mission in great detail. A few studies have directly and briefly addressed the issue of the PLA internal mission, noting the PLA's refocus on external missions since Tiananmen, as well as efforts to enshrine the PLA/PAP internal security mission in law. A short but particularly clear characterization of the PLA's declining focus on its internal mission is David Shambaugh, *Modernizing China's Military: Progress, Problems, and Prospects*, Berkeley, CA, University of California Press, 2002, esp. pp. 12-14; See also James Mulvenon, "China: Conditional Compliance" in Muthiah Alagappa, ed., *Coercion and Governance: The Declining Political Role of the Military in Asia*, Stanford, CA: Stanford University Press, 2001, pp. 317-335; and Thomas Bickford, "A Retrospective on the Study of Chinese Civil-Military Relations Since 1979: What Have We Learned? Where Do We Go?," in James Mulvenon and Andrew N. D. Yang, eds., *Seeking Truth From Facts: A Retrospective on Chinese Military Studies in the Post Mao-Era*, Santa Monica, CA, RAND Corporation, 2001, pp. 1-38; Andrew Scobell "The Meaning of Martial Law for the PLA and Internal Security in China After Deng," in James C. Mulvenon and Andrew N. D. Yang, eds., *A Poverty of Riches: New Challenges and Opportunities in PLA Research*, Santa Monica, RAND, 2003, pp. 169-191; and Dennis Blasko, *The Chinese Army Today: Tradition and Transformation for the 21st Century*, London and New York, Routledge, 2006, pp. 156-158. On the reorganization of the PAP to strengthen its internal security role, see Shambaugh,

Modernizing China's Military, pp. 170-173; also Dennis J. Blasko and John F. Corbett, Jr., "No More Tiananmens: The People's Armed Police and Stability in China, 1997," *China Strategic Review*, Spring 1998; Andrew Scobell and Brad Hammet, "Goons, Gunmen and Gendarmerie: Toward A Reconceptualization of Paramilitary Formations," *Journal of Political and Military Sociology*, Volume 26, No. 2, Winter 1998, pp. 213-227; Tai Ming Cheung, "Guarding China's Domestic Front Line: The People's Armed Police and China's Stability," *China Quarterly*, June 1996, pp. 525-547; and Murray Scot Tanner, "The Institutional Lessons of Disaster: Reorganizing China's People's Armed Police After Tiananmen," in James Mulvenon, ed., *The People's Liberation Army as Organization*, Washington, DC, RAND Corporation, 2002, pp. 587-635.

3. Dennis Blasko and John Corbett, in their excellent 1998 article on the People's Armed Police, note one of the most powerful public assertions of the PLA's desire to avoid ever again carrying out such a mission:

> Perhaps the most significant reference to the reluctance of the PLA to become involved in domestic security operations was made about 6 months earlier by Defense Minister Chi Haotian during the question and answer period after his speech at the U.S. National Defense University on 10 December 1996. The U.S. media that covered this event focused on Chi's unrepentant reiteration of the Party line defending the need to use deadly force - "So finally we had to adopt corresponding measures to disperse these people."[i] However, little editorial or critical mention was made of the words soon to follow - "I can also tell you here that such things will not happen again." (Emphasis added.) To a listener not surprised at hearing a senior Party official retell the same old, discredited story about Tiananmen, what Chi said sounded much like a promise not to use the PLA again in domestic stability operations. As an old soldier, General Chi understands the nuances that differentiate between combat against foreign enemies and operations to control a civilian disturbance.

Dennis J. Blasko and John F. Corbett, Jr., "No More Tiananmens: The People's Armed Police and Stability in China, 1997," *China Strategic Review*, Spring 1998, pp. 88-89.

4. Scobell and Hammet, "Goons, Gunmen and Gendarmerie," pp. 213-227.

5. Blasko and Corbett, "No More Tiananmens."

6. See, for example, Wang Mingwu *et al.*, *Feizhanzheng Junshi Xingdong* (*Noncombat Military Operations*), Beijing, China: Guofang Daxue Chubanshe, 2006; by comparison, see Yuan Jingwei, *Kongtian Yiti Zuozhan Yanjiu* (*Studies on Integrated Aerospace Combat*), Beijing, China: Guofang Daxue Chubanshe, 2006.

7. For an analysis of the Martial Law Law's content and background and the historical role of Martial Law in China, see Andrew Scobell's essay "The Meaning of Martial Law for the PLA and Internal Security in China After Deng," in James C. Mulvenon and Andrew N. D. Yang, eds., *A Poverty of Riches: New Challenges and Opportunities in PLA Research*, Santa Monica, RAND, 2003, pp. 169-191.

8. Article 10: Martial law enforcment institutions shall establish martial law command organs, which shall coordinate and enforce operations related to martial law enforcement, and implement martial law measures under a unified plan. PLA units enforcing martial law are commanded by a military institution designated by the CMC under a unified plan of the martial law command organs.

9. Article 3: To stop armed subversion and safeguard social stability. China's Constitution and laws prohibit any organization or individual from organizing, plotting or carrying out armed rebellion or riot to subvert the state power or overthrow the socialist system. China opposes all forms of terrorism, separatism, and extremism. Regarding maintenance of public order and social stability in accordance with the law as their important duty, the Chinese armed forces will strike hard at terrorist activities of any kind, crush infiltration and sabotaging activities by hostile forces, and crack down on all criminal activities that threaten public order, so as to promote social stability and harmony. Chap 2, p. 4.

10. For his assistance in acquainting me with this source, and for sharing with me his excellent research on the "historic

missions," I am grateful to my CNA colleague, Dan Hartnett. For a series of quotes from Hu's speeches that lay out much of his notion of the historic missions, see "Comrade Hu Jintao's Important Expositions (胡锦涛同志重要论述) at the National Defense Education Universe," *Guofang Jiaoyu Tiandi;* (国防教育天地) of Hebei province's Dongming National Defense Education Institute, *Dongming Guofang Jiaoyu Xuexiao;* 东明国防教育学校, *dongming.w187.bizcn.com/hbll1/zzll/zzll3.htm,* accessed January 2009.

11. Dennis Blasko, *The Chinese Army Today: Tradition and Transformation for the 21st Century*, London and New York, Routledge, 2006, pp. 156-158. (Quotation at p. 158.)

> When possible, anti-terrorist operations us high technology reconnaissance to gather information about the target and then seek to eliminate the terrorists quickly using speed, stealth, and violence while protecting the lives of any hostages or innocent civilians in the area . . . In contrast, anti-riot procedures require much larger formations of troops or police to intimidate rioters or demonstrators overtly by their mass and discipline, preferably without using deadly force.

12. Zhang Baoshu, *Lujun Junshi Xunlian Xue* (*The Study of Ground Forces Military Training*), Beijing, China: Junshi Kexue Chubanshe, 2006, esp. pp. 210-211, 220-225; Wang Mingwu, *et al.* These sources note the issuance of new PLA training materials on noncombat operations in the early 2000s.

13. *Ibid.*, p. 210.

14. *Ibid.*

15. *Ibid.*, p. 220-224.

16. *Ibid.*, p. 222.

17. *Ibid.*

18. *Ibid.*

19. Wang Mingwu, *et al.*, esp. p. 87.

20. I am especially indebted to the research of Andrew Scobell and Thomas Bickford for sensitizing me to these challenges of developing paramilitary forces that can serve a wide array of missions and leadership systems.

21. For an example of police strategies at this time, see the analysis of "prevention" and "handling" of protests and other social order emergencies in Hu Guanwu, *Jinji Zhi'an Shijian yu Duice* (*Emergency Social Order Cases and Countermeasures*), Beijing, China: Zhongguo Renmin Gongan Daxue Chubanshe, 1996, esp. pp. 101-106.

22. Tanner, "Chinese Communist Party Strategies for Containing Unrest."

23. Wang Zhimin, "*Dui xibu dakaifa zhong ruhe weihe shehui wending tiji youzhi fuwu de sikao*" ("Thoughts on How to Maintain Social Stability and Provide Excellent Service in the Process of Developing the West"), Police Science Society of China, ed., *Xibu Dakaifa yu Gongan Gongzuo Lunwenji* (*Collected Essays on Public Security Work in the Great Opening of the Western Regions*), Beijing, China: Chinese People's Public Security University Press, 2002, pp. 251-257.

24. Information obtained by the author from CPPSU course information listings.

25. Xu Nailong, *et al.*, *Quntixing Shijian de Yufang he Chuzhi* (*Preventing and Handling Mass Incidents*), Beijing, China: Chinese People's Public Security University Press, 2003, esp. pp. 111-115. *Quntixing Shijian de Yufang yu Chuzhi*, p. 117.

26. Wang Caiyuan, *Quntixing Zhi'an Shijian*, pp. 85-87, 96-99, 101, 116, 124; Zhang Shengqian, *Zhi'an Shijian Chuzhi*, pp. 63-67; Xu Nailong, *et al.*, *Quntixing Shijian de Yufang he Chuzhi* (*Preventing and Handling Mass Incidents*).

27. In a January 2006 article in the MPS flagship journal, *Gongan Yanjiu*, Guangdong Public Security Bureau Chief Liang Guoju issued the following rather absolute prohibition on firing on mass protestors:

[I]n handling mass incidents, we absolutely must not carry weapons of the type that could wound or slay people, *sha shang xing wuqi*, and at absolutely no time should we open fire on the masses, *renhe shihou buneng xiang qunzhong kai qiang*. This is an iron rule of discipline that public security organs must follow while handling incidents of unrest, *Zhei shi chuli quntixing shijian zhong gongan jiguan wu bi yange zunshou de yi tiao tie de jilu.*

Liang Guoju, "*Guanyu Yufang he Chuzhi Quntixing Shijian de Sikao*" ("Reflections on the Prevention and Handling of Public Order Incidents"), *Gongan Yanjiu* (*Policing Studies*), No. 5, 2006, pp. 9-14.

28. Wang Caiyuan, *Quntixing Zhi'an Shijian Jinji Chuzhi Yaoling* (*Outline of Emergency Handling of Mass Social Order Incidents*), Beijing, China: Zhongguo Renmin Gongan Daxue Chubanshe, 2003, p. 190.

29. Qiangba Puncog (Champa Phuntsog, in the standard Tibetan romanization) chose to interpret these facts as proof positive of a coordinated international conspiracy. Comments by Qiangba Puncog in "State Council Press Office Holds A Press Conference on the Recent Situation in Tibet," April 9, 2008, full text in Chinese at *www.china.com.cn/zhibo/2008-04/09/content_14577761. htm?show=t*; "Life in Lhasa in Returning to Normal," *Ming Pao* Special Report, cited in *Ming Pao* San Francisco, April 9, 2008, *www.mingpaosf.com/htm/News/20080409/st3.h.*

30. Jim Yardley, "Monk Protests in Tibet Draw Chinese Security," *New York Times*, March 14, 2008, at *www.nytimes. com/2008/03/14/world/asia/14china.html?th=&emc=th&pagewante d=print*; "Second day of protests in Lhasa: monks dispersed by tear-gas" International Campaign for Tibet (ICT) report, March 11, 2008.

31. *Ibid.* The ICT March 11 report, citing a Tibetan blog, describes some of the vehicles involved in the response as "military" or "army" vehicles, but in context these could very easily refer to the PAP.

32. "Troops 'Seal Tibet Monasteries'," *BBC World Service*, March 14, 2008, *news.bbc.co.uk/2/hi/asia-pacific/7295753.stm*; Jill Drew, "Tibet Protests Turn Violent, Shops Burn in Lhasa," *The Washington Post*, March 14, 2008, *www.washingtonpost.com/wp-dyn/content/article/2008/03/14/AR2008031401448_pf.html*; also information from discussions with Western experts on China and Tibet, Winter 2008.

33. Jane Macartney, "Riot in Tibet as Chinese Police Clash with Protesters," *Times Online*, March 14, 2008, *www.timesonline. co.uk/tol/news/world/asia/article3551219.ece*; *Ming Pao*, April 10, 2008; Drew.

34. *China Daily*, March 15, 2008, p. 1. Macartney; *Ming Pao*, April 10, 2008.

35. "Troops 'Seal Tibet Monasteries'"; Drew.

36. "Trashing the Beijing Road," *The Economist*, March 19, 2008, at *www.economist.com*.

37. Robert Barnett, "Thunder Out of Tibet," *New York Review of Books*, Vol. 55, No. 9, May 29, 2008, at *www.nybooks.com/ articles/21391*. For another account that tracks very closely with Barnett's, see Drew.

38. "Trashing the Beijing Road."

39. James Miles, "The Illusion of Calm in Tibet," *The Economist*, July 10, 2008, at *www.economist.com/world/asia/displaystory. cfm?story_id=11706247*. The thesis of a deliberate loss of control would seem to require that not only Tibetan and Central leaders be in on the plan, but also that they decided rather quickly to "take advantage" of the sudden outburst near the Ramoche, and also that a considerable number of rank and file police who were sent as reinforcements know this was the goal. This explanation, though certainly possible, seems rather complex to the present author.

40. Interviews, Beijing, China, March and April 2008.

41. I am grateful to June Dreyer for pointing this out, and for a trenchant discussion on this section which, it is hoped, has improved this analysis.

42. *China Statistical Yearbook, 2007,* China Statistics Press, 2008, p. 294. Law enforcement expenditure figures officially include public security, courts, procurators, justice departments, and, according to some sources, state security expenditures. After Tibet, the province with the second lowest law enforcement expenditure is Ningxia with 975,860,000 yuan).

43. *Ibid.*

44. Su Deliang, Ningxia Prov PSB Chief, "*Yi Kexue fazhanguan Tongling Gongan Gongzuo he Duiwu Jianshe . . .,*" *Gongan Yanjiu,* 2006, No. 3, p. 24, gives figure as "6000 plus, yu)." Su claims this is smallest per capita ratio (per 10,000) in entire country, less than 1/20th of some major cities/provinces, even less than one half of some provinces/autonomous regions/cities in China's west. On Sichuan, see *Gongan Yanjiu,* 2004, No. 6, p. 15. Source is Sichuan provincial PSB. Precise figure is for "total police manpower" (*zong jingli*).

45. Li Yingming, ed., *Zhongguo Renmin Wuzhuang Jingcha Dajiegou* (*The Structure of the Chinese People's Armed Police*), Taipei, Taiwan: Yang-Chih Book Co, Ltd., 2003, p. 68. I am indebted to Tom Bickford for drawing on his own excellent PAP research to assist me with generating these rough manpower estimates, though Dr. Bickford is in no way responsible for any inaccuracies.

46. Jim Yardley, "As Tibet Erupted, China Security Forces Wavered," *New York Times*, March 24, 2008.

47. "Transcript: James Miles interview on Tibet," *CNN.com.*

48. *Ibid.*

49. "I think the effort of the authorities this time was to let people let off steam before establishing a very strong presence with troops, with guns, every few yards, all across the Tibetan quarter. It was only when they felt safe I think that there would not be massive bloodshed, that they actually moved in with that decisive force." *Ibid.*

50. Interviews, Chinese security and military officials and experts, Beijing, China, Washington, DC, and Honolulu, HI, 2008.

51. Yardley, "As Tibet Erupted . . ."

52. Interviews, senior Chinese security and foreign policy specialists, 2008.

53. "Transcript: James Miles interview on Tibet," CNN.com:

> It was only during the night at the end of the first day that this cordon was established around the old Tibetan quarter. But even within it, for several hours afterwards, people were still free to continue looting and setting fires, and the authorities were still standing back. And it was only as things fizzled out towards the middle of the second day that as I say they moved in in great numbers.

54. Miles describes the forces in these APC as "riot police." "Trashing the Beijing Road."

55. "Tibet Gripped by Violent Clashes," *The Guardian*, March 14, 2008.

56. "Lhasa Calm after Riot, Traffic Control Imposed," *Xinhua* in English, March 15, 2008.

57. Interviews, Summer 2008.

58. "Transcript: James Miles interview on Tibet"; "Trashing the Beijing Road." Barnett reports that at an indeterminate time on the night of the 14th "Later, the PAP moved in, shooting from time to time, leading to an unknown number of casualties." Robert Barnett, "Thunder Out of Tibet," *New York Review of Books*, Vol. 55, No. 9, May 29, 2008, at *www.nybooks.com/articles/21391*.

59. "Tibet Official Gives Government Account of Unrest," *Reuters*, Beijing, China, March 17, 2008. In the opening statement to his press conference, Qiangba Puncog went a bit further, stating

that "in responding to the incident, our public security officers and armed policemen showed great restraint and performed their duty in accordance with the law and in a civilized manner. *None of them carried or used any lethal weapon in the process.*" "Opening Statement at the Press Conference on the Incident of Beating, Destruction of Property, Looting and Arson in Lhasa by His Excellency Qiangba Puncog . . ." March 17, 2008, at *www.fmprc.gov.cn/ce/ceun/eng/xw/t416058.htm*; James Yardley, "Tibetans Clash with Chinese Police in Second City," *New York Times*, March 16, 2008, *www.NYTimes.com*. According to this report, Tibetan exile government sources reported that they could confirm 30 Tibetans dead with unconfirmed deaths reported as high as 100. Chinese government sources denied that live fire had been used against protestors.

60. Lindsay Beck and Chris Buckley, "China Says its Police Shot Tibetan Protestors," Reuters, March 20, 2008.

61. "Trashing the Beijing Road."

62. Miles reported that:

> authorities chose to move in gradually with troops with rifles . . . they occasionally let off with single shots, apparently warning shots, in order to scare everybody back into their homes and put an end to this . . . I did hear persistent rumors while I was there during this rioting of isolated clashes between the security forces and rioters. And rumors of occasional bloodshed involved in that. But I can do no more really on the basis of what I saw than say there was a probability that some ethnic Chinese were killed in this violence, and also a probability that some Tibetans, Tibetan rioters themselves were killed by members of the security forces. But it's impossible to get the kind of numbers or real first hand evidence necessary to back that up.

"Transcript: James Miles interview on Tibet."

63. "Tibet Official Gives Government Account of Unrest," *Reuters*, March 17, 2008; "Riot Death Toll Raised to 13 as Protests Spread in Tibet," *International Herald Tribune*, March 17, 2008.

64. Edward Cody, "Backstage Role of China's Army in Tibet Unrest Is a Contrast to 1989," *The Washington Post,* April 13, 2008, p. A17.

65. Miles noted "I saw numerous, many military vehicles, military looking vehicles with telltale license plates covered up or removed. And also many troops there whose uniforms were distinctly lacking in the usual insignia of either the police or the riot police. So my very, very strong suspicion is that the army is out there and is in control in Lhasa." *CNN.com* interview transcript.

66. "Tibetan Riots Spread to Provinces; Protesters Torch Police Station; PLA Moves In," Choi Chi-yuk in Lhasa and Agencies, *South China Morning Post*, Monday, March 17, 2008, reposted to *www.sinodefence.com*.

67. Jim Yardley, "As Tibet Erupted, China Security Forces Wavered," *New York Times*, March 24, 2008, at *www.NYTimes. com*.

68. Cody, p. A17.

69. The fact that these troops had bayonets does not clarify whether they were PLA or PAP.

70. Interviews, March-April 2008; also "Trashing the Beijing Road"; "Fears of Contagion from Tibet," *The Economist*, March 21, 2008, at *www.economist.com*.

71. Lou Chen, Yi Ling, "China Focus: Fears and Tears in Holy Plateau City Wracked by Turmoil," *Xinhua* in English, March 15, 2008.

72. "China Covers Up Sending Elite Troops to Tibet," March 20 posting to Tibet Will Be Free blog, citing Kanwa Defence Review report, *blog.studentsforafreetibet.org/2008/03/20/china-covers-up-sending-elite-troops-to-tibet/*.

73. "Protestors Call for Olympic Boycott, Media and UN Access to Tibet" VOA News, March 22, 2008, *www.voanews.com/ english/2008-03-22-voa7.cfm*.

74. "Seven Killed in Tibetan Protests: China," Australian Broadcasting Corporation, ABCNews, March 15, 2008, *www.abc.net.au/news/stories/2008/03/15/2190418.htm*.

75. Part of the issue is no doubt traceable to the deliberately understated official Chinese euphemism for most protest suppression operations — "handling" the incident (*chuzhi*) — or the frequently fatal "decisively handling" an incident (*guoduan chuzhi*). Part of the confusion is fanned by reports such as that issued by the VOA that employs strong-sounding but vague language that seems to imply, without unambiguously asserting, PLA front line involvement in the violent suppression of the riots. The issue also underscores the importance of analysts being careful in their summary of other analysts' reports, so as not to attribute to them more of an assertion than is actually there. None of the reports reviewed for this chapter, however, has provided detailed or first-hand evidence eyewitness or photographic/video evidence that it was PLA troops — rather than PAP or Public Security — who were among those forces alleged to have fired upon or beaten civilians in streets and alleyways during any of the several reported shooting incidents from March 10 to March 16.

76. "Tibet Official Gives Government Account of Unrest," *Reuters*, Beijing, China, March 17. 2008.

77. David Lague, "Chinese Leader Blames Dalai Lama for Tibet Violence," *International Herald Tribune*, March 18, 2008, *www.iht.com/articles/2008/03/18/asia/18tibet.php*.

78. Jim Yardley, "Chinese Forces Say They've Secured Tibet's Capital," *New York Times*, March 15, 2008, *www.nytimes.com/2008/03/15/world/asia/15cnd-tibet.html?hp*; "China Sets Tibet Protest Deadline," *BBC World Service*, March 15, 2008, *news.bbc.co.uk/2/hi/asia-pacific/7297911.stm*; Janet Ong and William Bi, "Chinese Army Won't Quash Tibet Protests, General Says," *Bloomberg.com*, March 15, 2008, *www.bloomberg.com/apps/news?pid =20601087&sid=aN26bO28Kiz1&refer=home*.

79. Andrei Chang, "Elite PLA Army Units Enter Lhasa," *Kanwa Daily News*, March 21, 2008, *www.kanwa.com/dnws/showpl.php?id=353*. Chang's report appears to have initially

been published by UPI Asia under the same title, *www.upiasia.com/Security/2008/03/21/elite_pla_army_units_enter_lhasa/4132/*; Chang makes similiar arguments, with some noteworthy additional points, in a later article published by UPI entitled "Analysis: Controlling Tibet—-Part I," *www.upi.com/Security_Industry/2008/07/02/Analysis_Controlling_Tibet_ – _Part_1/UPI-88751215000000.*

80. Chang, "Elite PLA Army Units Enter Lhasa."

81. For analysis and photographs of the vehicles mentioned in this section, see *www.sinodefence.com/army/armour/default.asp*, especially section *www.sinodefence.com/army/armour/zsl92.asp*.

82. Chang "Analysis: Controlling Tibet—-Part I."

83. Chang, "Elite PLA Army Units Enter Lhasa."

84. *Ibid.*

85. The author obtained these photos from a careful and respected scholar who obtained them from the person who took them. My "forensic" analysis of uniforms, vehicles and photos builds upon the tremendous work of my CNA colleagues Dennis Blasko and Tom Bickford. Although they provided me with a crash course in this work, they are in no way responsible for my conclusions.

86. Unfortunately, despite the editors' best efforts, publishing considerations preclude the photo's publication in this chapter. The photo, sourced to Agence France Presse/Getty Images, is widely available online, including in Jim Yardley's March 16, 2008 *New York Time*'s article "Tibetans Clash with Chinese Police in Second City," at *www.nytimes.com/2008/03/16/world/asia/16tibet.html.*

87. The author and CNA have electronic copies of these photos, and the author is indebted to Dennis Blasko and Tom Bickford for providing him with them.

88. See, for example, the exchange on this point on the military and weapons bulletin board at *wenwen.soso.com/z/q96813260.*

htm?rq=105939986&r1=2. The author does not regard the comments on this or any bulletin board as a highly reliable source, merely one more indicator confirming information independently published by official Chinese press sources.

89. Yardley, "Chinese Forces Say They've Secured Tibet's Capital"; "China Sets Tibet Protest Deadline," BBC World Service, March 15, 2008, *news.bbc.co.uk/2/hi/asia-pacific/7297911.stm*; Ong and Bi.

90. Financial Express, March 20, 2008; the total official figure of over 1,000 is from Barnett, "Thunder from Tibet."

91. Comments by Qiangba Puncog in "State Council Press Office Holds A Press Conference on the Recent Situation in Tibet," April 9, 2008, full text in Chinese at *www.china.com.cn/zhibo/2008-04/09/content_14577761.htm?show=t*; "Life in Lhasa in Returning to Normal" (拉薩生活回復正常), Ming Pao Special Report, cited in *Ming Pao* San Francisco, April 9, 2008, *www.mingpaosf.com/htm/News/20080409/st3.h.*

92. Financial Express, March 20, 2008; the total official figure of over 1,000 is from Barnett, "Thunder from Tibet."

93. "OSC Observations of CCTV-1 Special on 14 Mar. Tibet Unrest," CCTV, April 18, 2008, documents number PSB, PAP, and unidentifed plainclothes officers, videorecording civilians involved in demonstrations.

94. Comments by Qiangba Puncog; "Life in Lhasa in Returning to Normal."

95. Bryan Krebs, "Cyber Attacks Target Pro-Tibet Groups," *Washingtonpost.com*, March 21, 2008.

CHAPTER 4

CHINA'S EXPANDING PRESENCE
IN UN PEACEKEEPING OPERATIONS
AND IMPLICATIONS FOR THE UNITED STATES

Bates Gill and Chin-hao Huang*

Introduction.

Since the establishment of the People's Republic
of China, (PRC) the People's Liberation Army (PLA)
has maintained a relatively cautious and ambivalent
stance toward exchanges with foreign militaries.[1]
Supporting an independent foreign policy largely free
of binding security-related commitments, and steeped
in the tradition of self-reliant wariness toward outside
powers, the PLA minimized high-profile contact with
foreign counterparts.

However, since the beginning of the reform period,
and especially since the mid- to late-1990s, the PLA has
altered its reclusive approach and actively participated
in a broadening range of bilateral and multilateral
military engagements throughout the region and
around the globe. This effort by the PLA is part and
parcel of the larger "new security diplomacy" exhibited
by Beijing across a range of international political and
security matters.

Among the most interesting and high profile aspects
of this shift is China's increasingly active participation
in United Nations (UN) peacekeeping operations.
The deployment of Chinese peacekeepers to UN

*The authors are deeply grateful to Matthew Boswell and Melissa
Colonno for their excellent research assistance in the completion
of this chapter, especially in the generation of data and graphics.

99

missions has seen a dramatic 20-fold increase over its contributions of less than 100 peacekeepers in early 2000. As of December 2008, China was the 14th largest contributor to UN peacekeeping missions, providing more civilian police, military observers, and troops to UN missions than three other permanent members of the UN Security Council, namely Russia, the United States, and the United Kingdom. Nearly three-fourths of China's contributions are concentrated in Africa, and Beijing plans new and even more significant increases to its contributions in such strife-torn countries as Darfur/Sudan, the Democratic Republic of the Congo, and Liberia.

In spite of these developments, deeper thinking and analysis about the motivations and broader implications of China's engagement in peacekeeping initiatives remain at an early stage.[2] These trends should lead us to larger, critical questions: What are the principal motivations behind Chinese peacekeeping activities? To what extent do UN peacekeeping missions factor into the PLA's modernization agenda and priorities? How does increasing PLA interaction with other foreign militaries in peacekeeping missions contribute to broader Chinese foreign and security policy? What implications can be gleaned from these developments for Washington's regional and global security interests, especially at a time when military-to-military relations between the United States and China remain lukewarm at best?

To shed some light on these questions, and to understand Chinese peacekeeping as a potential "mission beyond Taiwan," this chapter will first highlight some of the major recent developments in Chinese peacekeeping activities, providing a broad descriptive and comparative overview. Second, the chapter looks into the current debate, motivations, and decisionmaking processes behind the PLA's expanding engagement in UN peacekeeping activities. The chapter concludes with a number of implications and recommendations which emerge from the analysis, with a focus on U.S.-China relations. The conclusions recommend the United States engage with China on peacekeeping-related issues, ensure greater convergence between Chinese and other international interests on questions of regional security, and encourage more effective international peacekeeping operations.

China's Expanding Engagement in UN Peacekeeping Activities.

Following its admission to the UN in 1971, the PRC took little to no action in the Security Council related to peacekeeping affairs. This ambivalence subsided from the 1980s onwards, with Beijing taking an increasingly active stance following the end of the Cold War. Beijing cast its first vote on peacekeeping in 1981, supporting UN Security Council Resolution 495 which extended the ongoing UN Peacekeeping Force in Cyprus (UNFICYP). The following year China made its first official payments toward UN peacekeeping operations. Subsequently, it applied for membership and was accepted into the UN Special Committee on Peacekeeping Operations. At the time, Ambassador Yu Mengjia, then Chinese Representative to the UN, publicly called for the international community to give "powerful support" to peacekeeping activities.

In 1989, 20 Chinese civilian officials took part in the UN Transition Assistance Group (UNTAG) to help the UN monitor elections in Cambodia. In 1990, five military observers were dispatched to support the UN Truce Supervision Organization (UNTSO) in the Middle East. These were the first contributions of their kind from China. Shortly thereafter, in another first, China sent military units—two separate deployments of 400 engineering troops each, accompanied by 48 military observers—to Cambodia over an 18-month period from 1992 to 1993.

Since the mid-1990s, China's contributions to UN peacekeeping activities steadily increased and diversified. According to the Peacekeeping Affairs Office, which was established in 2001 under the Chinese Ministry of Defense to oversee management and coordination of the PLA's participation in all UN peacekeeping operations, China has contributed more than 7,500 peacekeepers to the UN peacekeeping operations since 1990. As of December 2008, there were 2,146 Chinese peacekeepers serving in 11 UN missions, and China ranked as the second largest contributor to UN peacekeeping operations among the permanent members of the Security Council. Since 2000, as contributions from the United States, United Kingdom, and Russia have declined or remained static, China's contributions of troops, police, and military observers has expanded about 20-fold. Figures 1, 2, and 3 provide further detail on China's contributions to UN peacekeeping operations and compare them to contributions of India, France, Russia, the United Kingdom, and the United States.[3]

1989	1990	1991	1992	1993	1994	1995	1996	1997	1998
20	5	44	488	65	60	45	38	32	35
1999	2000	2001	2002	2003	2004	2005	2006	2007	2008
37	98	129	123	358	1036	1059	1666	1824	2146

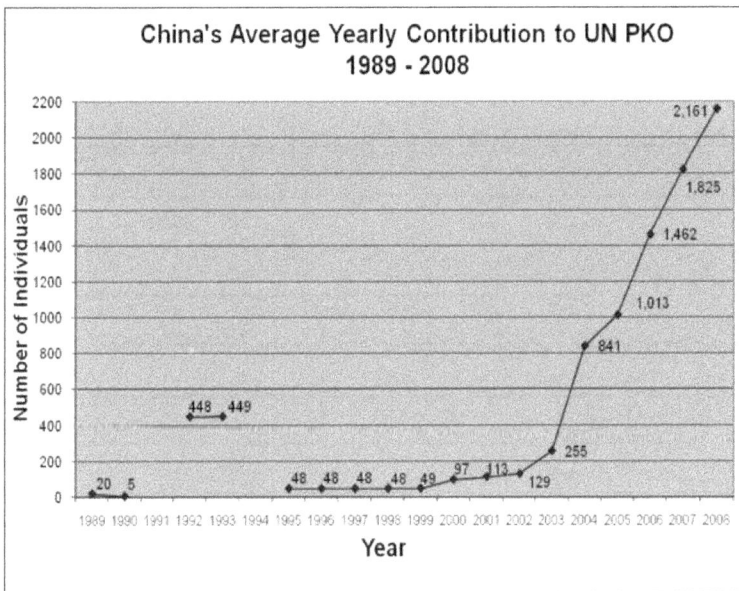

Figure 1. China's Average Yearly Personnel
Contribution to UN PKO, 1989-2008.

China, P5 & India

Contributions to UN PKOs 2000-2008 (yearly averages)

	2000	2001	2002	2003	2004	2005	2006	2007	2008
China	98	129	123	358	1036	1059	1666	1824	2146
France	489	540	452	326	506	598	1,067	1,978	1,950
Russia	294	320	362	328	340	305	267	295	294
UK	579	656	694	594	556	393	358	367	355
US	886	814	700	525	451	365	339	315	296
India	3,871	2,446	2,929	2,827	3,075	6,309	9,033	9,401	9,079

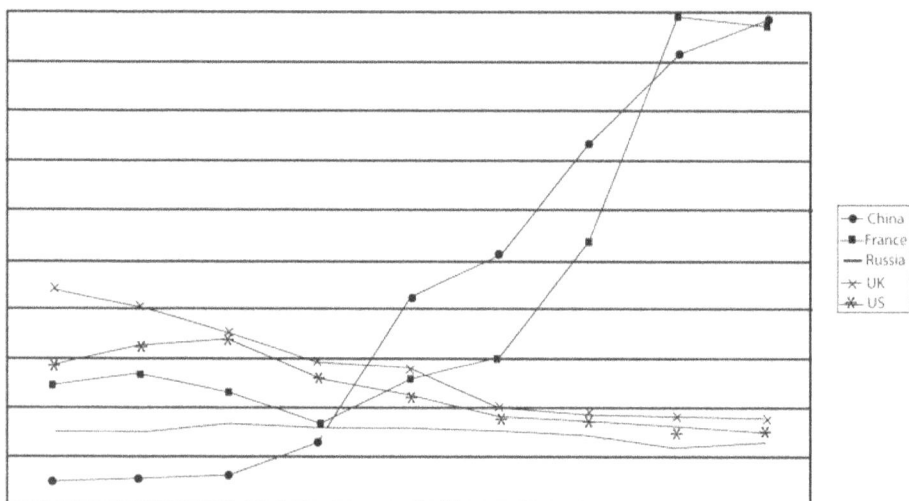

Figure 2. Average Yearly Contributions
of Peacekeepers to UN Missions by China, India,
France, Russia, United Kingdom, and United States,
2000-08.

Figure 3. China's Contribution to UN Peacekeeping Operations by Individual Mission, January 2006 to June 2008.

Month	TOTAL	UNTSO (Truce Supervision Organization)	UNOCI (Operation in Côte d'Ivoire)	UNMIT (Integrated Mission in Timor-Leste)	UNOTIL (Office in Timor-Leste)	UNMIS (Mission in the Sudan)	UNMIL (Mission in Liberia)	UNMIK (Interim Administration Mission in Kosovo)	UNMEE (Mission in Ethiopia & Eritrea)	UNIOSIL (Integrated Office in Sierra Leone)	UNIFIL (Interim Force in Lebanon)	UNAMID (Hybrid Operation in Darfur)	UNAMA (Assistance Mission in Afghanistan)	ONUB (United Nations Operation in Burundi)	MONUC (Organization Mission in the DRC)	MINUSTAH (Stabilization Mission in Haiti)	MINURSO (Mission for Referendum in Western Sahara)
Jan-06	1,060	4	7		7	35	595	18	7				1	3	230	134	19
Feb-06	1,052	4	7		6	35	595	18	7				1	3	230	127	19
Mar-06	1,137	4	7		6	35	595	18	7		85		1	3	230	127	19
Apr-06	1,271	4	7		6	65	596	18	8		187		1	1	232	127	19
May-06	1,413	4	7		6	204	596	18	7		187		1	1	232	131	19
Jun-06	1,663	4	7			473	596	19	7		187			1	230	130	9
Jul-06	1,648	3	7			473	576	18	7		187				232	130	15
Aug-06	1,663	2	7			473	593	19	7		187				232	130	13
Sep-06	1,648	3	7			473	593	1	7		187				232	130	15
Oct-06	1,664	3	7			467	593	18	7		190				232	130	14
Nov-06	1,659	3	7	2		461	594	18	9	1	190				230	130	14
Dec-06	1,666	4	7	1		469	593	19	9	1	190				230	129	14
Jan-07	1,861	4	7	2		469	588	19	7	1	392				230	129	13
Feb-07	1,814	4	7	2		469	589	18	7	1	343				230	129	13
Mar-07	1,809	3	7	3		469	586	18	7	1	343				231	129	13
Apr-07	1,820	3	7	3		468	588	18	7	1	343				234	136	13
May-07	1,828	3	7	13		469	587	18	7	1	343				234	133	13
Jun-07	1,830	3	7	13		465	587	15	7	1	343				234	135	19
Jul-07	1,830	3	4	13		468	587	15	7	1	360				234	134	13
Aug-07	1,828	3	7	13		468	570	18	7	1	343				234	134	13
Sep-07	1,811	3	7	13		468	570	18	6	1	343				234	134	13
Oct-07	1,819	4	7	13		468	580	15	6	1	343				234	134	14
Nov-07	1,820	4	7	13		468	582	15	6	1	343				234	134	13
Dec-07	1,824	5	7	13		468	581	15	7	1	343				234	134	13
Jan-08	1,963	4	7	27		466	581	2	7	1	343	143			234	134	13
Feb-08	1,962	4	7	27		466	581	2	7	1	343	143			234	134	13
Mar-08	1,978	4	11	25		466	581	20	2		343	147			234	134	10
Apr-08	1,981	4	13	25		466	581	18	2		343	147			234	134	14
May-08	1,977	4	10	25		466	580	18	2		343	147			234	134	14
Jun-08	1,955	4	6	18		466	580	18	2		343				231	127	13
Total/Avg	1,834	4	7	13		468	585	16	6	1	302	146			232	132	13

105

The majority of Chinese troop contributions play a supportive role in engineering, transportation, and medical services. Chinese peacekeepers document that they have built more than 7,300 kilometers of paved roads and 200 bridges, treated more than 28,000 patients, and cleared more than 7,500 explosives.

In addition, China has become the thirteenth largest contributor of civilian police to UN peacekeeping operations. China first sent police in 1999 to serve in the UN mission to East Timor. In 2004, China dispatched the first group of Chinese riot police to support the mission in Haiti to help maintain law and order and to train the local police force, even though the two countries do not have formal diplomatic ties. According to Guo Baoshan, the deputy director-general of the international cooperation department of the Chinese Ministry of Public Security, UN peacekeeping police should shoulder greater responsibilities beyond the usual tasks of enforcing ceasefires. Guo noted that they should also assist with reconstruction of the local legal system, law enforcement, help protect civilian rights, and provide humanitarian relief efforts.[4]

Broadly speaking, beyond simple "boots on the ground," China has also exhibited greater commitment to peacekeeping activities by increasing Chinese administrative and leadership personnel involved in UN peacekeeping and by placing its troops in more dangerous situations. Chinese military officers working in the Chinese permanent mission at the United Nations in New York are becoming increasingly involved both in providing information and expertise on peacekeeping for policymakers in Beijing and in representing Chinese military and peacekeeping-related policies at the United Nations. Additionally, within the UN Department of Peacekeeping Operations

(UNDPKO), there are now at least three Chinese nationals serving in the Force Generation Unit, Military Planning Service Office and the Operations Office for the Asia and Middle East Division. In September 2007, the UNDPKO announced the appointment of General Zhao Jainmin as the force commander for the UN Mission for the Referendum in Western Sahara (MINURSO). More recently, on such sensitive issues as Darfur, Beijing has adopted a more active approach, embracing the need for political reconciliation and a hybrid African Union/United Nations peacekeeping force to address the humanitarian crisis. In mid-July 2008, China deployed an additional 172-member engineering battalion, bringing its contributions to a total of 321 troops in Darfur to help prepare the way for the larger UN force envisioned by the international community.

Key Factors Shaping China's Evolving Approach to UN Peacekeeping.

It appears China will continue this more active approach to UN peacekeeping. A reading of recent Chinese actions, statements, and writings suggests a number of interrelated factors and motivations for the PLA and the Chinese leadership that shape and drive this new approach: enhance multilateral security cooperation to help secure a stable international environment; reassure neighbors about China's peaceful intentions; and balance U.S. and Western influence while gradually but more firmly establishing China's Great Power image within the international community. It is less clear from the open-source literature whether involvement in UN peacekeeping missions is seen in China as having a more direct impact on the PLA's military modernization effort, though an indirect linkage can be made.[5]

According to Pang Zhongying, an academic who has commented widely on China's peacekeeping operations, the Chinese leadership has gradually realized that participation in peacekeeping missions can help reduce tensions and conflicts in global hot-spots, "which works in China's national interest as the country begins to build a sound external environment for its long-term economic growth and social development." This view was also expressed by a senior Chinese foreign policy official at the Munich Conference on Security Policy in 2007: "China's increasing involvement in UN peacekeeping missions reflected China's commitment to contribute to global security, given the country's important role within the international system and the fact that its security and development are closely linked to that of the rest of the world."[6] The link between international developments and China's own security as a core national interest is one important factor for the Chinese leadership's decision to adopt a more constructive role in peacekeeping missions abroad.

In addition, participation in peacekeeping operations is seen as a way to assuage China's neighbors' concerns with the PLA's growing military capabilities. Beijing is increasingly attuned to and seeks to dampen regional concerns that a rising China would pursue a hegemonic path and destabilize regional and international peace and security.[7] As such, Chinese strategists argue that one of the most urgent diplomatic tasks for Beijing today is to assure the world of its positive intentions and goodwill.[8] By participating in UN peacekeeping operations, Beijing seeks to put forward the "good side" of the PLA and China's increasing military capability, sending a message that China is further integrating into the international community, becoming more responsive to regional and global expectations, making positive and tangible contributions to global peace and security, and acting as a more responsible major power.[9]

An interesting aspect of this is how Beijing has become more flexible in its approach to peacekeeping on matters where Taiwan is concerned. On past occasions, on UN Security Council votes involving peacekeeping activities in countries which diplomatically recognized Taiwan, Beijing would typically take obstructionist positions. This approach has changed in recent years as Beijing has sought to burnish its credentials as a more responsible power (and has taken a more nuanced approach in its efforts to isolate Taiwan). For example, Beijing chose first to veto a proposed peacekeeping mission to Guatemala in 1997 owing to the country's diplomatic relations with Taiwan. China subsequently reversed its vote, allowing the mission to proceed. More recently, Beijing supported the UN peacekeeping mission to stabilize Haiti, and even signed on to provide Chinese police, even though Haiti formally recognizes Taiwan. As one senior minister in the Ministry of Public Security commented, "China's active involvement in peacekeeping missions of the United Nations, especially in Haiti, which has not set up a diplomatic relationship with China, fully exhibits a peace-loving and responsible image of the country."[10] Some have also speculated that such steps would help China bring Haiti into China's diplomatic camp over time.

In another example, China has agreed to take part in highly sensitive and potentially dangerous missions to deflect international criticism and position itself as a responsible power. China's approach to peacekeeping in Darfur is the most prominent example of this development. By bringing pressure on the Sudanese government to follow through with its international agreements and by committing PLA troops to one of the most politically volatile and unstable regions in Africa, China demonstrates a willingness to shoulder greater responsibilities while also hoping to defuse international criticism about its relations with Khartoum.[11]

Chinese scholars also claim that the positive image generated from participation in peacekeeping operations could help solidify and consolidate its Great Power status and balance against American and Western influence in global hotspots.[12] As one Chinese author opined, "China could use its symbolic power in the UN to its advantage."[13] In Beijing's view, closer integration with the UN system, and the UNDPKO in particular, means that China can play a more prominent role in shaping the future direction of UN peacekeeping missions. China has taken an official position to criticize "the lack of officials from developing countries . . . who occupy high posts in the UNDPKO."[14] It has also expressed concern that peacekeeping missions around the world remain largely dominated and directed by "some Western powers and military alliances such as NATO" and argued that developing countries should have a greater say in the decisionmaking process in the UNDPKO.[15]

Finally, there is some evidence that China's increased peacekeeping activity is intended to help the PLA and Chinese police forces improve their readiness for other missions. In June 2007, the PLA convened the first major internal peacekeeping work meeting. Over the course of the 4-day meeting, senior representatives from the Ministry of Foreign Affairs, Ministry of Finance, and the Ministry of Public Security gathered to discuss the current situation of Chinese participation and contribution in UN peacekeeping operations and to put forth specific measures and suggestions for strengthening and improving Chinese peacekeeping activities. Lieutenant General Zhang Qinsheng, deputy chief of the General Staff of the PLA, was subsequently quoted in the Chinese press that the meeting helped gather further insights "to raise the peacekeeping capabilities of China's armed forces . . . and [to] gradually expand peacekeeping exchanges and cooperation with the outside world in a planned and focused manner."[16] Mindful of the persistent challenges China faces in its peacekeeping capabilities, Zhang also commented that China "must vigorously strengthen building of the peacekeeping ranks and forge a high-caliber peacekeeping contingent."[17]

Echoing these views at an international seminar on multilateral peace operations in 2007, PLA Senior Colonel Zhang Ping further categorized China's increasing external exchanges and peacekeeping training exercises into three important levels. First, as part of the "going out to learn" phase, the PLA has sent more than 100 officers to take part in professional training and exchanges organized by more than 10 Southeast Asian and European countries. Chinese participation, either as observers or active participants, in peacekeeping training exercises organized by the French Reinforcement of African Peacekeeping Capabilities (RECAMP) as well as those sponsored by the British defense and security establishments have all provided valuable insights into joint coordination mechanisms involving various military units and civilian departments from which the PLA can draw during its own training processes.[18]

Second, it has also extended invitations to foreign military counterparts for additional help and more rigorous peacekeeping training programs. According to the Chinese Peacekeeping Affairs Office, it has in the recent past invited peacekeeping specialists from the UNDPKO and foreign military officers from the United Kingdom, for example, to assist and inspect China's predeployment contingents. And third, China has increasingly taken on the role of hosting and organizing international seminars on peacekeeping affairs. Together with London, it has been coordinating the "UK-China Seminar on Peacekeeping Operations" since 2004. It has also arranged similar seminars with Sweden, Norway, and the Association of Southeast Asian Nations (ASEAN), giving the PLA a better understanding of the standard training manuals and courses commonly used by other countries' peacekeeping training programs. The International Committee of the Red Cross (ICRC) has also been able to work with the PLA to develop and integrate seminars and predeployment briefings for Chinese peacekeepers on such issues as human rights and customary norms in international humanitarian law.

The increase in Chinese military engagements abroad has prompted some Chinese academics to call for a clearer legislative basis to govern such activities. Such debate and thinking indicates that there is greater acknowledgement and perhaps approval of PLA's increasing "nonwar" activities such as peacekeeping. It also indicates a growing recognition of the need for a stronger "legal basis" to govern such practical issues as,

> the administration of the exit and entry of military personnel and their weaponry, the signing procedures

of foreign-related agreements, expenditures and backup methods of military actions, the legal responsibility and jurisdiction of military personnel involving in foreign-related nonmilitary actions, rescue and treatment of causalities, and compensation responsibility.[19]

Over the last few years, China has invested in the necessary facilities within China to improve the training and preparedness of its peacekeepers, which will in turn make them better able to translate their international experiences into useful lessons for missions other than peacekeeping. For example, in 2000, the Civilian Peacekeeping Police (CIVPOL) Training Center was established in Langfang, a city about 25 miles (40 kilometers) southeast of Beijing. It has the capacity to train more than 200 officers at one time. The training programs offer extensive courses on such necessary skills as map reading, handling of weapons, radio communication, conducting investigations and arrests, and enforcing laws for Chinese police officers who will be dispatched to serve in UN missions abroad. According to senior officials at CIVPOL, the center has received funds amounting to $13 million for further expansion and modernization. Similarly, the International Relations Academy in Nanjing, associated with the PLA defense intelligence services, has been active in preparing Chinese officers on such topics as peacekeeping principles, the UN Charter, conducting medical and communications procedures in international settings, and foreign language study. In addition, Chinese officials expect that a new peacekeeping training center in Huairou will become operational during 2009 to help the PLA's Peacekeeping Affairs Office centralize and better coordinate Chinese peacekeeping.

Expanding peacekeeping-related contact with foreign counterparts presumably provides benefits for the PLA as it seeks to modernize its mobilization, organization, and deployment capabilities. However, it is difficult to clearly identify a direct linkage. Western scholars and officers at the Chinese National Defense University confirm that the sharpened skills and know-how acquired through foreign training as well as the hands-on experience of serving in peacekeeping missions provide valuable follow-on benefits. Each peacekeeping contingent can share valuable experiences and insights to help benefit and modernize the larger main force and military region to which it belongs upon the completion of its peacekeeping assignment abroad.[20]

Implications and Recommendations.

This brief analysis of the activities and motivations of Chinese peacekeeping points us to a number of important implications and recommendations for the international community and for the United States more specifically. In short, China's expanding engagement in peacekeeping activities offers new opportunities to strengthen China's commitment to regional stability and security-building and improve its international peacekeeping capacity, while also opening potentially beneficial areas of military-to-military cooperation between China and its major security partners, especially the United States.

At the international level, while it is clear Beijing is keen to ramp up its peacekeeping activities, it will do so on a case-by-case basis and within certain persistent limitations. On the one hand, China's increasing commitment to UN peacekeeping activities opens a new avenue for engagement between the international community and Beijing, and offers an opportunity to deepen China's commitment to global norms of security-building, conflict resolution, and post-conflict reconciliation and reconstruction. The continued deployment and redeployment of Chinese units throughout Africa, for example, means that over time they will accrue operational knowledge and a better understanding of the political and security dynamics and complexities on the ground. At the same time, Beijing's increasing interaction with other militaries in blue helmet missions has, to a certain degree, opened the window for a better understanding of the strengths and weaknesses of the PLA. Generally speaking, it appears Beijing is prepared to shoulder some greater responsibilities and to play a more significant role in supporting the UN peacekeeping system. Certainly such an approach would be welcomed within the UN system as the UNDPKO's increases its reliance on Chinese contributions and support.

On the other hand, China's willingness to fully engage in UN peacekeeping operations will face a number of constraints, and expectations within the international community should be modest but cautiously optimistic. The traditional view of state sovereignty and noninterference will continue to be the most important concern for Chinese policymakers. In addition, practical matters of political, military, and bureaucratic will and capacity will also be factors slowing Chinese responsiveness in peacekeeping affairs. To date, China has not provided its planning data sheet to the UN Standby Arrangements System. The data sheet provides, among other details, a list of major equipment, unit organization, and movement data to the UN. Furthermore, Beijing has yet to provide a formal commitment to contribute standby troops to the UN under the standard response timeframe. In private, Chinese officials at the UN explained that there is a perennial shortage of well-trained peacekeeping officers with the necessary language and technical skills. The lack of sufficient air- and/or sea-lift capacity has also inhibited its capabilities to commit to rapid deployment of significantly large number of troops over long distances. Moreover, China's financial contribution toward peacekeeping operations represents around 2 percent of the overall UNDPKO budget and would need to be augmented if Beijing wants to play a larger role commensurate with its growing influence globally and within the UN system.

Beijing remains generally cautious toward the use of peacekeepers and on the broader issue of intervention by the international community. In such cases as Zimbabwe and Myanmar, China has thus far resisted calls from human rights advocacy groups and some Western governments to pursue intervention based on humanitarian justifications. It should be noted, however, that in 1999, China accepted a UN-sanctioned humanitarian justification for using force in East Timor. It also subsequently dispatched a civilian police contingent to support the mission in East Timor. Likewise, in 2003, in response to growing instabilities in the Congo and Liberia, then Chinese Ambassador to the UN Zhang Yishan argued that the "United Nations should intervene in the areas of conflict faster, sooner, and in a more forceful manner."[21] In short, Beijing prefers to review the "reality of conflicts on a case-by-case basis."[22] There will be limitations, and it is unlikely that Beijing will take the initiative, offering active support under circumstances where the international community remains divided and where sovereign governments are adamantly opposed to the intervention of such UN forces.

Over time, it is possible China would aim to counterbalance Western influence gradually and take a more active role in shaping the norms and responses regarding UN peacekeeping operations in ways consistent with Chinese foreign policy principles and national interests. To be sure, such influence could accrue over time, but it would also require greater Chinese commitment in several key areas, including better trained troops, a more capable military that can deploy effective rapid-response teams, a willingness to dispatch active combatant units, demonstrate leadership capabilities at the UNDPKO in New York and throughout the peacekeeping missions around the world, and provide greater financial contribution commensurate with its status as a permanent member of the Security Council and a rising global power.

Given these developments, the United States should implement policies aimed at deepening these encouraging trends related to Beijing's involvement with UN peacekeeping operations. There has been some thinking in this direction. As former U.S. Secretary of Defense William Cohen indicated in a speech in Beijing in 2000: "U.S. and Chinese service members may one day find themselves working side by side in peacekeeping missions."[23] More recently at a track-1.5 dialogue on U.S.-China security issues, former U.S. Secretary of Defense William Perry also suggested that the two armed forces should cooperate more closely on humanitarian operations and peacekeeping missions.[24]

Working on peacekeeping training activities and capacity-building thus provides a useful platform to build confidence and greater understanding between the two militaries. The United States is in the midst of an expansive phase on peacekeeping training and capacity-building engagements with foreign militaries, with the Global Peace Operations Initiative (GPOI) as a flagship initiative in this regard. In 2004, in response to the Group of Eight (G8) Summit agreement to address the continued shortage of available peacekeepers, then-U.S. President George W. Bush announced the establishment of GPOI, a 5-year program managed by the State Department's Bureau of Political-Military Affairs to enhance peacekeeping training for UN missions as well as partner countries' overall peacekeeping capacity-building.[25] The goal is to train as many as 75,000 military peacekeepers by 2010, mostly in Africa. There is an emerging interest at the policymaking level within the State Department to explore future prospects for working with China to help build African peacekeeping capacity. This would include, for example, working with Chinese contractors and drawing on Chinese assistance in infrastructure and hardware support in the initial build-up stage of peace operations.

While Africa remains a focal point in the program, GPOI's outreach includes all the major regions around the world. In the Asia-Pacific front, for example, GPOI programs include: Cobra Gold Exercise; train-the-trainers (TTT); command post military exercise (CPX); and field training military exercise (FTX). The latter two exercises have been largely integrated into the multinational Khan Quest Exercises based in Mongolia. These exercises follow most of the UN standard peace support operations' training, techniques, and procedures, and have sought to enhance multinational interoperability, expand confidence-building and military-to-military relationships, and simulate multinational cooperation experienced in UN peacekeeping missions. Since China is not a GPOI partner country, however, it has only taken part in the Cobra Gold and Khan Quest exercises as an observer.

The prospects for U.S.-China collaboration on peacekeeping activities face considerable obstacles at this stage. The congressionally mandated restrictions on U.S.-China military-to-military ties outlined in the Defense Authorization Bill for fiscal year 2000 places strict limitations on the scope and scale of bilateral military exchanges, which includes advanced combined-arms and joint combat operations, advanced logistical operations, surveillance and reconnaissance operations, and force projection operations, among many other areas.[26] Official exchanges on peacekeeping training and coordination between the two sides are not explicitly restricted in the bill, but it will require strong political will at the senior policymaking level to make the case that such interactions with the PLA do not pose a threat to U.S. national security. Absent strong political will, and as long as the limitations remain the law of the land, there will be continued caution in the level of interaction between the two militaries. This is especially true as long as concerns remain about the opacity of China's longer-term military intentions and how they contrast with U.S. regional and global security interests.

The Defense Department's *Quadrennial Defense Review* expresses concerns about the pace, scope, and future direction of China's military modernization effort. But, on the other hand, the report also recommends military exchanges, visits, and other forms of engagement as useful tools in promoting transparency as long as they bear substance and are fully reciprocal. It further identifies that regularized exchanges and contacts have the significant benefit of building confidence, reducing the possibility of accidents and other unintended confrontations, and providing lines of communication that are essential for the two militaries.[27]

As the new U.S. administration looks to build a productive relationship with Beijing, Washington should take steps to engage China on peacekeeping-related issues with an aim to deepen China's commitment to global and regional stability, further the development of effective international peacekeeping operations, and help shape China's expanding peacekeeping activities in ways consistent with U.S. interests. Such steps could include:

- *Intensify bilateral and multilateral dialogue and policy coordination with China on mutual security concerns such as Afghanistan and Zimbabwe, and on the prospects for multilateral peacekeeping support and deployment.* In recent years, Beijing's support for and interest to take part in UN peacekeeping operations in East Timor, Haiti, and Darfur all point to more flexible views toward intervention by the international community. When there is broad international consensus around a specific intervention, China has tended to lend its support. The critical part of gaining Chinese involvement and cooperation will thus require Washington to work assiduously with the broader international community to forge greater consensus to enlist Beijing's support and help shape Chinese policies in a constructive direction.
- *Expand military-to-military relations to encompass forms of peacekeeping training and capacity-*

building. To the extent possible under the Defense Authorization Bill for 2000, Washington should seek to encourage greater Chinese participation in future peacekeeping training exercises under the GPOI framework. It could also work with China to explore the prospects of supporting peacekeeping capacity-building in GPOI partner countries in Africa, where both the United States and China have increasing areas of common interest. In Liberia, for example, the United States is involved with the training of the Liberian armed forces. China has also come in to complement this work in constructive ways by assisting with hardware and refurbishing buildings, facilities, and other infrastructures, and there has been ongoing communication between the defense attachés from both embassies in Liberia. Over time, China should be more fully engaged on such issues as security sector reform (SSR), disarmament, demobilization, and reintegration (DDR), and election observations.

• *Work with other countries that have substantial interests in peacekeeping affairs to increase peacekeeping-related military interactions with Beijing and support greater Chinese involvement in the UNDPKO and other peace operations.* In recent years, many countries with strong support for UN peacekeeping operations such as Australia, Bangladesh, Canada, France, India, Norway, Sweden, and the United Kingdom have seen more expansive interactions with the PLA on peacekeeping training exercises and seminars. Washington should encourage this trend and work with these partners to explore ways in which China could play a more active part in the planning, coordination, leadership, and financial contribution roles at the UNDPKO and possibly beyond.

- *Build on growing Chinese interests in peacekeeping affairs to encourage greater openness and transparency in the PLA.* Washington and its partners should continue to communicate to the Chinese that a greater degree of openness is needed to sustain a collaborative relationship. Collaboration in relation to peacekeeping, humanitarian intervention, and other related forms of military-to-military exchange would usefully contribute to building greater openness and transparency within the PLA.

CHAPTER 4 - ENDNOTES

1. See, for example, Michael Yahuda, "China's Search for a Global Role," *Current History*, Vol. 98, No. 629, September 1999; Gilbert Rozman, "China's Quest for Great Power Identity," *Orbis* Vol. 43, No. 3, Summer 1999; Evan S. Medeiros and M. Taylor Fravel, "China's New Diplomacy," *Foreign Affairs,* Vol. 82, No. 6, November/December 2003; Bates Gill, *Rising Star: China's New Security Diplomacy,* Washington, DC: Brookings, 2007, especially chaps. 2 and 4.

2. Some earlier work on this topic includes Bates Gill and James Reilly, "Sovereignty, Intervention, and Peacekeeping: The View from Beijing," *Survival,* Autumn 2000; Stefan Staehle, *China's Participation in the United Nations Peacekeeping Regime,* M.A. thesis, George Washington University, May 2006; M. Taylor Fravel, "China's Attitude Toward UN Peacekeeping Operations Since 1989," *Asian Survey*, Vol. 36, No. 11, November 1996; He Yin, *China's Changing Policy on UN Peacekeeping Operations*, Stockholm, Sweden: Institute for Security and Development Policy, 2007.

3. Data generated from multiple sources, including the web site of the UN Department of Peacekeeping Operations (UNDPKO), available from *www.un.org/Depts/dpko/dpko/contributors*.

4. "Chinese Police Forces Second Largest among UN Peace Missions," People's Daily Online, July 24, 2007, available from *english.peopledaily.com.cn/90001/90776/6222369.html*.

5. Some work to appear in recent years from Chinese writers on peacekeeping issues are Pang Zhongying, "China's Changing Attitude to UN Peacekeeping," *International Peacekeeping,* Spring 2005); Yin; Wang Jianwei, "Managing Conflict: Chinese Perspectives on Multilateral Diplomacy and Collective Security," in Yong Deng and Fei-Ling Wang, eds., *In the Eyes of the Dragon: China Views the World,* Lanham, England: Rowman & Littlefield, 1999; Zhuang Maocheng, "A Synopsis of the Beijing International Seminar on Challenges of Peace Operations: Into the 21st Century," presented at the Partners Meeting in British Defense Academy, March 1, 2005.

6. "China Bolsters Peacekeeping Commitment," *Jane's Defence Weekly*, February 21, 2007.

7. See, for example, "PLA Must Improve Capabilities, Safeguard Party's 'Ruling Status' in New Era," *Zhongguo Junshi Kexue*, October 20, 2007, translated in Open Source Center: CPP20080618436001; Du Nongyi, "Peacekeeping Diplomacy: Main Theme of Military Diplomacy in the New Phase of the New Century," *Military Science*, Vol. 10, No. 4, 2007.

8. He, p. 49.

9. See Wang Yizhou, "Conducting a Multiinsight Study of China's Relations with Key International Organizations," in Wang Yizhou, *Construction in Contradiction: A Multiple Insight into Relationship between China and Key International Organizations,* Beijing: China Development Press, 2003.

10. "China to Send Anti-riot Peacekeepers for Haiti," Xinhuanet, June 4, 2004, available from *www.chinaview.cn*.

11. For more, see Chin-hao Huang, "U.S.-China Relations and Darfur," *Fordham International Law Journal,* Vol. 31, No. 4, April 2008, pp. 827-842.

12. Tang Yongsheng, "China and UN Peacekeeping Interactions," in Wang Jisi, ed., *World Politics: Views from China – China's Foreign Affairs,* Hong Kong: Peace Book Publisher, 2006.

13. Pang, "China's Changing Attitude to UN Peacekeeping," p. 96.

14. "Position Paper of the People's Republic of China on the United Nations Reform," Chinese Ministry of Foreign Affairs, June 7, 2005, available from *www.fmprc.gov.cn/ce/ceun/eng/xw/t199101.htm.*

15. *Ibid.*

16. "Chinese Deputy Military Chief on Raising Army's Peacekeeping Role," *Zhongguo Xinwen She,* June 22, 2007, translated in BBC Monitoring International Reports: CPP20070622968151.

17. *Ibid.*

18. Presentation notes by Senior Colonel Ouyang Wei and Senior Colonel Xu Weidi from the PLA National Defense University at a conference on UN peacekeeping operations in Oslo, Norway, on October 9, 2007.

19. "Speeding up Legislation on PLA's Nonwar Military Actions," *Jiefangjun Bao Online,* October 28, 2008, translated in Open Source Center: CPP20081028710005.

20. See, for example, Roy Kamphausen, "PLA Power Projection: Current Realities and Emerging Trends," in Michael Swaine et al., eds, *Assessing the Threat: The Chinese Military and Taiwan's Security,* Washington, DC: Carnegie Endowment for International Peace, 2007. See also presentation notes by Senior Colonel Ouyang Wei and Senior Colonel Xu Weidi from the PLA National Defense University at a conference on UN peacekeeping operations in Oslo, Norway, on October 9, 2007.

21. "China Takes on Major Peacekeeping Role," *Jane's Intelligence Review*, November 1, 2003.

22. He, p. 52.

23. "Chinese Military Students, Family Member Query Cohen," U.S. Department of Defense, July 14, 2000, available from *www.defenselink.mil/news/newsarticle.aspx?id=45322.*

24. "China, U.S. Armed Forces Vow to Enhance Cooperation," Xinhuanet, June 30, 2008, available from *news.xinhuanet.com/ english/2008-06/30/content_8466881.htm.*

25. "Global Peace Operations Initiative," U.S. Department of State, April 1, 2004, available from *www.state.gov/t/pm/ppa/gpoi/.*

26. See Kenneth Allen, "U.S.-China Military Relations: Not a One-Way Street," Henry L. Stimson Center News Advisory, December 13, 1999, available from *www.stimson. org/?SN=ME20011221208.*

27. *Quadrennial Defense Review Report,* Washington, DC: U.S. Department of Defense, February 6, 2006, available from *www. defenselink.mil/pubs/pdfs/QDR20060203.pdf.*

CHAPTER 5

PLA MISSIONS IN FRONTIER SECURITY AND COUNTERTERRORISM

Robert O. Modarelli III

China's 2006 national defense white paper (NDWP), officially entitled *China's National Defense of 2006*, states that China's defense policy is intended to guarantee maintenance of the country's "security and unity, and realizing the goal of building a moderately prosperous society." In a subsequent detailed outline of the key elements of a security strategy to accomplish this, the Chinese People's Liberation Army (PLA) is tasked with "performing its historical missions" of "providing an important source of strength for consolidating the ruling position of the CPC [Communist Party of China, hereafter referred to as the Chinese Communist Party or CCP]," providing a secure environment for sustained national development, providing support to safeguarding national interests, and playing a "major role" in maintaining world peace and development.

In recent years it has become increasingly common for observers to conclude that the principle concern, and top priority, of national security strategy in China is the preservation of the legitimacy of the CCP as the sole governing power, a legitimacy that in turn depends primarily on the maintenance of social stability and public order. External threats, while clearly addressed and given much weight in Chinese strategic writings, are often discussed in terms of their ability to destabilize internal social order. Chinese history and traditional strategic thought have long recognized the dangers of foreign threats coupled with domestic unrest (内忧外患 *neiyou waihuan*) as a classic recipe for regime failure, and this meme continues to permeate much contemporary writing on this subject. In this context, an argument can be made that from a strategic perspective, the "main front" in China's attempt to achieve national security goals is internal and aimed at stability within China and its near abroad. The NDWP seems to support this interpretation, for though it does discuss the threats and challenges China faces from more traditional state actors, in general it concludes that China's security situation with regard to outside powers is basically "sound."[1]

On the other hand, the NDWP provides considerable discussion of more "nontraditional" threats to China's continued security, including such factors as threats to domestic social stability. While there is no explicit discussion of the relative "weights" assigned to these traditional and nontraditional threats in the Chinese strategic calculus, it seems likely that social stability (especially in the less ethnically homogenous frontier regions) and counterterrorism (CT) issues will remain strategic priorities, and thus sources of PLA missions, well beyond potential resolution of such traditional "external" matters like the Taiwan issue, regardless of how such resolution might be achieved. While highly visible, extremely neuralgic from China's point of view, and of great concern to the United States and its regional allies as the only security concern that has the realistic potential at present to involve the United States in direct conflict with China, it is important to remember that preparing for a Taiwan scenario is not the sole focus of PLA planning or modernization efforts, nor is it the PLA's *raison d'etre*. That surely derives more from the broader strategic imperatives of regime security and national stability.[2]

PURPOSE

Much has been written elsewhere about the implications of this strategy for the PLA in terms of more traditional missions, force structure and equipment requirements, and modernization programs.[3] The primary purpose of this chapter is to identify key missions for the PLA in the areas of frontier security and CT, and to understand how it pursues missions in security cooperation with other countries in these areas, primarily through the mechanism of combined exercises. In doing so, the chapter will concentrate on identifying and analyzing these missions from a strategic perspective in terms of how they integrate with overall Chinese strategic priorities. It will also take a look at some potential implications of these missions and their importance for the PLA. The chapter will touch only briefly on consideration of lower-level tactical type missions such as patrolling, building fences, etc. — these sorts of missions are generally quite obvious, and detailed listings of such are easily found in a number of sources.

There are numerous primary sources available to assist in determining the broad outlines of PLA missions in these areas, beginning with the NDWP of 2006, and including publications from both PLA and People's Armed Police (PAP) publishing houses, schools, and professional journals. By surveying these sources and seeking to place them within the context of overall Chinese national strategy, we can get a sense of how the PLA and PAP leadership interpret this guidance and derive their own specific missions (in other words, the outcomes of their own "mission analysis" process).[4] It is also possible to develop some theories as to what level of importance these missions may have in the PLA's overall strategic calculus, and how these missions might be affected, if at all, by potential resolution or prolongation of the Taiwan Straits situation.

TERMS

Attempts to study this topic are complicated by the fact that Chinese publications use a variety of terms somewhat interchangeably when discussing many of these issues. Nevertheless, in the area of border security it is clear that they generally conceive of two basic fields of action: actions taken to promote security and stability within the region around the border, including on both sides of international borders; and physical defense of the internationally-recognized border of the People's Republic of China (PRC) in the event of armed incursions by foreign enemies. For purposes of this discussion, the former will be referred to as "frontier security" and the latter as "border defense." Concerning the "frontier," it is also important to note that the depth of this area does not appear to be doctrinally fixed or standard, but varies depending on local conditions, including ethnic makeup and distribution of population, geography and topography, and so on.

Under current Chinese policy, numerous forces and agencies are involved in these missions, and overlapping responsibilities and chains of command can also lead to confusion as to which units are referred to when Chinese sources use nonspecific terms like "armed forces" or "border security forces." Most sources are, however, consistent in using the term 'PLA' to refer solely to those units identified explicitly as belonging to the PLA (such as PLA Border Defense

Battalions). These units will also often be referred to as "border defense" units. The PAP, militia, and other public order units assigned to frontier security missions are considered separately and referred to as "frontier security forces." This chapter will follow these conventions.

It is important to note that Chinese authors recognize that in areas such as frontier security or CT, considered to be "nonwar actions," the implications of "mission" are often very different than would be the case in more traditional combat-related instances.[5] For example, criteria for determining mission success, appropriate courses, levels and intensity of action, distribution of responsibility and involvement across varying levels of command, and so on are often unique to specific situations and cannot automatically be assumed to follow patterns assumed by traditional "missions."[6] The PLA emphasizes that commanders and planners must understand this to effectively carry them out; scholars attempting to understand these missions and their implications must likewise do so.

BORDER DEFENSE AND FRONTIER SECURITY

It has become commonplace to observe that in a post-Communist world, the CCP can no longer derive its legitimacy or "mandate" from Marxist ideological roots, but instead must demonstrate its effectiveness at achieving the twin goals of delivering economic prosperity and protecting national sovereignty as the primary means of retaining its legitimacy.

Because the frontier regions of China for the most part are economically underdeveloped and potentially vulnerable to foreign violations of sovereignty, protection of these regions becomes a matter of strategic importance to the CCP and the government of China. In this context, it is not at all surprising to see the subject of border security receive the detailed level of treatment it does in China's 2006 NDWP. The inclusion of a detailed discussion on this topic, given much more specific attention than in the 2004 Paper, likely reflects a growing awareness on the part of the PRC leadership of the critical importance of this mission to China's overall strategic priorities.

China's assessment of its current security environment as outlined in the 2006 NDWP demonstrates a sophisticated analysis of the regional and global security picture that emphasizes recognition of the "growing interconnections between domestic and international factors and interconnected traditional and non-traditional factors" influencing the nature of existing or emergent threats to its national security.[7] It concludes that the overall security environment "remains sound," especially in terms of its relations with neighboring states along its land frontiers.[8] China nonetheless recognizes serious threats from what are often characterized as the "Three Forces" (三股势力 *san gu shili*), or occasionally the "Three Evil Forces" (三股邪恶势力 *san gu xie'e shili*), of terrorism, ethnic separatism, and religious extremism.[9]

It follows logically that any element of Chinese national security strategy or planning aimed at combating these three "forces" must in turn focus on security of the frontier and China's borders—especially China's extensive interior land border. Not only does this frontier stretch over 22,000 kilometers and border 14 different countries, but, more significantly, it is drawn through regions characterized by religion, ethnicity, and levels of economic development often markedly different from that of the majority of China "proper."

These frontier regions are thus perceived to be prime areas for the flourishing of the "three forces."

In addition, Chinese writers have expressed concern that the international aspect of the frontier offers further opportunity for foreign elements to take advantage of, influence, or even instigate the arousal of these "forces" to challenge China's stability and security. These concerns have ensured that stability and security of the frontier remain core strategic interests for China, in support of a national strategic objective of maintaining domestic and international stability to create an environment amenable to continued economic growth.[10]

The imperatives in turn implied by these objectives mean that border defense and security remain a source of important missions for China's military forces, including the PLA and PAP, as well as civilian security organs. In his 2007 study of China's frontier defense doctrine, M. Taylor Fravel argues that "frontier defense remains a core mission for China's armed forces," particularly when understood from the perspective that defending the territorial integrity of the PRC is *the* core mission of that nation's armed forces.[11]

As mentioned above, it is clear from professional journals and official PRC government documentation that Chinese military thought conceives of "border defense" as only one aspect within the larger context of "frontier security." The former deals with the more traditional and limited scope of preventing invasion or violation of the sovereignty and integrity of the countries' borders; the latter more comprehensively applies to maintaining internal political and societal stability within the frontier regions of China's periphery.[12] These concepts differ in terms of the missions the PLA has under each, as well as the apparent relative importance of the PLA and the military arm in general, in forming a part of the national response to the task.

In brief, the PLA's missions in China's frontier security strategy appear to be as follows:

- In the event of major border incursions, assume the lead role in defeating invading forces and restoring order to the frontier regions. This mission implies assuming overall command of border defense efforts; delaying and shaping enemy penetrations using light forces, militia and PAP; counterattacking and destroying enemy forces, and restoring territorial integrity, primarily through maneuver of PLA main force units deployed from the interior.

- In peacetime, support local civilian and PAP authorities' efforts to promote and maintain social stability in frontier regions. This mission entails operating as a junior partner under the combined command of the interagency Commissions on Border Defense; acting as a deterrent to both internal upheaval and foreign interference; and assisting in the training, administration, and equipping of border defense forces including the militia and the PAP.

Each of these will be discussed in greater detail below.[13]

In addressing the challenge of frontier security, China appears to understand the importance of promoting economic growth, encouraging ethnic co-existence and cultural integration and combating cross-border criminal activities as key components of building stability, and thus enhancing security, in frontier areas.[14] In addition, many authors stress the importance of pursuing constructive relations with neighboring states, and in particular emphasize security cooperation activities as a means of stabilizing conditions along frontiers and anticipating the transnational and cross-border nature both of potentially destabilizing forces and of the measures that will be necessary to combat them.[15]

While recognizing the importance of these tools in creating a secure frontier environment, China's leaders nonetheless also continue to emphasize the critical importance of more traditional instruments of national and Party power in maintaining stability near, in and across borders. They acknowledge the complex interplay of the PLA, the PAP, and the Public Security Bureau (PSB), as well as civil government officials and organs (particularly at the local level) required to effectively pursue this goal. As a result, a substantial part of the NDWP, as well as a large volume of contemporary literature by PLA and PAP writers, in addition to Western analysts, is devoted to analyzing and attempting to understand the complexities of these relationships.

The NDWP outlines a hierarchical structure from the State Council and CMC down to the prefecture and county level that coordinates and administers frontier security under "an administration system of sharing responsibilities (分工负责 *fengong fuze*) between the military and local authorities." Within the context of this approach to border defense, the conceptual distinction between "border defense" and "frontier security" entails differing and distinct missions for the PLA. In its simplest form, the division of responsibilities is expressed through designation of the PLA as "the main force for defending China's borders and coasts," while the border public security force is tasked with "safeguarding security and maintaining social order in border and coastal areas."[16]

135

At the highest level, the Central Military Commission (CMC) exercises command over the military forces; in conjunction with the State Council, it also provides the administrative leadership, including specifically "administration of border, coastal, and air defenses." This is done through the State Commission of Border and Coastal Defense, a combined civilian-military group made up of the "relevant departments of the State Council and the PLA." This Commission is headed by the Minister of Public Security, underscoring the conception that frontier security is primarily the responsibility of the public security forces, with the military in a support role. This model of joint civil-military commissions is replicated at every level of command down from military regions to the county level. Military units remain under command of their next higher military headquarters, but at the provincial level and below this command is described as being exercised in a "dual leadership" with civilian and Party officials. As far as border defense missions, the key tactical headquarters is at the military subdistrict, or prefectural, level. According to the NDWP, prefectural commands in border areas are "in charge of the military, political, logistical, and equipment work of border defense troops as well as border defense duties, talks and meetings, and border management, protection, and control."[17]

Certain missions are inherent in the border defense role, though these are perhaps missions which the PLA is ultimately less likely to be called upon to perform. Other missions deriving from the PLA's frontier security mission, in which it plays primarily a supporting role, are far more likely to be executed and indeed could be argued to be ongoing tasks the PLA is performing on a daily basis in some form or other.

In defending China's borders and coasts from external threats, the PLA is expected to be the "main force" in preventing any major incursion or invasion by foreign elements. Previous research has done an excellent job of synthesizing the various Chinese doctrinal publications that outline how the PLA would likely respond operationally and tactically to such an incursion event. The current posture, composition and location of PLA units—an emphasis on lightly armed border defense units closer to the frontier, with heavier combined arms units concentrated in the interior of the country—lends itself to an interpretation as an essentially defensive, reactive approach. Under this configuration, any enemy incursion would be met first by the border security forces, composed of primarily PAP border security troops supported by light PLA units and militia troops, initially under a local command structure. While this border security element delays the enemy, PLA main force units (under centralized control at the Military Region (MR) level) would be deployed to eventually counterattack and destroy the enemy incursion, and presumably return the border to its antebellum configuration.[18]

It is important to note that many Chinese sources emphasize that border defense operations are conducted "in the service of national strategic priorities," and strongly imply national-level control of the operation in both time and space.[19] This means that the PLA may be ordered to cease operations when diplomatic objectives have been achieved, regardless of perceived tactical or operational military objectives in the actual zone of operations. In addition, in spite of invoking the concept of active defense as a key source for planning, discussion of PLA border defense operations consistently emphasizes the defensive nature of such missions and does not portray them as a means of expanding or annexing territory.[20]

In the broadest terms, this concept of confronting the threat of a heavy armed cross-border incursion with a "defense in depth" based on a frontier/interior lines force array is a fairly traditional approach and the types of missions and capabilities required of the PLA to execute such an operation would include the kinds of general capabilities any modern military force should be expected to accomplish with a degree of competency – ability to conduct delaying actions in time and space, establishment and maintenance of communications networks between services and between military and civilian agencies, as well as vertical networks from tactical units through operational headquarters to the national command authorities, ability to create, secure, and sustain movement corridors for rapid deployment of mobile reserves, and so on. These kind of tactical and operational-level missions are fairly "standard," and it is unlikely the border defense mission alone would generate a unique set of tactical or operational missions for the PLA that it would not otherwise prepare for.

Strategy for defense of maritime borders (encompassing coastal waters and shoreline) and airspace appears to be grounded in the same sort of division of labor. Unfortunately, open source literature is much more limited in discussing these aspects of China's frontier security strategy, often devoting whole chapters to land security and dismissing maritime or air frontiers as "special cases" that cannot be considered in the same way. Nevertheless, it would seem there are at least three important trends worth noting.

First, the basic division of responsibilities between PLA and PAP appears to mirror that along the land frontier, although the force structures are different. It is important to note that the command structure may very well be different, as provincial or prefectural joint commissions would likely not be the best mechanisms for handling situations that are much more likely to be politically sensitive, involve assets above the provincial level, and have strategic implications, even if they possess the technical capability and technology to do so. Nevertheless the focus on PLA defense as a supplement to PAP security work still seems to be the primary paradigm.

Second, development of China's coast, coupled with its expanding interests and capabilities, has pushed its maritime "frontier" farther out to sea, so that maritime frontier security is no longer synonymous with "coastal defense." As a result, it has been argued that the PLA's mission needs to change from "coastal defense" (近岸防御 *jin'an fangyu*) to "offshore defense" (近海防卫 *jinhai fangwei*). Defense and security of this more remote sea frontier will require surface, air and subsurface assets only the PLA Navy (PLAN) possesses.

Third, China recognizes that the likelihood of serious hostile intrusion by enemy naval forces is less than in previous years, but the threat posed by criminal elements and other nontraditional threats is greater. This calls for greater capability and emphasis on PAP and maritime law enforcement and policing in waters near the shore. It also has led Chinese authors to call for a "transition from a system emphasizing military defense to a system that emphasizes both civilian administration and military defense equally."[21]

In considering the overall role of the PLA in China's frontier security strategy, it is interesting to note how the less-traditional, but arguably more likely, frontier security challenges recognized by China as emergent in the 21st century would be addressed by the various actors in this "shared" approach, and in particular what additional nontraditional missions the PLA may be required to prepare for in implementation of this strategy.

The NDWP specifies that "stability and development of border areas are the foundation for border and coastal defense." Thus the PLA, as the "main force" for border defense in time of war, has a clear interest in being an active agent in securing the stability and development of border areas in peacetime. The NDWP further specifies that the PLA, along with other border security forces, "... maintain[s] social stability in border areas and unity among ethnic groups, and take[s] an active part in the economic development of border areas."[22]

The PLA therefore appears to have a specific mission to combat nontraditional threats (such as the "Three Forces" or cross-border criminal activity) in addition to being prepared for the more traditional threat of a foreign incursion. In assessing these less traditional threats, however, it does seem clear that China's strategy views them as more properly considered "frontier security" challenges rather than matters of border "defense." Thus, while the PLA has an active role in combating these threats, it is expected to do so as a supporting element, while the primary responsibility lies with the border security forces, namely the PAP, militia, and civilian governments and police.

Some such missions, like assisting in the development of the frontier regional economy through physical or technological infrastructure development, obviously are doubly beneficial, as they both serve the immediate mission of building a stable social environment in the region, while also providing the kind of infrastructure the PLA would need to support rapid escalation of assets and effort in the event of a more conventional border defense scenario.[23] One major concern of PLA and PAP writers in discussing the challenges of conducting border defense operations is the concern about providing a secure rear-area for operations by PLA and PAP forces in undeveloped, frontier zones dominated by potentially unfriendly ethnic or religious groups—obviously the peacetime "security" mission of building social unity and economic development in frontier zones also serves the PLA well in the event of possible future border defense contingencies.

It also remains the case that if internal civil or social unrest escalates to such a level that local Border Security Commissions are no longer able to manage the problem with only the PAP, PSB, and militia units available, the PLA may be expected to be able to conduct counterinsurgency operations to prevent further escalation and spread of unrest. Such an event would likely have to be very extreme and protracted to trigger such a shift in responsibilities, and the mechanism for how this would be effected is unclear, as is discussed below.[24]

In addition, the PLA must be prepared for the hypothetical case wherein a foreign force decides to take advantage of a deteriorating internal frontier situation to launch an incursion, so that from China's perspective the mission transitions from frontier security to border defense. Successful conduct of such a transition would require development in peacetime of clear lines of authority, chains of command, mechanisms for exercising command, and clear guidelines for the timing, authorization, authentication, and implementation of transfer of command and control, which would almost certainly take place under conditions of extreme stress and probably of much more intense public scrutiny than would have been the case in the past.

One of the most difficult aspects of the "shared responsibility" system to understand clearly is the mechanism for distributing, and if necessary transferring, command authority between civilian and military authorities. While command is generally described as "unified" (统一 *tongyi*) or "joint" (联合 *lianhe*) in theory, in practice it seems that the civilian authorities (including police forces and the PAP under civilian control) play the "lead role" up to a certain point. There is presumably, however, a "pivot point" at which the severity, political sensitivity, or scale of the problem becomes too great, and primary leadership transitions to being exercised through the military elements of the "shared responsibility" architecture. For example, in the government response to the Sichuan earthquake in May 2008, it very rapidly became clear that military headquarters were the key actors in allocating and deploying units and assigning missions.[25] On the other hand, in response to widespread outbreaks of unrest in Tibet in March 2008, officials explicitly denied PLA involvement in the subsequent crackdown, though they do concede the PLA was brought in "after the riots" to help clean up and maintain order — if true, this indicates an employment of both PAP and PLA in roles seemingly completely consistent with that envisioned by the "shared responsibility" model.[26]

It is possible that the lack of detail available on how such a handover is effected may reflect the fact that the Chinese themselves have not yet clearly defined a standard means by which such transitions are triggered and managed. The decision is likely made at the national level by the CMC and State Council, and is probably situation-dependent and driven by considerations such as those outlined above. Nevertheless it seems that the system remains somewhat ad hoc and thus potentially vulnerable to confusion in crisis, especially given the interplay of personalities and traditional relationships among local and national officials, and among civilian and military officials. For example, PAP or PLA units at the sub-district level that have been conducting frontier security missions for long periods under local government authorities can be expected to have built habitual command and cooperation relationships, especially among key officials and leaders. The opportunities for considerations of "*guanxi*" or habitual relationships to interfere with smooth implementation of sudden changes to the command hierarchy could be considerable. Such complexities would logically give rise to the kinds of inefficiencies and ambiguities that are frequently mentioned as problems by Chinese professional writers on this topic.

Since China's frontier security challenges involve complex interactions of domestic and foreign actors across a wide spectrum of potential activities, it is perhaps not surprising that the system described above, while logical in theory, appears to have some inadequacies in practice. These inadequacies have occasionally been thrown into sharp relief at least in training exercises, and there has been some significant discussion of the problems with the current system and proposals for remedies in professional journals of the PLA and PAP.[27]

The majority of the difficulties in Chinese frontier security operations mentioned in recent publications center on the challenges of coordination between multiple military, police and civilian headquarters and units. One publication by officers of the Yunnan Provincial Committee on Frontier Defense complains

143

of the disjointed, uncoordinated nature of current frontier security processes, which suffer from unclear authority structure and a blurred division of responsibilities. In particular, operations are said to be highly fragmented, especially between military and local goverenment jurisdictions, and to create an environment that discourages innovation.[28] In the Far West, staff officers place heavy emphasis on the problems of discordant authority, lack of integration among units and problems in communication.[29]

Among the remedies recommended by PLA and PAP officers alike, the most common is an emphasis on joint and combined training involving all the key stakeholders in the frontier security mission.[30] These are principally the PLA, the PAP, the local militia units, and local civilian authorities, but can include many other "social stability" organs. At least one exercise conducted in 2007 in Guangxi was hailed as "an innovative construction" of an "experimental" joint training model for combined military, police, and militia units. This example in particular is illustrative of several points, namely: the "innovative," "experimental," solution was developed at the military sub-district level, under authority and directive from the provincial military district headquarters; PLA border defense units, as well as PAP border security units, were expected to use their superior resources and organization to train the less developed militia units. This was viewed as a distinct break from previous form, which was based on the approach that "each carries out its own duties and trains its own soldiers."[31] This singular example illustrates the PLA execution of at least two distinct missions in support of frontier security (including border defense)—in this case, PLA headquarters at provincial and prefectural level assumed the mission of improving joint operations, and PLA units undertook the mission of providing training support to militias and frontier security partners.

Some commentators also note the need to strengthen the effectiveness and leadership capability of the Border Commissions at all levels and the need for greater clarity in regulations to spell out detailed, specific division of responsibilities among various agencies involved. The article by the Yunnan Frontier Defense Commission members notes that (as of 2007) China "still does not have comprehensive border defense laws and regulations," which is directly affecting the country's ability to continue developing frontier security. The most common complaints are lack of clarity in command relationships and division of responsibility—a subject obviously of crucial importance in a system that theoretically depends upon clear understanding of such divisions among subordinate actors to work properly.[32]

In addition to these concerns at the interagency level, as a supporting element the PLA needs to develop and sustain certain capabilities to fulfill its mission as a partner in the frontier security mission. Chief among these is the need to develop communications networks and systems that facilitate information and intelligence sharing both horizontally and vertically, as well as to enable command and control between military and civilian headquarters. It clearly will also require emphasis on political officers and cadres to develop civil affairs capabilities to conduct the kind of public outreach and civil-military relations activity necessary to build unity within the border regions, especially in those dominated by non-Han ethnic minorities. In terms of force structure, it requires large numbers of units with specific capabilities—manpower intensive, light enough to operate in difficult terrain and climate conditions, and well trained in civil-military operations as well as public affairs. These units will also need high quality personnel and leaders, conscious of the fact that they operate in an increasingly "open" environment. The "strategic corporal" may not yet be a feature of Chinese military understanding, held at bay by an authoritarian command structure and rigidly controlled official information environment. Nonetheless, there is recognition of the idea that lower-level commanders will be required to make decisions that could have strategic consequences, especially given the repeated emphasis on the need for flexibility and innovation in frontier security operations in the current environment. The degree to which the PLA is successful in cultivating this kind of leader, or units capable of this kind of flexibility, will depend in large part on how training programs are modified to develop and encourage these skills, and whether or not professional development courses, as well as career progression and personnel policies, emphasize the importance of demonstrating such skills.

Understanding the application of the "shared responsibility" concept also appears to be the key to understanding PLA missions in response to another threat category currently of great concern to Chinese national defense planners — namely, the threat of terrorism. As one of the three "evil forces" threatening stability and social order, terrorism in the Chinese assessment presents another significant national-level threat that requires an advanced, sophisticated and multiagency approach to be successfully countered.

COUNTERTERRORISM

Chinese discussion of the terrorist threat acknowledges the international nature of terrorist threats in the post-September 11, 2001 (9-11) world, but it is evident that perceptions of the nature, goals, and characteristics of the threat are quite different than those prevalent in the United States. Analyses in Chinese sources tend to focus on the threat of domestic terrorism, aimed at destabilizing Chinese society, usually for purposes of furthering "separatism" along ethnic, religious or national lines. As is the case in frontier security planning, the fundamental chain of Chinese strategic security planning is quite clearly evidenced — economic growth is essential to government stability; social stability is essential for economic growth; terrorism directly attacks social stability, hence terrorism is a strategic threat to the nation. Practical experience with the negative impact of terrorism on economic development in Xinjiang has been cited as an example of this.[33] Terrorism also threatens national territorial integrity by demonstrating the government's inability to protect its people and by potentially inciting secessionist sentiment. Thus, terrorism is perceived as representing a direct challenge to the two primary strategic pillars of Chinese governmental legitimacy.

There is widespread recognition on some characteristics of the terrorist threat that are clearly in synch with Western perceptions: that the threat is "globalized" or transnational; that terrorists operate in a decentralized manner, able to function disparately yet remain coordinated through technology; that technology in general greatly enables terrorist actions; that there is increasing threat of terrorists employing unconventional attack means such as

147

cyber attack or weapons of mass destruction (WMD); that terror networks are often deeply interlinked with other transnational criminal activities such as drug smuggling; and that these and other traits in turn can result in their linkage to governments or governing organs through corrupt or sympathetic officials. Very importantly, China also quite clearly perceives the threat that hostile governments can utilize terrorist cells, or the disruption they cause, to threaten social stability and perhaps create conditions favorable for foreign interference in Chinese domestic affairs.

There is also a general agreement in Chinese discussion of the necessary characteristics of an effective CT program. They recognize the importance of preventing terrorism as the centerpiece of a comprehensive CT program, which is pursued by removing incentives and attacking terrorist recruitment sources through economic development as well as promotion of ethnic and national harmony and unity through propaganda and public relations campaigns. They also call for close cooperation with neighboring countries, especially in the area of intelligence sharing, which is often identified as one of the most important yet least developed means of international cooperation against cross-border terrorism.

The NDWP specifically assigns the mission for CT to the PAP. As in the approach to frontier security, there appears to be a system for organization and direction of domestic CT operations in China that divides responsibilities and assigns the PLA the mission of playing a supporting role in what is primarily a PAP responsibility. At the national level, the National Leading Small Group for Counterterrorism Coordination was established in 2001 to coordinate the many government organizations that have a role in a comprehensive national CT effort. This structure is replicated down to the provincial level, and membership reportedly includes civilian police, PAP, foreign affairs offices, the Ministry of State Security (MSS), and the military. A recent CT exercise held in Tibet was overseen by CCP and government officials, including representatives of the "Autonomous Region Counterterrorism Working Group" — some military units were listed as participants, but do not appear to have exercised primary control of the event.[34] This is a similar pattern to that observed in various other CT exercises in China. For example, the PLA has been reported as participating in only two of the past five "Great Wall" series national-level Chinese CT exercises.[35]

Because CT operations are politically sensitive, extremely time-sensitive, involve complex command and coordination requirements, and require highly specialized techniques in virtually unpredictable circumstances for direct action against specific terrorist targets, reliance on small, highly trained and specially equipped CT units remains the most common prescription. The primary PLA units for this are the various Special Operations Groups at the MR level (the "Flying Dragons," "Divine Swords," etc.). In the PAP, Special Police Units, probably organic at the provincial or municipal level, fulfill this function. In addition, at the national level the PAP has formed the elite "Snow Leopards" unit, which has become a highly publicized standard bearer for China's CT preparedness, especially in the run up to the Beijing Olympics.[36] Such units are not limited to direct action teams, but also appear to include specialized support units such as aviation. For example, at least one report regarding security arrangements for the Beijing Games discussed an elite "special flight brigade," equipped with helicopters and surveillance optics, crewed by pilots "all trained at undisclosed locations overseas."[37]

Some authors have argued that all specialized CT units (presumably including PLA ones) should be placed under PAP/PSB authority when deployed operationally, and that except in a small number of unique cases (such as Tibet or Xinjiang), the PLA "should not unduly take on counterterrorism missions at the risk of causing too much harm for too little gain."[38]

An important mission for the PLA in support of PAP-led CT missions is in the area of unconventional terrorist attack, specifically those involving maritime, air, or WMD (nuclear, biological, or chemical) attacks. This is also almost certainly because the PLA possesses the capabilities, specialized units and equipment, and training necessary for dealing with these contingencies. In the lead up to the Beijing Olympic Games in August 2008, Chinese reports specified that the PAP was responsible for general security and preventing terrorism "on the ground" while the PLA had primary responsible for air, maritime, or WMD events. It should be noted, however, that the Olympics may have been a special case, and that even under special circumstances the PLA seems more often to be expected to fulfill supplementary missions in support of the PAP. Maritime CT drills conducted in Qingdao before the games were run by the "marine police," under control of the Ministry of Public Security (MPS).[39] The PAP likely possesses at least some capability to deal with the initial phases of WMD attacks, as they would almost certainly be the "first responders" before the PLA arrives. For example, Exercise "Great Wall 3," held in Qingdao in 2006 but coordinated from Beijing, had a scenario built around a "biochemical attack," but the only participants mentioned in available sources are the PAP and Qingdao PSB.

In essence, then, it appears the PLA's missions in China's domestic counterterrorism strategy are similar in nature to those it has under the frontier security strategy, namely:

- Work in cooperation with local civilian and police authorities to deter domestic terrorism by helping promote and maintain social stability;
- Augment police forces in responding to terrorist attacks, including by sustaining, deploying, and controlling specialized CT units as needed;
- Assume a key role in preventing, defending against, or responding to terrorism attacks in maritime or air environments, or attacks involving WMD.

Much remains unclear about the exact implementation of this strategy in practice.

It would seem there is still much work that could be undertaken to improve interagency coordination and address command, control, and coordination problems similar to those that occur in the area of frontier security. For example, there is recognition that, as in the case of frontier security, there is a need for more detailed CT laws and regulations to clearly delineate the division of labor and responsibility within agencies for CT operations.[40]

We have seen that Chinese planning considers that CT operations should be primarily a job for security forces, especially domestically. Yet Chinese authors make clear that the nature of globalized terrorist threats are such that terrorist threats against China could, and likely would, emerge outside of China. Under the theory of active defense, the PLA still recognizes the need to be able under the right conditions to operate preemptively if necessary, which raises several questions. How would this be done when the operation involves crossing international boundaries? Clearly, preparing for these contingencies requires a high degree of cooperation and coordination with the CT and border security forces of foreign countries, and if China's CT exercises with foreign countries are any indicator, it appears the PLA has a much more prominent role in conducting CT operations in an international context.

SECURITY COOPERATION/ COUNTERTERRORISM EXERCISES

As Chinese frontier security and counterterrorism planning both recognize the importance of international cooperation against transnational threats, it is perhaps no surprise that the past decade has seen a dramatic increase in the number, scale, and type of PLA exercises with foreign militaries, both within China and outside its borders. Since 2002 alone, over 30 different exercises have been identified or reported.[41] While some of these exercises have been conducted with Western countries or allies, the clear majority share two common themes — they have been conducted with countries directly bordering the PRC, and they have featured at least a declared theme or emphasis on CT.

The clear majority of these exercises have taken place within the member countries of the Shanghai Cooperation Organization (SCO), and almost always they have been publicized as "counterterrorism" exercises. Exercises are often described as practicing cross-border coordination of operations, multinational direct action operations against "terrorist" units, and involving border defense and frontier security units from one or more participant countries, in addition to national-level CT forces. The frequent involvement of frontier security units, coupled with CT-based scenarios and troops, further underscores the importance of these missions in supporting China's national security strategy by addressing the threats it perceives along its frontier.

Bilateral and multilateral exercises with foreign militaries, both inside and outside of China, serve a variety of strategic and political functions including demonstrating capabilities, fulfilling national "great power" aspirations, and signaling other countries. In terms of PLA missions and mission readiness, however, there are three main aspects worth highlighting: first, they provide the PLA an opportunity to observe and learn from foreign militaries lessons that can then be used to improve its own capabilities; second, they improve the PLA's capabilities to operate outside of China and in cooperation with other forces; and, third, they support the mission of promoting stability and social order by providing a highly visible deterrent to potentially destabilizing forces. This latter aspect is enhanced by the visible propagandizing and publicity given by Chinese media, both to these exercises and the elite units participating in them.

Determining exactly what types of units participate in the individual exercises is sometimes difficult, but many of the exercise scenarios appear to involve combined "direct action" missions against "terrorist" bands who have seized important hostages or building complexes. It is likely that in the event of such an occurrence, especially outside China, the PLA would be the primary provider of any armed Chinese contribution to the CT force, and indeed, most often these exercises involve PLA units such as elite CT units of the MRs, as well as specialized PLA supporting elements for transport, logistics, and communications. This in turn implies a division of responsibility for domestic and international CT efforts between the PAP and PLA, a division that would mirror the overall apparent strategic orientation of both forces. In accordance with China's concept of "active defense," even within the context of CT operations, it seems clear that the PLA has a mission to respond to terrorist actions outside China in cooperation with friendly foreign militaries. It remains unclear if this mission encompasses actions taken "proactively" (i.e., on the basis of shared intelligence and perceived threat, but before any actual terrorist action has taken place), or unilaterally (without cooperation or invitation of a foreign government). The exercise scenarios and public reports do not give any explicit indications of this, but it clearly warrants closer study.

In 2007, Exercise "Cooperation 2007" in Russia featured participation by the PAP's "Snow Leopard" CT unit, the first publicly reported instance of this level of PAP involvement in exercises outside China.[42] The inclusion of the PAP in this exercise is an exception, but this may have other functions — some PAP professional publications have noted the importance of training with foreign elite units to remain current on the latest techniques, equipment, and experience of these units, to assist in developing China's own domestic capabilities. It is more likely that PAP international participation is thus aimed at improving the PAP's own capabilities to operate domestically, rather than expanding its role to operations outside China.

Still, while CT remains the stated mission for many, if not most, of these exercises, there is no question that China clearly capitalizes on the international currency of the CT issue in a post-9-11 world to pursue other security cooperation objectives in its interaction with foreign militaries. Most of these involve signaling to outside powers, especially the United States, that China remains interested and engaged in regions around its periphery, especially Central Asia, and has the capability to project power (in a limited, albeit developing way) into those regions, especially with the assistance of friendly SCO partners. It also intends to assuage the concerns of smaller neighboring states about China's rise, by establishing the image of China as a cooperative security partner focused on addressing issues of shared concern, such as cross-border operations of terrorist groups.

In this sense, the PLA clearly has a mission of supporting the demonstration and credibility of the strategic "messages" through organizing and executing these types of combined exercises. Decisionmaking authority for approval and conduct of such exercises is no doubt retained at the national level with the CMC in conjunction with the State Council, due to the diplomatic and national level factors involved, but planning and execution of the actual exercises clearly involve MR headquarters and probably also provincial level commands where appropriate, judging from the types of commanders and officers generally interviewed, cited, or referenced as observing or participating in the various press reports.

CONCLUSIONS AND IMPLICATIONS

It is thus quite evident that the PLA has significant missions in support of Chinese national security strategic goals beyond the preservation of territorial integrity through deterring Taiwan independence or potentially compelling unification. In the areas of frontier security, CT, and international security cooperation, we have seen PLA missions spelled out, with varying degrees of clarity, in official government publications (such as the NDWP) as well as acknowledged, analyzed, and explained in extensive discussion in professional journals and in analysis by Western scholars.

In all of these cases, PLA missions fulfill a largely supporting role in the overall national defense strategy. Both frontier security and to a large extent CT are primarily the responsibility of the public security forces, especially the PAP. While the international aspects of CT appear to be primarily a PLA responsibility, it is nevertheless important to realize that China evidently perceives its primary terrorist threat to be a domestic challenge. It is likely that this is as much a result of recent events as it is of China's current physical security environment, which at present features relatively peaceful, constructive relations with almost every country along its long land frontier.[43] Both factors, coupled with China's strategic priority to project a nonthreatening image to the world as part of its "peaceful rise" strategy, strongly militate against a highly visible military role in such actions as border policing and CT.

Finally, as noted above, it is likely these missions would remain a core part of the overall PLA mission regardless of the development of the Taiwan issue. Some have argued that China's adoption of an essentially defensive posture along its land borders, emphasizing diplomatic efforts to resolve long-standing border disputes coupled with increased cooperation and a de facto "demilitarization," is designed to create strategic space for an offensive posture eastward, towards Taiwan and China's maritime "frontier."[44] While this analysis may very likely be correct, it does not necessarily follow that upon resolution of the Taiwan issue (especially if in China's favor, i.e., through reunification or at least neutralization), China would fundamentally change the PLA's role, mission, or orientation in terms of land border defense, nor transition to a more "offensive" or aggressive land security posture. Of more interest perhaps would be consideration of how the strategy of "frontier security" missions would apply, and whether or not the "shared responsibilities" system would remain the model for promotion of social stability and security in the "newly acquired" frontier province of Taiwan.

On the other hand, unfavorable resolution of the Taiwan issue (from China's point of view), presumably including military defeat and independence for the island, would probably severely destabilize China domestically and further heighten the regime's fears of foreign interference along its land borders, possibly leading to a rebalancing of focus among the PLA's various missions. In such a case, a "remilitarization" of China's land frontier and border missions, as the reaction of both a wounded national pride and a regime that perceives itself as under threat from within and without, would seem a very possible, though not inevitable, outcome.

The importance of these missions in PLA planning, and even more perhaps their prominence in the national defense strategy of the PRC, has significant implications for U.S. policymakers in coming years. China's focus on frontier security as a strategic priority increases the potential risk of incidents between Chinese border security forces and foreign forces. This is especially likely along disputed and less well-defined maritime and air frontiers, as incidents like the April 2001 collision between a Chinese fighter and a U.S. EP-3 aircraft and its aftermath clearly demonstrate. Because of the very high level of importance attached to the frontier security issue in Chinese strategic conceptions, such incidents are likely to have much more significant diplomatic and political implications, and greater risk of serious conflict, than might be anticipated by other countries involved who do not view the incident in the same light or as being of the same level of seriousness.

At the level of strategic diplomacy, China's frontier security focus implies that U.S. policymakers should expect China to continue to emphasize building constructive relationships with neighboring states, especially those along land borders, using bilateral diplomacy as well as multilateral mechanisms in which China is a dominant partner, such as the SCO. China can also be expected to increase its ability to secure what it sees as its maritime frontier, most likely by pursuing a two-pronged policy of seeking diplomatic and legal recognition of its maritime claims while continuing development of military capabilities to secure and defend such claims, or at least deter intrusion by foreign powers into waters or airspace considered by China to be part of its "frontier."

In the area of CT, U.S. planners should expect China to continue to use CT as a convenient rationale for continued and expanded military cooperation and exercises, especially within the SCO. It provides China with a useful narrative within which to expand influence in Central Asia and present an alternative security architecture for the region that does not include the United States. The United States should expect China to continue to promote this approach to counter perceived expansion of U.S. influence and power in the region.

Finally, it is essential that U.S. analysts and policymakers continue to improve their understanding of China's conceptions of "frontiers," its doctrine for defending them, and above all the place and prioritization of such missions in overall national defense planning. In the changing world of the early 21st century, security dynamics are in constant flux. Frontiers are no longer simply land borders or even maritime lines or zones. Clearly there are now frontiers in both space and cyberspace, in physical security as well as economics and trade, in demographics, environmental challenges, and health issues. When are such frontiers considered "violated" by another power? When are such violations a threat to national security? What is the threshold across which such a violation merits a military response? China and the PLA already recognize these questions, even if they have not yet defined their answers. The United States must not only answer these questions for itself, but must also strive to monitor and, if possible, influence this discussion or risk danger of miscalculation in any future confrontation with China.

CHAPTER 5 - ENDNOTES

1. Information Office of the State Council, *China's National Defense in 2006*, Beijing, PRC: December 29, 2006. As it is most commonly referred to as the *National Defense White Paper*, it is hereafter referred to as *NDWP 06*.

2. Professor Andrew Scobell's introduction to this volume proposes a four-celled "matrix" for classifying potential scenarios for Chinese management of the Taiwan issue. For purposes of this chapter, the issue of frontier security is considered within the conditions roughly analogous to Scobell's "A" or "B" cells, which reflect the current status quo with a tendency towards nonconflict resolution in the long term. Specific implications for frontier security that are dependent on which of these outcomes prevails are discussed more fully at the end of this chapter.

3. Among current scholarship on these issues, one of the best recent examples is M. Taylor Fravel, "Securing Borders: China's Doctrine and Force Structure for Frontier Defense," *Journal of Strategic Studies*, Vol. 30, No. 4-5, August-October 2007. Specific lists of tactical missions performed by PLA border defense units are listed in Li Xing, ed., *Bianfang Xue* [*The Science of Border Defense*], Beijing, China: Junshi Kexue Chubanshe, 2004, pp. 304-306. Numerous discussions and lists are also available in English-language sources. Likewise, this chapter will not concern itself with discussing unit sizes, troop numbers, equipment, and so on—these have been thoroughly covered in excellent detail in a number of other works, and need no elaboration or recounting here. See, for example, Dennis Blasko, "PLA Ground Force Modernization and Mission Diversification: Underway in All Military Regions," in Roy Kamphausen and Andrew Scobell, eds., *Rightsizing the PLA: Exploring the Contour's of China's Military*, Carlisle, PA: U.S. Army War College, Strategic Studies Institute, 2007, pp. 281-373.

4. The author is deeply indebted to Matthew Boswell, whose support as research assistant on this project was invaluable, particularly in the survey and initial translation of primary source materials.

5. Chinese sources recognize that nontraditional threats likely require nontraditional responses, sometimes referred to as "nonwar" actions to distinguish them from more traditional military missions. See Gao Taicun, "Zhongguo feichuantong anquan mianlin de tiaozhan yi sikao" ["Challenges and Reflections on Non-Traditional Security in China"], *Journal of the People's Armed Police Academy*, Vol. 23, No. 1, January 2007.

6. Guo Yan, "Clearly Recognizing Basic Characteristics of Non-War Action," *Zhongguo Guofang Bao* Online Edition, August 14, 2008, pp. 1-3.

7. *NDWP 06*, p. 3.

8. This is itself viewed as the product of deliberate Chinese strategy, including diplomatic efforts in recent years aimed at peaceful resolution of all remaining border territorial disputes with neighboring states. Each of these has been greeted with great

publicity and propagandistic fanfare, including recent resolutions finalized with Russia.

9. This expression is repeatedly cited throughout relevant literature, from *NDWP 06* down, as an apparent "official" or at least "officially sanctioned" formulaic expression of the principle potential sources of social disorder.

10. See Wang Guosheng, "On Relations to be Correctly Handled in Strengthening Border Area Defense," *Zhongguo Junshi Kexue*, Vol. 19, No. 2, 2006, pp. 7-10. Major General Wang wrote as Chief of Staff of the Lanzhou MR. Wang also makes the point that border defense and frontier security are mutually reinforcing missions.

11. Fravel, p. 706.

12. *Ibid.*, p. 709.

13. One further mission the PLA must be assumed to have under Chinese strategic planning in the context of frontier security is the mission of deterrence against violations of the border by hostile powers. Clearly, providing a credible demonstration of capability to respond effectively to neutralize threats, whether they originate externally or internally, is an ongoing mission for the PLA. See Blasko, pp. 292-293.

14. There is also recognition that promoting development in the frontier can pose difficult challenges through what appear to be contradictory imperatives — for example, promoting economic growth often requires facilitating easier cross-border movement, while countersmuggling or criminal cross-border activity may require tighter controls.

15. See, for example, Gao, pp. 7-8. An earlier discussion of this topic in the same journal occurs in Wang Hongjun, "Woguo fankongbu douzheng duice yanjiu" ["Research into China's Countermeasures in the Struggle Against Terrorism"], *Journal of the People's Armed Police Academy*, Vol. 20, No. 5, October 2005, pp. 83-86.

16. *NDWP 06*, p. 21. Interestingly, the English translation of this term by China is "shared responsibilities," while the actual Chinese seems to convey "divided responsibilities." In application, the latter appears more accurate; use of the former in this chapter is a reflection only of the fact that this appears to be the "official" Chinese government translation.

17. *Ibid.*, pp. 6-8.

18. A particularly excellent summary of current Chinese operational doctrine for border defense is found in Fravel, pp. 718-722. The author draws on a number of PLA sources to analyze a typical PLA "border defense campaign" plan.

19. *Ibid.*, p. 718.

20. To be sure, sources discuss the principles of "active defense," and clearly the PLA conception of mission here includes strikes across borders at targets in neighboring countries. Such strikes are contemplated using a variety of means, including missiles, aircraft, or deployed troop units. Such operations, however, are typically characterized as defensive in nature and aimed at neutralizing targets before they can violate Chinese territory, not as a means of annexing territory from neighboring countries.

21. Li, pp. 197-205.

22. *NDWP 06*, p. 23.

23. Some analysis of the response to the Tibet unrest in March 2008 has noted the presence of "out of area" PAP units in photographs, and the rapid deployment of reinforcing elements (especially if it included PLA main force units) from other regions would certainly have demonstrated the security forces' ability to benefit from recently improved infrastructure linking Tibet to the rest of China.

24. Fravel, p. 715. The use of the term "counter-separatist military action" (*fan fenlie junshi xindong*) for this mission may indicate that it is only expected to be required in the case of a large-scale separatist guerilla event presumably marked by ethnic or

religious separatism, and is not conceived of as a potential option against economically or otherwise motivated social upheaval, i.e., violence against the system but that does not necessarily advocate *separatism*. It is, however, likely that this distinction is a largely semantic one.

25. James Mulvenon, "The Chinese Military's Earthquake Response Leadership Team," *China Leadership Monitor*, No. 25, Summer 2008, available from *www.hoover.org/publications/ clm/issues/20100024.html*. While this was not a frontier security situation, it does demonstrate one attempt at coordinating civil-military joint efforts on a massive scale.

26. "Lethal Weapons Not Used in Tibetan Unrest," *South China Morning Post*, March 18, 2008. Some analysts cite photographic evidence of PLA involvement in the earlier "suppression" phase of the operation, but what is available in public sources does not seem to be conclusive.

27. It will be useful to monitor various Chinese sources in the wake of actual incidents such as the domestic unrest in Tibet or the rash of attacks against PAP and police units in Xinjiang in August 2008 to see if more detailed and candid internal assessments of the effectiveness of government responses are forthcoming.

28. Shi Hongguang and Fang Xingguo, "Yunyong kexue fazhanguan zhidao bianfang jianshe chuangxin fazhan" ["Using Scientific Development to Bring About New Ideas in Border Defense"], *Guofang*, 2007, No. 1, pp. 54-56.

29. Cheng Bing, "Jiji tuijin 'Guanbian kongbian jianbian' jizhi chuangxin shiying xin shiqi bianfang gongzuo xuyao" ["Actively Promote the Innovative System of 'Manage, Control, and Develop the Border' to Adapt to the Border Defense Requirements of the New Era"], *Guofang* 2006, No. 8, pp. 61-63. Major General Cheng writes as Chief of Staff of Xinjiang Military District (MD).

30. A good representative source is Lu Meizhang, "An Analysis of PAP and Military Border Defense Joint Training Organization," *Guofang* 2004, No. 12. Lu wrote as Chief of Staff of a Military Sub-District in Yunnan Province, and provides a good summary of

specific goals to be addressed in joint training, as well as threats and scenarios to be used.

31. Yuan Wei, "Complementing Advantages, Linked Training, Coordinated Operations—Chongzuo Military Sub-District Constructs Military/Police/Militia Joint Defense Joint Training Mechanisms," Guangzhou *Zhanshi Bao*, March 8, 2007, p. 3. The publication is an official daily put out by the political department of the Guangzhou MR.

32. Cheng, p. 62; Shi and Fang, p. 55.

33. Wang Hongjun, p. 86. The author is identified as Deputy Director of the Theoretical Teaching and Research Section, Security Department, PAP Academy.

34. Liu Junwu, "Tibet Autonomous Region Conducts Counterterrorist Exercise with Real Units," originally published in *Xizang Ribao*, August 5, 2008, accessed from Renminwang at *leaders.people/com/cn/GB/7612526.html on 28AUG08*. These "drills," referred to as "Sky Road 08," and "Grand Hawk 08," were held on August 2 and 4, 2008, and centered on the Lhasa airport and train station respectively. Participants included not only the local PAP and PLA headquarters, but elements of the PLA Air Force (PLAAF), fire departments, propaganda departments, sanitation/health office, foreign affairs bureau, environmental protection office, communications office, civil aviation, and others. The simple fact of the inclusion of so many disparate units would seem to indicate a thorough analysis of the threat implications, and a good attempt to include as comprehensive as possible a list of participants who could be expected to have a role in response to a real world incident.

35. James Bellacqua, *Terrorism in China: Perceptions of Vulnerability, Countermeasures*, Alexandria, VA: CNA Corporation, July 2008, p. 14.

36. While specifics on these units are naturally difficult to come by, China does publicize some aspects of these units' training and capabilities for both propaganda and likely deterrent purposes. A good overview can be found at *sinodefence.com*, *www.sinodefence. com/organisation/armedpolice/special-police.asp* (for PAP units) and

www.sinodefence.com/organisation/groundforces/specialoperations.asp (for PLA units).

37. "Snow Leopards, Blue Swords Ready to Keep Games Safe," available from *China.Org.Cn, www.china.org.cn/china/ national/2008-07/09/content_15977501.htm.*

38. Wang Hongjun, p. 86. It should, of course, be noted that Wang is employed by the PAP Academy and writing in a PAP publication, and so might be expected to support this view.

39. "Marine Police Stage Anti-Terror Drills for Olympics," Xinhua News Agency, July 14, 2007, available from *www.china. org.cn/china/national/2007-07/14/content_1217065.htm.* The same article, however, notes that the PLAN is "responsible for security of maritime venues" for the games, without explaining the apparent contradiction. Such ambiguity and contradictory statements are distressingly common.

40. Bellacqua, p. 17. The author cites numerous Chinese sources, including Li Wei, Deputy Director of the National Leading Small Group for CT Coordination, as specifically acknowledging these needs.

41. Total numbers vary depending on criteria used to define "exercise," such as whether "observer-only" participation qualifies an exercise as "multinational." Since 2002, at least 36 exercises have occurred involving actual deployment of troops from more than one country as exercise participants.

42. "China's 'Snow Leopard' Commandos to Train with Russian Commandoes," *People's Daily Online*, August 29, 2007, available from *english.people.com.cn/90001/90776/6250873.html.*

43. It is perhaps instructive that in the case of two countries that are arguably least stable/predictable, North Korea and Burma/ Myanmar, the PLA assumption of its border defense mission in 2003 was highly publicized and portrayed as the PLA "taking over the border defense." Some evidence seems to indicate the PLA was deployed to strengthen the PAP presence, rather than replace it—in other words, exactly as the "shared responsibility" system would envision. But the characterization of "PLA takeover" may

have indicated a change in command relationships. More study of this particular incident is needed.

44. A good example of this argument is Ji You, "Defending China's Land Borders: The 1.5 War Scenario," *OpinionAsia*, July 24, 2007, available from *www.opinionasia.org/DefendingChinasLandBorders*. The author is a Senior Lecturer at the University of New South Wales in Australia.

CHAPTER 6

STRATEGIC DETERRENCE BEYOND TAIWAN

Brad Roberts

As other chapters in this volume amply attest, "beyond Taiwan" means something substantial to the on-going development of the Chinese People's Liberation Army's (PLA) capabilities. This is as true of China's strategic deterrent as of other elements of the PLA. To gain insights into the missions of China's strategic forces "beyond Taiwan," this chapter begins with a review of China's strategic posture. The central element of this posture is China's force of ballistic missiles tipped with nuclear weapons. But this is not the only element of China's strategic deterrent force, and a broader view is needed. This chapter summarizes the historical development of this force with an eye to highlighting evolving operational capabilities for different missions. The chapter then turns to a discussion of the Taiwan mission itself as it relates to China's strategic deterrent, on the argument that the Taiwan mission accounts for many of the operational characteristics of China's strategic deterrent, but not all of them. The chapter will then explore the roles of China's strategic deterrent vis-à-vis other conflicts around China's periphery. The chapter closes with a discussion of conclusions and implications.[1]

As a point of departure, it is important to note that relatively little has been written about the roles and missions of China's strategic forces by authoritative Chinese sources. The PLA academic community has produced a small but growing body of material that provides general characterizations of Chinese thinking about deterrence and the role of nuclear weapons in China's national security strategy, but this literature makes few or no apparent distinctions between the "Taiwan mission" and other missions.[2] There is very little authoritative information about the roles and missions of specific strategic forces, the nature of ongoing modernization activities and the problems they are intended to address, or the resourcing enabling such modernization. The scholarship by experts outside of China on China's nuclear posture and strategic force, whatever its many virtues, does not add many significant new insights into the mission space "beyond Taiwan."[3] Accordingly, the conjectural nature of this work requires analytical caution.[4]

To help locate this analysis within the larger framework employed by this volume, two further introductory points are useful. First, this chapter is framed within "cell A" of the introduction, i.e., it assumes that there is no conflict over Taiwan, but also no resolution and that the status quo persists. The concluding section of this chapter includes a discussion of how China's strategic deterrence posture might be affected by some of the other "outcomes" elaborated in the editor's matrix of possible outcomes. Second, this chapter follows the definition of roles and missions introduced earlier. The role of China's nuclear force is strategic deterrence and toward this end it maintains and is developing various capabilities, but its missions are defined in terms of specific political-military end states in the various scenarios that concern China's military planners.

CHINA'S STRATEGIC POSTURE

The U.S. defense community has a relatively strict and indeed simple notion of what constitutes a nation's strategic posture that equates strategic with intercontinental range nuclear strike capabilities. U.S. experts tend not to recognize the degree to which this notion reflects the unique strategic circumstance of the United States, separated as it is from potential adversaries by two oceans and having arrived at an arsenal after 60 years as a nuclear power that is devoid of medium-range delivery systems and nearly devoid of shorter-range tactical systems. Accordingly, experts in the United States tend to misperceive the nature and scope of China's strategic posture by limiting their focus to nuclear weapons deployed on intercontinental missiles.

China's strategic posture is different in part because, like that of the United States, it reflects its own geographic circumstances and history. In contrast to America's two wide oceans and two friendly neighbors, China has more countries around its periphery than any other country in the world, and a long history of conflict along that periphery that leaves many unsettled issues. Accordingly, its nuclear forces are not just long range. In contrast to the continuing deemphasis of nuclear weapons in the U.S. strategic posture since the end of the Cold War, China has perceived a need to adapt and update its posture to address changing requirements. Accordingly, it has modernized those forces and also increased their numbers. Moreover, China has begun to integrate additional military capabilities into its strategic posture. These include ballistic missiles tipped with conventional rather than nuclear weapons, counterspace attack capabilities, and even nonkinetic means for damaging critical nodes at very long distances. In an objective sense, China's strategic posture also includes the capacity to protect China from strategic attack, a capacity unlike that of the United States in its emphasis on passive defense. (The United States has emphasized active defense in the form of ballistic missile protection, whereas China has pursued a very ambitious civil defense program aimed at protecting national leadership and key capabilities in underground facilities.) Any strategic posture also includes the capabilities to command and control strategic weaponry, and the supporting intelligence, surveillance, and reconnaissance systems. China has not publicly articulated a concept for its strategic posture that identifies all of these elements, yet they objectively are part of its capacities to wage a confrontation at the strategic level of war.

But too little is known about the broad elements of China's strategic posture to enable an informed and coherent exploration in this space. Accordingly, the focus here is on China's nuclear weapons and their delivery means, including primarily the land-based forces under the control of the Second Artillery but also nuclear delivery forces in the PLA Navy and Air Force. In Hu Jintao's words, "The Second Artillery Corps is a strategic force directly commanded and used by the Party Central Committee and the Central Military Commission and is our core force for strategic deterrence."[5]

Three Phases of Force Evolution.

It is useful to think of the evolution of this force in roughly three main phases. The purpose here is not to review each phase exhaustively; rather, it is to provide enough information about each to illuminate findings and conclusions relevant to the mission space "beyond Taiwan."

Phase 1. The first phase was the period of China's strategic infancy, as it moved to plan, create, and field its first-generation strategic force.[6] This phase lasted from the initiation of China's nuclear weapons development program to the achievement of a capability to deliver nuclear weapons at intercontinental range—that is, from 1955 when Mao launched Project 02 to 1980 when China successfully tested the DF-5.[7] As a testament to the closing of this phase of strategic infancy, in 1981 China conducted a massive combined arms exercise aimed at demonstrating its full preparedness for nuclear war, and in 1983 it showcased its array of nuclear missile capabilities in its annual military parade through Tiananmen Square.[8] Mao embraced nuclear weapons as essentially "a political weapon" (a term that remains in use today),[9] useful for standing up to "bullying" by other powers. The principles of no first use and minimum retaliation followed. Mao also embraced nuclear weapons as helpful for restoring national self-esteem following decades of turmoil and civil war.[10]

In this period, China deployed weapons platforms for delivering nuclear weapons at increasing range. Bombers and short-range missile systems came first, along with tactical weapons intended to cope with a potential Soviet invasion of China.[11] Two years after exploding its first nuclear device in 1964, China achieved initial operational capability of a missile with a range sufficient to strike Korea and Japan (and U.S. bases there). Additional missile systems were deployed over the coming decade capable of reaching Okinawa, the Philippines, Vietnam, the Russian Far East, and

India. In 1980, China deployed the DF-4 with a range sufficient to reach Moscow and Guam.[12] China also had a largely unsuccessful effort in this period to develop a sea-based missile force and ultimately fielded only one submarine armed with 12 medium-range ballistic missiles, which reportedly has not sailed outside China's territorial waters and reportedly has never conducted a deterrence patrol.[13]

As argued above, this phase of strategic infancy culminated in the early 1980s with the deployment of a broadly diverse set of nuclear strike capabilities. This allowed Deng Xiaoping to argue in 1983 that China's success in building its deterrent "had forced the superpowers not to use" nuclear weapons against China.[14] Then Defense Minister Zhang Aiping argued further in 1986 that "we have built a powerful national defense and possess a nuclear strike capability. The enemy no longer dares to strike [the first blow] or to underestimate us."[15]

What does this history imply about the differentiation between Taiwan and non-Taiwan missions? U.S. observers generally believe that the evolution of China's strategic capabilities in this first phase was driven more by technological factors than by guidance to target specific countries in specific contingencies. By this argument, China built weapons capable of reaching a broadening set of targets because it could do so and generally sought an effective deterrent. As John Lewis and Hua Di argued, China's nuclear weapons program in this period "proceeded without such strategic guidance" and "until the early 1980s, there were no scenarios, no detailed linkage of the weapons to foreign policy objectives, and no serious strategic research."[16] Lewis and Hu note a possible exception in a decision following the 1968 Ussuri River clash with the Soviet Union to extend the range of the DF-4 to bring Moscow within range.[17]

Other observers have surveyed the available evidence and come to a different conclusion. Bates Gill, James Mulvenon, and Mark Stokes have argued as follows:

> This story, along with others in the narrative about the sequential development of missiles capable of hitting the Philippines, Guam, Hawaii, and the U.S., suggest that someone, somewhere at a central level was making decisions about strategic purpose and direction of various missile systems, which was then reflected in the seemingly logical pattern (defined as matching geographic location with range of target) of base and missile deployments.[18]

Without further transparency from China, it is impossible to assess definitively which interpretation is correct. Whatever strategic analysis might have guided the development of China's deterrent in this first phase, there is little evidence to suggest that the potential for military confrontation over Taiwan served as the primary guiding principle in the development of China's strategic posture. Nor did any other specific regional contingency appear to guide that development. Rather, Beijing was concerned broadly with creating a strategic force sufficient to enable it to resist coercion by any foreign power.

Phase 2. As the initial phase wrapped up in the early 1980s, a new phase in the development of China's strategic posture began. This one lasted approximately a decade or so.[19] This phase was marked by the declining centrality of people's war as a central organizing concept for the PLA and also by China's initial opening to the world following Mao's death. During this period, some initial modernization of China's strategic forces began, with the pursuit of solid-fuel and road-mobile land-based systems and improved command and control capabilities. China's weapons designers were given guidance to diversify China's strategic arsenal to cover a broader spectrum of potential contingencies and were given a decade or more to accomplish the shift to second-generation forces.[20] Improvements were sought to the range, payload, and accuracy of missile systems. Renewed concern about Soviet military power and ambition fueled the decision to develop a modernized strike capability against Moscow with the capability to penetrate its missile defense system as well as improved tactical weapons that might be useful to turning back a Soviet armored invasion of China (i.e., an enhanced radiation device, or "neutron bomb"). During this period, an expert community of strategic analysts emerged within the PLA, along with "a systematic elaboration of China's concept of deterrence."[21]

In this phase, it is possible to see some further differentiation of China's capabilities for specific operational requirements. The need for effective nuclear deterrence of the Soviet Union seems to have remained as the central organizing concern of China's evolving force posture.[22] It is difficult to discern any specific role for China's strategic posture vis-à-vis the Taiwan contingency in this period.

Phase 3. Phase 3 began in the early 1990s. The driver of this new phase was the broader national ambition to adapt the PLA more generally to the changing national and international context, as reflected in what was essentially a new military strategy in 1993. That strategy took the form of the Military Strategic Guidelines for the New Period promulgated by Jiang

Zemin on January 13, 1993. As David Finkelstein has argued, the guidelines "represent the national military strategy under which the PLA has been operating" ever since.[23]

The need for a new strategy was dictated by changes in China's security environment. With the demise of the Soviet Union and the end of cold war confrontation, the emerging set of strategic relationships gained prominence in China, along with the associated military challenges and contingencies. The first Gulf War had also provided a vivid illustration of how much the so-called revolution in military affairs was changing the nature of warfare, leading to renewed calls to adapt PLA capabilities to new requirements through dramatic shifts in operational art and technical capacity. As David Finkelstein has argued, these requirements and assessments are both "capabilities based and contingency based."[24]

The guidelines establish five major tasks for the PLA: (1) defending national territory and sovereignty, (2) securing the nation's maritime rights and interests, (3) maintaining the unity of the motherland, (4) ensuring internal stability, and (5) maintaining a secure and stable external environment, especially on China's periphery.[25] Jiang summarized the salient strategic guidance as follows:

> In terms of strategic guidance, we have long since transferred the key preparations from being based on fighting early, fighting large, and fighting nuclear weapons, to dealing with local war. Now, on the basis of developments and changes to the international system, we must give priority to preparations for dealing with local wars under modern high-tech conditions. This is a further development and perfection of our army's strategic guiding thought.[26]

With the national military strategic guidelines as the starting point, further guidance was provided to specific elements of the PLA for planning and action. The Second Artillery emerged as prominent in the leadership vision of how to implement the desired transformation of the PLA. In 1993, Jiang Zemin argued that "with regard to our building up of national defense and with regard to our whole strategy, the Second Artillery is of considerable importance."[27] Along with the other services, it was directed to undertake "building efforts." The Second Artillery was specifically directed to "have a stronger nuclear deterrent and conventional strike capabilities."[28]

Before reviewing these Second Artillery "building efforts," it is useful to understand the key concepts that drove such planning. The 1993 guidelines instigated a broad and ambitious PLA effort to "put its intellectual house in order," with updated doctrine appropriate to the new requirements of local wars under modern high tech (and "informationalized") conditions.[29] This effort led to the release in January 1999 of a new and comprehensive set of guidelines for the conduct of military operations, emphasizing "campaigns and battles and all levels and all scales" and "unifying the operational thinking of the whole military."[30] Each of the armed Services then prepared its own study of the application of new doctrine to their operational arts, and the Second Artillery produced in 2004 *The Science of Second Artillery Campaigns*, a volume which "through abstract summaries . . . focuses on revealing the general laws of Second Artillery corps campaigns, systematically expounds the basic theories of Second Artillery Corps campaigns, and strives to enhance the theoretical, innovative and practical qualities."[31] In an effort "to overcome the thinking barrier of sticking to old ways and following the beaten path," the document highlights the need for transformational approaches, and the first such transformation it envisions is "to shift the footing of theoretical research of Second Artillery Corps campaigns from dealing with a nuclear war in the past to participating in a high tech local war under the conditions of nuclear deterrence."[32]

These efforts have led to a much clearer articulation about the roles and functions of the strategic deterrent than evident in the prior phases. As argued in *The Science of Military Strategy:*

> Warfighting and deterrence are two major basic functions of the armed forces. What is termed deterrence is the military conduct of a state or a political group in displaying force or showing the determination to use force to compel the enemy to submit to one's volition and to refrain from taking hostile actions or escalating the hostility. As part of military strategy, strategic deterrence refers to strategic behavior performed for deterrence on the overall strategic situations. Strategic deterrence and strategic operations are dialectically unified. Strategic operations secure the strategic objective through direct engagement with the enemy on the battle field, with a view to winning the war or to curbing the war by war, while the objective of strategic deterrence is to contain the outbreak of war or to limit the scope and the escalation of war, with a view to curbing the war... Strategic deterrence is based on warfighting. . . . The more powerful the war-fighting capability, the more effective the deterrence.[33]

> The main types of strategic deterrence are as follows: First, nuclear deterrence. It means the deterrent action and posture of taking nuclear force as backup power to shock and contain the opponent by threatening to use nuclear weapons or determining to carry out nuclear counterattack. The essence of nuclear deterrence is to warn the opponent in advance the possibility of using nuclear weapons or carrying out nuclear counterattack

and the likely grave consequences as a result of taking this advantage, for the purposes of bringing about the opponent's dreadful mentality by his weighing the advantages against the disadvantages and the gain against the loss, so as to force him to obey the deterrer's volition or to give up his original attempts.[34]

The employment of nuclear deterrence is based on the development level of nuclear strength owned by the nuclear nations. At the moment, nuclear deterrence is generally classified into three gradations. The first is the maximum nuclear deterrence. It is designed to threaten the opponent by disarming him with just the first massive nuclear strike for attaining the aim of containing and coercing him under the condition of the deterrer's possession of quantitative and qualitative superiority of nuclear force. The second is the minimum nuclear deterrence. It depends on a handful of nuclear weapons to threaten the opponent by striking his cities for making up nuclear deterrence to him. The third is nuclear deterrence of moderate intensity. It relies on "sufficient and effective" nuclear strike forced to threaten the opponent by incurring him an unbearable destruction to a certain extent so as to attain the objective of one's deterrence.[35]

Nuclear deterrence is not almighty and it has many limitations. . . . With the development of post-war history, the limitations of nuclear deterrence are increasingly exposed, and the effect of conventional deterrence is gradually valued.[36]

This document goes on to explore the many ways in which "conventional deterrence is merged into the overall deterrence" and argues that deterrence by means of a "space military force" and "information deterrence" is increasingly important in a comprehensive view of deterrence.[37]

Deterrence Concepts.

These concepts go well beyond the simple view of minimum deterrence typically invoked by the community of U.S. experts interested in China's nuclear strategy. They reflect a concerted Chinese effort to better understand the use of military power to shape China's security environment in peacetime and war. In this regard, these concepts mirror efforts of the Bush administration to think through the problems associated with dissuasion, deterrence, and defeat in the 2001 *Quadrennial Defense Review* (QDR).

The Second Artillery's own study of campaign science adapted these concepts to the problems of waging "high tech local war under the conditions of nuclear deterrence." A few concepts from this document are cited below:

> The Second Artillery Corps is a strategic missile force with nuclear power as its mainstay. With the formulation of the strategic principles for the new era, the strategic missions of the Second Artillery Corps have shifted from the single undertaking of guided missile nuclear assault to nuclear and conventional "dual deterrence and dual operations."[38]

> The goal of campaign deterrence is to force an enemy to accept our will or to contain an enemy's hostile acts. The campaigns large formation undertakes the task of deterrence. Once deterrence has lost its effectiveness, the campaign large formation can quickly transit to actual combat.[39]

> Second Artillery campaign deterrence is carried out in peacetime, in pre-combat period, and during war time. Local wars under informationalized conditions often begin with campaign deterrence, which forces the adversary to accept certain conditions.[40]

The conventional missile strike campaigns of Second Artillery will be implemented under the nuclear deterrence conditions. Even if the future warfare mainly will be conventional localized warfare, the major militarily powerful nations possessing nuclear weapons had never promised not to use nuclear weapons first. In the most recent localized warfare, there were several implementations of nuclear deterrence. Therefore, under the informationalized conditions, the implementation of conventional missile strike campaigns of Second Artillery will definitely receive nuclear deterrence from powerful countries. This kind of nuclear deterrence is even more practical in regional conflicts or localized wars that could happen in areas surrounding our country. Therefore, no matter whether it is nuclear counterattack campaigns or conventional missile strike campaigns, it will receive serious threats from nuclear weapons. Second Artillery must do well on the long-term preparation of nuclear strikes and stand firm on implementing operations under nuclear conditions or nuclear deterrence conditions.[41]

Second Artillery missile units . . . aim mainly to fully demonstrate their role in nuclear deterrence and prevent the war from moving toward widening or spreading, and to deter the enemy from initiating nuclear war, and thereby controlling the war by keeping it localized, limited and bearable in scope.[42]

During conventional operations, missile units must be prepared to carry out nuclear deterrence or even nuclear counterattacks.[43]

This doctrine has guided the "building efforts" of the Second Artillery in the years since the Guidelines were issued in 1993. In the words of one PLA source from 1996, two concerns dominated the effort to adapt China's strategic deterrent to the requirements of the new military strategic guidelines:

After more than three decades of arduous pioneering work, the accomplishment that the Second Artillery has achieved is great. However, based on facts, there are still some problems that exist in the development and building up of the Second Artillery. These problems are mainly reflected in two most basic gaps. One is that there exists a fairly large gap between China's strategic requirements of gaining mastery by striking only after the enemy has struck and the operational capacity of the Second Artillery with regard to nuclear counterattack. The other is that there exists a fairly large gap between the requirements of the times to win victory in high-tech local war and the current conventional operational capacity of the Second Artillery.[44]

To address the second main concern about a capability for strategic but non-nuclear means of warfare, the Second Artillery was given a requirement in the early 1990s to develop a force of conventionally-tipped missiles, along with the associated modernized command and control capabilities.[45] Over the last 15 years, it has moved aggressively to do so and, as noted above, to integrate conventional missile operations into its doctrine and operational art.

The first concern, survivability, was not new to China. In 1984, China began round-the-clock alerts in response to rising concerns about survivability.[46] But it took on added potency with the shifting assessment of the international security environment and especially rising concern about the precision strike capabilities displayed by the United States in the first Persian Gulf war. The requirement was highlighted in a speech reportedly given in 2000 by Jiang Zemin setting "the five musts" guiding the building up of Second Artillery capabilities. In his words, China must:

1. "own strategic nuclear weapons of a definite quality and quantity in order to ensure national security";

2. "guarantee the safety of strategic nuclear bases against the loss of combat effectiveness from attacks and destruction by hostile countries";

3. "ensure that our strategic nuclear weapons are at a high degree of war preparedness";

4. "be able to launch a nuclear counterattack and nuclear re-attack against an aggressor who launches a nuclear attack against us"; and

5. "pay attention to the global situation of strategic balance and stability and, when there are changes in the situation, adjust our strategic nuclear weapon development strategy in a timely manner."[47]

In 2004 *The Science of Second Artillery Campaigns* summarized the programmatic impact of doctrine as follows.

> Second Artillery has developed new techniques and new equipment non-stop in the recent years. It is predicted that, around 2010, Second Artillery will be equipped with a new generation strategic nuclear missile series that can realize global firepower control with high launch precision and advanced technology. . . . After the 1990s . . . it continuously added conventional missile forces, electronic warfare forces, and cruise missiles forces. . . . In the future, there is a plan for the computer network forces, psychological warfare forces, and space warfare forces. . . . It will eventually make Second Artillery an armed service with multiple forces.[48]

The results of China's efforts to date are uncertain. China's strategic posture is clearly in transition. It is on its way to becoming more technologically sophisticated. It is on its way to becoming more capable of operations integrated with conventional military campaigns. It is on its way to higher readiness, as it moves from fixed land-based to mobile systems. It is revitalizing some of the elements of the original strategic posture that matured less fully than the land-based missile force – i.e., the sea-based force (with the deployment of a small fleet of new ballistic missile submarines) and air-delivered capabilities associated with modernized bombers. There has been a dramatic, huge build-up in short-range ballistic missiles deployed across the Taiwan strait and the number of deployed missiles has reached a point (generally assessed at more than 1,000 missiles) to raise a basic question about what types of missions other than strategic bombardment are associated with China's short-range missiles. Of note, some of these missiles are understood to be capable of carrying nuclear weapons. China is modernizing and replacing its force of medium- and intermediate-range ballistic missiles, while also reportedly significantly increasing the network of deployment sites for the new road-mobile systems.[49] By one authoritative report, between 2006 and 2008 China built up its force of road-mobile solid-fueled CSS-5s (DF-21) from 19-50 to 60-80. As of 2008, China's force of land-based nuclear-tipped missiles capable of reaching targets around its periphery (that is, its medium- and intermediate-range ballistic missiles but not the short-range systems or intercontinental ones) consists of 20 liquid-fueled CSS-3s, between 15 and 20 liquid-fueled CSS-2s, and the CSS-5 force.[50] This is in addition to whatever JL-1 missiles might be available for launch from the old *Xia* class fleet ballistic missile submarine (SSBN) as well as air-launched cruise missiles deliverable from modernized bombers.[51]

What does this suggest about the importance of missions "beyond Taiwan" in this third phase of development of China's strategic deterrent? Even as the Taiwan contingency loomed very large in the thinking of China's military planners and political leadership, it appears that the top-level guidance given to China's military forces has emphasized the generic challenges of local wars under modern high-tech conditions rather than, as a first order priority, success in a Taiwan contingency. In the vernacular of the 2001 U.S. QDR, China's leaders have dictated a shift from threat-based planning to capabilities-based planning. In other words, in a security environment where they cannot confidently predict the specific types of conflicts that might involve their military forces in the decades ahead, they are working to create a suite of capabilities that would be useful across a broad set of contingencies. In the specifically nuclear domain, China's military planners contemplate the possibility of localized wars involving nuclear powers with varying degrees of nuclear and conventional military power, not just a canonical war involving Taiwan and the United States.

With these three phases encompassing the history of China's development of its strategic posture, what about its future? Recent Chinese defense white papers have described the modernization of the Second Artillery as integral to the modernization of the PLA more generally. The 2006 White Paper described desired future developments of the PLA in the following way:

> China pursues a three-step development strategy in modernizing its national defense and armed forces, in accordance with the state's overall plan to realize modernization. The first step is to lay a solid foundation by 2010, the second is to make major progress around 2020, and the third is to basically reach the strategic goal of building informationized arms forces and being capable of winning informationized wars by the mid-21st century.[52]

How these benchmarks correlate with the future development of China's strategic posture is not elaborated in the report and remains a topic of debate and controversy. The 2006 white paper addresses also the role of naval forces in strategic deterrence, stating that "the Navy aims at gradual extension of strategic depth for offshore defensive operations and enhancing its capabilities in integrated maritime operations and nuclear counterattacks."[53] On future nuclear capabilities more generally, the report noted that:

> China upholds the principles of counterattack in self-defense and limited development of nuclear weapons, and aims at building a lean and effective nuclear force capable of meeting national security needs. It endeavors to ensure the security and reliability of its nuclear weapons and maintains a credible nuclear deterrent force. China's nuclear force is under the direct command of the Central Military Commission. China exercises great restraint in developing its nuclear force. It has never entered into and will never enter into a nuclear arms race with any other country.[54]

Members of China's expert community interested in nuclear policy and strategy argue energetically that the modernization of China's nuclear forces is in service of stability and maintaining a status quo in the strategic military realm, now being threatened by developments in the U.S. strategic posture. They argue that the ambitions set out in the 2001 U.S. Nuclear Posture Review for the addition to the U.S. posture of missile defense, non-nuclear strike, and advanced intelligence, surveillance, and reconnaissance systems all jeopardize the credibility of China's deterrent, thus justifying adaptations in China's arsenal aimed at denying the United States such a one-sided advantage.[55] As Senior Colonel Yao Yunzhu of China's Academy of Military

Science has argued, "China's nuclear modernization is to keep valid its long-standing nuclear policy."[56]

Others see more ominous developments. As Mark Schneider of the National Institute for Public Policy has argued, "This assessment [that China is modernizing to maintain the status quo] may be too benign. The same thing was said about the Soviet Union a year before its nuclear buildup that became evident in 1966."[57]

These different assessments reflect profound uncertainty about the future roles and missions of China's deterrent. It is possible to build a best case on available evidence and project greater continuity than change. But it is possible also to build a worst case on available evidence that projects significant departures in China's strategic capabilities and intentions. It seems reasonable to expect that there will be continued refinement of Chinese military thinking about the specific missions associated with China's strategic force now that a modernization program compels specific decisions about the operational characteristics of future forces — i.e., the ranges and payloads of delivery systems, the effects associated with different warheads, the capabilities of the enabling systems (command, control, intelligence, surveillance, and reconnaissance), and the scale and diversity of the overall posture.

In sum, China's strategic deterrent has developed in three main phases, with the future now stretching out before us as either an extension of the third phase or a fourth phase marked by significant shift in China's capabilities and objectives. In the first phase, the Taiwan mission seemed not particularly prominent, and, indeed, there is little evidence of contingency planning driving force development. In the second phase, there was some apparent mission differentiation, but the Taiwan mission seemed not dominant. In the third phase, a broader set of contingencies have driven Chinese planning, though Taiwan has an obviously central role. But there has been an emphasis on the development of capabilities useful across the broader set of contingencies and against countries with very different conventional and nuclear capabilities relative to China's.

DEFINING THE TAIWAN MISSION

To further illuminate the different missions that have informed the development of China's strategic deterrent, it is useful to have a clear notion of the roles of that deterrent in the Taiwan contingency. Towards this end, it is useful to begin with a short summary of what would likely be China's primary objectives in a conflict over Taiwan involving the United States. China would have multiple strategic objectives in such a conflict. It would want to induce capitulation by Taipei and create a fait accompli before outside intervention can buttress the defense of Taiwan; make the United States reluctant to intervene with the hope that this will prevent it from doing so or at least doing so in a timely way; and if the United States does enter the war, induce U.S. restraint in using the tools of escalation available to it; and induce Japanese restraint, whether to prevent its entry into war or limit the support it provides to U.S. forces. China would also have multiple operational goals, including to inflict rapid defeat on Taiwan's military forces; delay or defeat U.S. power projection assets; and conduct attacks on U.S. bases and forces and possibly also the United States itself toward that end.

In seeking to achieve these strategic and operational objectives, China would marshal available military, political, and economic assets in a comprehensive strategy aimed at what it calls war control, whereby it manipulates the costs and perceived risks of others to induce outcomes favorable to China's interests.[58] From *The Science of Military Strategy:*

> War control is the war conductor's behavior to limit and restrain consciously the occurrence, development, scale, intensity and outcome of the war. The objective of war control is to prevent the occurrence of war, and once the war is inevitable, it is necessary to control its vertical and horizontal escalation and do utmost to reduce the negative consequences or to gain a major victory at a minor cost.[59]

That document goes on to articulate "fundamental principles of armed conflict control" (as opposed to the crisis preceding armed conflict), including "to make decisions swiftly and strive for initiative" and "to regulate military actions strictly on the basis of requirements of political and diplomatic struggles." Furthermore, it argues that "when the opponent deliberately takes advantage of a favorable opportunity to create disturbances and instigate an armed conflict, action should be taken quickly and resolutely to inflict a retaliatory strike on the instigator, but at the same time attention should be paid to avoiding over-reaction leading to enlargement of the incident."[60]

This framework is suggestive of how China may conceive the virtues of strategic forces in a conflict over Taiwan involving the United States. The strategic force would have warfighting benefits, in the sense that it could help achieve the operational objectives noted above. Indeed, the dramatic build-up of missiles across the Taiwan strait suggests that the PLA sees many important and, indeed unique, roles for missiles in achieving wartime objectives. But China's strategic forces would also be relevant to the achievement of the strategic objectives noted above—indeed, uniquely so. By signaling to U.S. allies in East Asia the potential for missile attack by conventional and nuclear means, China apparently hopes to create the "dreadful mentality" that induces caution, restraint, and early compromise. China may hope to achieve similar objectives vis-à-vis the United States by signaling its ability to attack forces in the zone of conflict, in the theater more generally, and even the United States itself, if the United States chooses to takes steps that China deems "disturbances" of peace requiring well-calibrated retaliation. As a general proposition, it seems obvious that missiles would play a central operational role in PRC military operations against Taiwan and the United States and potentially other forces coming to Taiwan's defense; it is less obvious that nuclear weapons would play any such role, beyond the long shadow that they cast.

There is very little evidence to suggest that China's expert community worries about the effectiveness of strategic deterrence in the way that their Western counterparts do.[61] The authors of *The Science of Second Artillery Campaigns* write confidently about the ability of the Second Artillery to wage campaign deterrence through operations intended to exert pressure, display resolve, demonstrate strength, and "adjust nuclear policies" in a way that reduces the nuclear deterrence threshold.[62] Western experts have had to come to terms with a variety of nuclear crises during the Cold War that raised basic questions about the ability of political and military leaders to employ the deterrent for desired purposes and, indeed, even to understand the facts associated with specific events or to be capable politically and bureaucratically of timely decisions.

This makes many Western experts skeptical about the controllability of nuclear crises. China's expert community seems not well informed about these Western experiences or perceptions. Although recent episodes such as the EP-3 incident appear to have heightened concern among some Chinese experts and authorities about China's capacity to manage political-military crises as it emerges onto the world stage,[63] there is no evidence to suggest that these concerns inform Chinese thinking about the processes of escalation and de-escalation that might occur in the strategic military realm if a Taiwan crisis were to erupt. Indeed, informal interactions with members of the Chinese expert community suggest a high degree of confidence in their predictions of how China could employ threats to induce restraint by the United States and Japan and military operations to inflict operational defeat on their forces with strategic means.[64]

BEYOND TAIWAN

That China's strategic posture seems now well-suited to the requirements of deterrence in the cross-strait contingency does not mean that it has been tailored solely for this purpose. As the guidance makes clear, China's leaders expect nuclear deterrence to play a role in many high tech local wars under modern conditions — because of the possession of nuclear weapons by some of its neighbors, or their protection under a nuclear shield extended from elsewhere. As one PLA expert has argued: "What, then, are the targets of the nuclear deterrence of China? The targets are countries with nuclear weapons."[65] And what countries other than the United States have nuclear weapons that are also a source of potential conflict with China? At the very least, Russia and India.

190

China's leaders voice optimism about strategic partnership with Russia and the long-term potential for cooperation to bring about a more multipolar world. But this has not prevented China from preparing a deterrent of possible utility against Russia. As noted above, deterrence of the Soviet Union was a key driver of the development of long-range Chinese nuclear strike systems, and of a theater force conceived as necessary for wearing down and ultimately reversing a Soviet armored invasion of China. China's first long-range missile was designed to target Moscow. It is useful to recall that Moscow is protected by a nuclear-tipped missile defense system, and thus that China has been concerned with the problem of penetrating missile defenses for decades. With the end of the Cold War and the drawdown of Russian nuclear forces, there has been no apparent change in China's nuclear posture vis-à-vis Russia—except its modernization. In the words of one PLA analyst, "Although Russia has promised us not to be the first to use nuclear weapons against China, we shall not let down our guard even for 1 day against the fact that the domestic political and economic situations of Russia are unstable and that a large number of nuclear weapons exist in that country."[66] As noted earlier, China has deployed medium-range missiles capable of reaching the Russian Far East and longer-range missiles capable of reaching Moscow, and it is now modernizing those systems. Although the specific mission assignments of China's medium-range forces are not known, the number of deployed land-based missiles with these ranges is approximately between 80 and 100.[67]

Few in China's expert community appear to see the prospect of armed conflict with Russia as in any way serious or imminent. As Yao Yunzhu has argued, "it would be too far-fetched to envision a military conflict between China and Russia, let alone one involving nuclear confrontation," in part because "the strategic partnership formed between China and Russia removed the prospect of a Russian nuclear first strike."[68] China's experts seem unworried that Russian military doctrine has reembraced first use of nuclear weapons or by Russian threats to withdraw from the Intermediate-range Nuclear Forces (INF) Treaty.

It is useful to note that some Russian experts do not view the balance of strategic military power along the Sino-Russian border with the same equanimity. Those experts speak privately of the dangerous implications of what they see as China's unilateral nuclear advantages in Asia. They argue that Russia lacks an intermediate-range system, cannot compensate with deployments of tactical weapons (given the absence of bases along the Chinese border), and cannot credibly counterbalance with long-range systems that are designed to counterbalance the United States. China's modernization of its theater nuclear missile systems is a key factor in Russia's case for withdrawal from the INF treaty. A deep underlying factor is the Russian expectation that China will grow stronger and more nationalistic over the coming decades and will seek to redress additional historic grievance against Russia by exploiting an imbalance of strategic military power.[69]

Regarding strategic partnership with India, China's leaders also voice optimism. Economic interactions are intensifying and political relations appear to be warm. But here, too, China has fielded forces capable of deterrence missions against India. No public disclosure of the number of such forces has been made by China. In the current situation, China's nuclear forces can target all of India and can also project power into the

192

Indian Ocean, whereas India cannot target all of China and hence is developing the *Agni 3* and associated light warhead to reach Beijing and other targets along China's northeastern seaboard. There are also reports that China is modifying its most modern bombers to carry long-range cruise missiles, some of which can be expected to carry nuclear warheads.[70]

Here too China's expert community seems largely untroubled by the mutual deterrence relationship. To again cite Yao:

> China formed with India a very credible mutual deterrent relationship the moment it went nuclear. Pakistan, a long time friend of China, has been locked into a mutual deterrent relationship with India as well. The pair of deterrent relationships brought about more earnest effort from both India and China for settling territorial disputes by political means.[71]

China, then, has a mutual deterrent relationship with India. China's experts attest that China is assured by India's no first use commitment. But the modernization of China's medium- and intermediate-range missile systems is improving the force it fields against India and the recent increases in road-mobile deployment sites noted above raise a question about the size of the future force that China has deemed or might deem necessary to counter India's rise. Of course, China has also helped build up a nuclear-armed Pakistan as a counterweight to India's nuclear power and counterfocus of its nuclear planning.

Chinese perceptions of strategic stability in the Sino-Indian relationship apparently differ from Indian perceptions just in the way Chinese and Russian perceptions differ. As one influential Indian analyst has argued:

The Chinese leadership comes from the Maoist tradition which asserts that power flows from the barrel of a gun. While calling nuclear weapons paper tigers, it went all out to get them at great cost to their people. It talked about joining the disarmament process if the U.S. and Soviet Union brought down their arsenals to half their original levels and has gone back on it. It talks about no-first use but tests tactical nuclear weapons which are essentially first-use weapons.[72]

Some Indian experts are also concerned about the potentially limited application of China's no-first-use principle.

Beijing, while insisting that its nuclear weapons are exclusively "defensive" in nature and focused only on deterring the possibility of nuclear coercion by other nuclear weapon states, has an added proviso that nuclear weapons have a role in preserving its sovereign territorial integrity, thereby extending their use in any military operation it may launch to wrest the territory it claims from India.[73]

Looking beyond Russia and India as potential foci of China's strategic deterrent, it is important also to consider those contingencies involving conflict between the forces of China, the United States, and/or Japan that may unfold but not involve Taiwan. Whether such contingencies are plausible, or could plausibly lead to potential escalation to the strategic domain, is highly debatable. But they cannot be ruled out of this survey of possible roles of China's strategic deterrent. The potential for such contingencies arises from China's increased focus on challenges in its maritime security environment. It has a strategy to "gradually extend the strategic depth for coastal defense."[74] As Taylor Fravel has argued, this implies the use of ballistic missiles and cruise missiles, in conjunction with other assets, to attack targets in the maritime setting; towards this end, China is developing the capabilities to launch anti-ship missiles from ships and submarines and from airplanes along with the capabilities to employ medium-range missiles against mobile targets at sea.[75] Implicitly, these contingencies could involve the United States and/or Japan and/or other powers projecting naval power in the region, including, for example, Russia and India. Whether and how China might seek to cast the nuclear shadow over such contingencies is an entirely open question based on available information. Available operational capabilities would give China a variety of options for doing so. This line of argument suggests the potential additional values that China might perceive in a stronger sea-based leg for its deterrent, which would enhance its capacity to project nuclear retaliatory forces into the Western Pacific, Indian Ocean, and elsewhere.

It is important to round out this survey of nuclear roles and missions with the observation that PLA authors generally emphasize that China's nuclear security environment took a decisive turn for the better with the end of the Cold War and their perception that new nuclear challenges around China's periphery are not also significant new threats. As one PLA author has argued, "China evaluates its overall nuclear security environment as improving instead of worsening."[76] But nor can it afford to ignore the realities that come from the nuclear shadows cast by the nuclear arsenals of other countries, or the value to China of casting its own nuclear shadow.

CONCLUSIONS AND IMPLICATIONS

Conclusions.

This analysis points to the following two main conclusions and a short list of implications. First, at this stage of its development, China's nuclear doctrine does not explicitly distinguish the two mission sets, "Taiwan" and "beyond Taiwan." China's scant but growing official literature on strategic warfare makes no explicit distinctions between the specific requirements of deterrence vis-à-vis Taiwan (and of the United States and its allies involved in a Taiwan contingency) and the broader mission set. This reflects the top-level guidance to develop capabilities to deal with the generic challenges of "high tech local war under the conditions of nuclear deterrence."

Second, at this stage in their development, China's strategic forces do seem to distinguish the mission sets. The roles and missions of China's strategic forces "beyond Taiwan" have had a substantial impact on the development of China' strategic posture. China has tailored, and continues to tailor, missile and other forces to its potential deterrence needs in the full range of military contingencies that might occur in an unpredictable security environment, and especially in those contingencies involving the slowly growing number of nuclear weapon states around its periphery. It has pursued a dramatic build-up of conventionally-armed (but apparently also nuclear-capable) short-range missiles across the Taiwan strait. It has sought to maintain both nuclear and conventional missile preponderance over India. It has deployed a more diverse strategic deterrent against Russia than Russia has deployed against it. Observing these differences,

Bates Gill, James Mulvenon, and Mark Stokes argued in 2000 that China pursues a differentiated strategy, one that seeks minimum deterrence vis-à-vis the United States but limited deterrence in its theater nuclear force posture and an offensively configured, preemptive, counterforce warfighting posture in its conventional missile forces.[77] Since they framed that analysis, the evidence supporting their propositions has only increased.

It is important to note that U.S. analysts tend to slight the salience of China's theater nuclear forces because they do not have intercontinental range. So far at least, China's requirements of its regional deterrent have resulted in a force structure larger and more diverse than the requirements of its intercontinental deterrent. That is, the number of theater systems capable of nuclear missions is significantly larger than the number of systems capable of such missions at intercontinental range. And furthermore, China's force modernization strategy has generated more new replacements for theater than intercontinental capabilities—so far.

At this point, it is useful to return to the matrix of possible outcomes over Taiwan presented in the introduction to this volume. How might China's thinking about the regional functions of its deterrent be shaped if the status quo across the Taiwan strait does not remain, but some alternative outcome appears to raise questions about the present development of PLA doctrine and force modernization plans? Of course, the short answer would seem to be that it would all depend on the role that nuclear weapons and strategic deterrence might play in the process of ending the status quo. If the Taiwan issue is resolved without conflict, China may well conclude that its build-up of strategic forces across the strait and efforts to maintain a credible deterrent vis-à-vis the United States were essential to this result and, accordingly, continue to emphasize these capabilities in PLA modernization strategies even as the expectation of conflict with the United States declines. If China attempts to brandish tools in its strategic toolkit but still "loses," it may deem more such strategic power as necessary — or, alternatively, as not promising of the desired result. If it brandishes such tools and wins, it may anticipate that others around its periphery, including an angry United States fearful of the implications of China's further rise, would sharpen their own strategic nuclear toolkit, in which case China could see a more robust strategic posture as in its interest, whatever its arms race consequences. It is obvious and trite to argue that if nuclear weapons are actually employed in a conflict over Taiwan to gain some operational or strategic advantage, the lessons would be hugely consequential and also highly difficult to predict.

Implications.

Four implications for U.S. policy follow from this analysis.

1. There are those in U.S. expert community who use the term in the title of this chapter, "strategic deterrent," and assume that they are invoking a concept that is shared and mutually understood by military planners, political leaders, and subject matter experts in the two countries. "Deterrence" is a word with many connotations, and it is important to be clear about the ways in which Chinese and U.S. concepts do not fully align. Many of the strategic concepts summarized above align closely with U.S. concepts — especially the value and importance of nuclear weapons in inducing

dread and restraint. But China emphasizes the value of its strategic force in negating the deterrence and compellance strategies of others more than the United States does. It invokes the term "counterdeterrence" to describe its strategy in a way the United States does not. By this logic, the deterrence of China attempted by China's opponents must be countered so as to enable China to do the right thing by its interests. And this requires "counterdeterrence operations" for the purposes of signaling resolve, including counterattack and reattack. China's emphasis on such operational roles for strategic weapons in achieving strategic results is unmistakable—and rather different from a United States that seems to rely simply on the long shadow of its vastly more numerous arsenal to induce restraint by potential adversaries.

2. The U.S. role is as a security guarantor in Asia and includes its alliance relationship with Japan and others in East Asia, its other commitments to Taiwan, and its relationships with countries with which it seeks strategic cooperation. These countries generally want to know how the United States can help them deal with the consequences of China's military modernization. Recipients of specific guarantees also want to know how those guarantees can remain credible in light of developments in that modernization. Their concerns impose an obligation on the United States to understand how the modernization of China's strategic military capabilities is affecting their interests, and to devise strategies to manage these challenges in mutually beneficial ways.

3. The United States and the international community need to reduce nuclear threats in Asia. The nuclear puzzle in Asia is complex and cannot be reduced to the single issue of potential China-U.S. strategic military

confrontation over Taiwan. More emphasis should be given to the interactions of force developments in the strategic military postures of Asia's nuclear powers. The situation is dynamic, not static. Shifting capabilities are likely to shift planning assumptions, leading to new capabilities better tailored to evolving strategic missions in Asia. Given shared interests in a stable security environment, and the common desire to ensure that nuclear competition does not erupt in Asia in a way that puts stability at risk, it is important to anticipate the sources of instability and implement an agenda of common action aimed at dampening them. Nuclear restraint in Asia is in America's interest, and it seems important to have a better understanding of the requirements of future restraint by Asia's nuclear actors—China first and foremost among them.

4. According to the "dual deterrence, dual operations" doctrine, the close integration of China's nuclear and non-nuclear strike systems and theater and intercontinental capabilities raises an important question about how separate and distinct the nuclear element remains. China's experts have raised alarm about the perceived lowering of the U.S. nuclear threshold associated with the 2001 U.S. Nuclear Posture Review (on the argument that a close integration of nuclear with non-nuclear missions means that nuclear weapons are increasingly likely to be employed against tactical targets). In fact, China is far more advanced in such efforts than the United States, and the impact of China's efforts to integrate conventional and nuclear missile missions may be felt unexpectedly in a moment of serious crisis instability. Efforts to address this problem should not await the potential moment of instability.

CHAPTER 6 - ENDNOTES

1. The author benefited from comments on earlier versions of this chapter by Ronald Christman, John Culver, Roy Kamphausen, Hans Kristensen, and Evan Medeiros, and by participants in the conferences hosted by the co-publishers. The author alone is responsible for the final contents. The views expressed here are his personal views and should not be attributed to any institution with which he is affiliated.

2. The single clearest statement of China's nuclear strategy is a short paragraph in the 2006 Defense White Paper. Other authoritative sources include Yu Jixun, ed., *The Science of Second Artillery Campaigns,* Beijing: PLA Press, 2004; and Peng Guangqian and Yao Youzhi, eds., *The Science of Military Strategy*, Beijing: Military Science Publishing House, 2005, especially chapter 9 on Strategic Deterrence, chapter 10 on Principles of Strategic Actions, chapter 12 on Strategic Offensive, and chapter 22 on Strategic Guidance of High-Tech Local War. PLA experts have also contributed chapters or journal articles on China's strategic deterrent to various sources. See for example, Pan Zhenqiang, "The Changing Strategic Context of Nuclear Weapons and Implications for the New World Order," Yao Yunzhu, "Chinese Nuclear Policy and the Future of Minimum Deterrence," and Yang Yi, "East Asia's Nuclear Future," in Christopher P. Twomey, ed., *Perspectives on Sino-American Strategic Nuclear Issues*, New York: Palgrave Macmillan, 2008. See also Sun Xiangli, "China's Nuclear Strategy," *China Security*, Vol. 1, Autumn 2005, pp. 23-27. See also "The Strategic Use and Development of the Second Artillery in the New Period," instructional materials, PLA National Defense University, Beijing, 1996 (further details on author and publication source not available); and Li Shaohui and Tao Yongqian, "Strength Foundation and Strategic Domain of Nuclear Deterrence," *Beijing Junshi Xueshu*, June 1, 2006, Open Source Center CPP20080228325001. See also Chu Shulong and Rong Yu, "China: Dynamic Minimum Deterrence," in Muthiah Alagappa, ed., *The Long Shadow: Nuclear Weapons and Security in 21st Century Asia,* Stanford, CA: Stanford University Press, 2008, pp. 161-187.

3. The most authoritative statements from U.S. sources are the annual Pentagon reports on China's military power. See also John Wilson Lewis and Xue Litai, *China Builds the Bomb,* Stanford, CA: Stanford University Press, 1988; Chong-Pin Lin, *China's Nuclear Weapons Strategy: Tradition within Evolution,* Lexington, MA: Lexington Books, 1988; John Wilson Lewis and Hua Di, "China's Ballistic Missile Programs: Technologies, Strategies, and Goals," *International Security*, Fall 1992, Vol. 17, No. 2, pp. 9-11; Litai Xue, "Evolution of China's Nuclear Strategy," in John C. Hopkins and Weixing Hu, *Strategic Views from the Second Tier: The Nuclear Weapons Policies of France, Britain, and China,* La Jolla: University of California Institute on Global Conflict and Cooperation, 1994; John Wilson Lewis and Litai Xue, *China's Strategic Seapower: the Politics of Force Modernization in the Nuclear Age*, Stanford, CA: Stanford University Press, 1994; Alastair Iain Johnston, "China's New 'Old Thinking': The Concept of Limited Deterrence," *International Security*, Vol. XX, No. 3, Winter 1995/96; Paul Godwin, "China's Nuclear Forces: An Assessment," *Current History*, September 1999; Mark A. Stokes, *China's Strategic Modernization: Implications for the United States,* Carlisle, PA: Strategic Studies Institute, U.S. Army War College, 1999; Bates Gill, James Mulvenon, and Mark Stokes, "The Chinese Second Artillery Corps: Transition to Credible Deterrence," in James C. Mulvenon and Andrew N. D. Yang, eds., *The People's Liberation Army as an Organization: Reference Volume v1.0,* 2001; Charles Ferguson, Evan S. Medeiros, and Phillip G. Saunders, "Chinese Tactical Nuclear Weapons," in Alistair Millar and Brian Miller, eds., *Tactical Nuclear Weapons: Emergent Threats in an Evolving Security Environment*, London: Brassey's, 2003, pp. 110-128; Michael S. Chase and Evan Medeiros, *China's Evolving Nuclear Calculus: Modernization and Doctrinal Debate,* in James Mulvenon and David M. Finkelstein, eds., *China's Revolution in Doctrinal Affairs: Emerging Trends in the Operational Art of the Chinese People's Liberation Army*, Alexandria, VA: CNA Corporation, 2005; Paul Bolt and Albert S. Willner, eds., *China's Nuclear Future*, Boulder, CO: Lynne Rienner, 2006; Hans M. Kristensen, Robert S. Norris, and Matthew McKinzie, *Chinese Nuclear Forces and U.S. Nuclear War Planning,* Washington, DC: Natural Resources Defense Council and the Federation of American Scientists, 2006; Jeffrey G. Lewis, *The Minimum Means of Reprisal: China's Search for Security in the Nuclear Age,* Cambridge, MA: MIT Press, 2007; Mark Schneider, *The Nuclear Doctrine and Forces of the People's Republic of China,* Fairfax, VA: National Institute Press, 2007;

Larry M. Wortzel, "China's Nuclear Forces: Operations, Training, Doctrine, Command, Control, and Campaign Planning," Carlisle, PA: Strategic Studies Institute, U.S. Army War College, 2007; Evan S. Medeiros, "Minding the Gap: Assessing the Trajectory of the PLA's Strategic Missile Forces," in Roy Kamphausen and Andrew Scobell, eds., *Right-Sizing the People's Liberation Army*, Carlisle, PA: Strategic Studies Institute, U.S. Army War College, 2007; Brad Roberts, "The Nuclear Dimension: How Likely? How Stable?" in Evan Medeiros, Michael D. Swaine, and Andrew Yang, eds., *Assessing the Threat: The Chinese Military and Taiwan Security*, Washington, DC: Carnegie Endowment, 2008; and Evan Medeiros, "China's Thinking on Escalation: Evidence from Chinese Military Writings," in Forrest Morgan, *et al.*, *Dangerous Thresholds: Managing Escalation in the 21st Century*, Arlington, VA: RAND, 2008, pp. 47-81.

4. The need for caution has been reinforced by the revelations about the quality of U.S. intelligence on weapons of mass destruction (WMD) that followed the intelligence failures vis-à-vis the WMD programs of Saddam Hussein. As argued by the Commission on the Intelligence Capabilities of the United States Regarding Weapons of Mass Destruction in its cover letter to the president of March 31, 2005, "we still know disturbingly little about the weapons programs and even less about the intentions of many of our most dangerous adversaries." This is a cautionary reminder of the need to treat information, even that which is provided by the U.S. Government, with an element of caution that admits the possibility that it may be wrong or misleading in some significant respects.

5. Xinhua News Service, July 2, 2005, in Foreign Broadcast Information Service (FBIS) Open Source Center, "Account of Party Central Committee's Care and Concern for Strategic Missile Units," *rccb.osis.gov*, July 5, 2006.

6. The following review of the first phase draws on Brad Roberts, *China and Ballistic Missile Defense: 1955 to 2002 and Beyond*, Institute for Defense Analyses Paper P-3826, Alexandria, VA: Institute for Defense Analyses, 2003.

7. Lewis and Litai, *China Builds the Bomb*. At a gathering of China's Central Military Commission (CMC) reportedly convened

in July 2000, the CMC vice chairman is reported to have described this initial period as lasting up until 1986 when decisions were taken to accelerate the replacement of older generation weapon systems. See Wen Jen, "Jiang Zemin Defines Position of China's Strategic Nuclear Weapons," *Hong Kong Tai Yang Pao,* Hong Kong, July 17, 2000, FBIS CPP20000727000021.

8. Lewis and Xue, *China's Strategic Seapower,* p. 213.

9. *The Science of Strategy,* p. 348.

10. Lin, *China's Nuclear Weapons Strategy,* pp. 105-136.

11. Beijing does not acknowledge the possession of tactical weapons. By one estimate in 1994, approximately one-quarter of China's arsenal of 400 or so nuclear weapons was understood to be devoted to tactical applications, including bombs for tactical bombardment, artillery shells, atomic demolition mines, and possibly short-range missiles. See Robert S. Norris *et al., Nuclear Weapons Databook,* Vol. 5, Boulder, CO: Westview Press, 1994, pp. 370-371. Norris has subsequently revised downward his estimate of the size of China's nuclear arsenal to 240. See Norris and Hans M. Kristensen, "China's Nuclear Forces, 2008," *Bulletin of the Atomic Scientists,* Vol. 64, No. 3, pp. 42-44.

12. Various sources, primarily Norris *et al., Nuclear Weapons Databook.* See also Lewis and Hua, "China's Ballistic Missile Programs," pp. 9-11.

13. Lewis and Xue, *China's Strategic Seapower.* See also "Taiwan Confirms China Building New Nuke Sub," *Washington Times,* December 8, 1999, p. A-16. Hans M. Kirstensen, "Chinese Submarines Patrol Rebound in 2007, But Remain Limited," as posted to the website of the Federation of American Scientists, *www.fas.org,* January 7, 2008.

14. As cited in Xue, "Evolution of China's Nuclear Strategy," p. 173.

15. *Ibid.*

16. Lewis and Hua, "China's Ballistic Missile Programs," pp. 6-7.

17. *Ibid.*, p. 17.

18. See Gill *et al.*, "The Chinese Second Artillery Corps: Transition to Credible Deterrence," p. 543.

19. Xue, "Evolution of China's Nuclear Strategy," pp. 173-178.

20. Chong-Pin, *China's Nuclear Weapons Strategy*, pp. 40-41; and Lewis and Hua, "China's Ballistic Missile Programs," p. 26.

21. Xue, "Evolution of China's Nuclear Strategy," p. 173.

22. *Ibid.*

23. Finkelstein, "China's National Military Strategy: an Overview of the 'Military Strategic Guidelines'," Kamphausen and Scobell, eds., *Right-Sizing the People's Liberation Army*, p. 95.

24. David Finkelstein, "Prologue," in Kamphausen and Scobell, *Right-Sizing the People's Liberation Army*, p. xi.

25. *Ibid.*, p. 109.

26. As cited in ibid., pp. 104-105.

27. Cited in *The Strategic Use and Development of the Second Artillery in the New Period*.

28. *Ibid.*, p. 125.

29. Mulvenon and Finkelstein, *China's Revolution in Doctrinal Affairs*.

30. As cited in David M. Finkelstein, "Thinking about the PLA's 'Revolution in Doctrinal Affairs'," in *ibid.*, p. 15.

31. From the Postscript, *The Science of Second Artillery Campaigns*, p. 323.

32. *Ibid.*, p. 27.

33. *The Science of Military Strategy*, pp. 213, 228.

34. *Ibid.*, p. 217.

35. *Ibid.*, p. 218. For a discussion of this gradation, see Chase and Medeiros, *China's Evolving Nuclear Calculus*, pp. 137-138.

36. *Ibid.*

37. *Ibid.*, p. 219.

38. *The Science of Second Artillery Campaigns*, p. 15.

39. *Ibid.*, p. 219.

40. *Ibid.*, p. 220.

41. *Ibid.*, p. 50.

42. *Ibid.*, p. 111.

43. *Ibid.*, p. 226.

44. From "The Strategic Use and Development of the Second Artillery in the New Period."

45. Stokes, *China's Strategic Modernization*, especially chapter 4, "Dawn of a New Age: China's Long-Range Precision Strike Capabilities," pp. 79-108.

46. Lewis and Xue, *China's Strategic Seapower*, p. 236.

47. As reported in "Jiang Zemin Defines Position of China's Strategic Nuclear Weapons," in *Tai yang pao*, Hong Kong, July 17, 2000, in *FBIS CPP200000717000021*.

48. *The Science of Second Artillery Campaigns*, pp. 54, 57-58.

49. By one count, 58 new launch sites have been identified. See Hans M. Kristensen, "Extensive Nuclear Missile Deployment Area Discovered in Central Asia," Federation of American Scientists, at *www.fas.org*, June 2008.

50. Hans Kristensen, "Chinese Nuclear Arsenal Increased by a Third Since 2006, Pentagon Report Indicates," posted at *www. fas.org/blog/ssp*, posted March 6, 2008.

51. *Military Power of the People's Republic of China, 2008*, pp. 24-25.

52. *China's National Defense in 2006.*

53. *Ibid.*

54. *Ibid.*

55. Strategic dialogues among the communities of experts in China and the United States working on nuclear policy and strategy have been sponsored in recent years by the U.S. Defense Threat Reduction Agency and the Department of State. For summaries of some of these recent dialogues, visit the website of the Center for Strategic and International Studies at *www.csis.org*.

56. Yao Yunzhu, "Chinese Nuclear Policy and the Future of Minimum Deterrence."

57. Schneider, *The Nuclear Doctrine and Forces of the People's Republic of China,* p. 28.

58. Lonnie D. Henley, "Evolving Chinese Concepts of War Control and Escalation Management," in Michael D. Swaine, Andrew N. D. Yang, and Evan S. Medeiros with Oriana Skylar Mastro, *Assessing the Threat: The Chinese Military and Taiwan's Security,* Washington, DC: Carnegie Endowment for International Peace, 2007, pp. 85-110.

59. *The Science of Military Strategy*, p. 197.

60. *Ibid.*, p. 208.

61. See Medeiros, "China's Thinking on Escalation: Evidence from Chinese Military Writings."

62. *The Science of Second Artillery Campaigns,* especially chapter 10 on Second Artillery Campaign Deterrence.

63. Michael Swaine and Zhang Tuosheng with Danielle F. S. Cohen, *Managing Sino-American Crises: Case Studies and Analysis,* Washington, DC: Carnegie Endowment for International Peace, 2007.

64. Roberts, "The Nuclear Dimension," pp. 213-242.

65. "The Strategic Use and Development of the Second Artillery in the New Period."

66. *Ibid.*

67. *Military Power of the People's Republic of China, 2008,* p. 24.

68. Yao, *Chinese Nuclear Policy and the Future of Minimum Deterrence,* p. 5.

69. Viewpoints collected during interviews in Moscow during June 2008. See also Dmitri Trenin, *Russia's China Problem,* Moscow: Carnegie Moscow Center, 1999.

70. Kristensen *et al., Chinese Nuclear Forces and U.S. Nuclear War Planning.*

71. Yao, *Chinese Nuclear Policy and the Future of Minimum Deterrence,* p. 5.

72. K. Subramanyam, "PRC Geopolitical Strategy, N-weapons Viewed," *Times of India,* October 23, 1996.

73. Vijai K. Nair, "China's Nuclear Strategy and Its Implications for Asian Security," *China Brief,* Vol. 4, No. 3, February 2004.

74. From *China's National Defense, 2006.*

75. M. Taylor Fravel, "China's Search for Military Power," *Washington Quarterly,* Vol. 31, No. 3, Summer 2008, pp. 133-135.

76. Yao, *Chinese Nuclear Policy and the Future of Minimum Deterrence*, p. 5.

77. Gill *et al.*, "The Chinese Second Artillery Corps."

CHAPTER 7

PROSPECTS FOR CHINA'S MILITARY SPACE EFFORTS

Dean Cheng

INTRODUCTION AND BACKGROUND

In thinking about the likely missions of the People's Liberation Army (PLA) beyond Taiwan, including the role of space operations, it is important to place Chinese military thinking in its context.[1] The forces and capabilities associated with a Taiwan scenario have constituted a contingency-based assessment. That is, certain capabilities were acquired to deal with the specific Taiwan situation. In a world beyond the Taiwan scenario however that might be achieved, what would be the PLA's basis for "army-building"?

Recent Chinese writings suggest that the PLA is already thinking along these lines. Jiang Zemin indicated, in a December 2002 speech to the expanded Central Military Commission (CMC), that space would be of growing importance in the context of the ongoing revolution in military affairs.[2] This increasing role of space is further noted among the new "historic missions," as set forth by Hu Jintao.[3] According to Chinese political and military writings, the "historic missions" for the PLA include:

- *To provide loyal support to the Chinese Communist Party (CCP). The PLA remains a "Party army."* Therefore, the first responsibility of the PLA remains to preserve the CCP's grip on power.
- *To help safeguard China's national development.* For the foreseeable future, national economic

development of the People's Republic of China (PRC) will remain the priority — but without a strong foundation of security, such efforts will always be potentially vulnerable. Therefore, the PLA has the responsibility for providing for China's national security, even as resource allocations remain focused on national economic construction.

- *To help safeguard China's expanding national interests.* Developments in high technology mean that the PLA must expand its focus beyond the traditional land frontiers, to the maritime, space, and electromagnetic spheres. It also means that it will have a role in nontraditional security missions. These include transnational concerns such as international crime and environmental degradation, as well as new national security problems attending the rise of the Chinese trading state, such as energy and shipping issues.

- *To help ensure world peace.* World peace and common development are prerequisites for China's continued national development, and therefore need to be maintained. For the PLA, this means greater engagement in such activities as United Nations (UN) peacekeeping operations.[4]

What these "historic missions" imply is that the PLA is now assuming a more capabilities-oriented perspective, rather than a contingency-based one, as it prepares to safeguard the security of the CPC and the PRC. Moreover, the areas of concern for national security have expanded. Where once the PLA was focused on defending China's land borders, and to a lesser extent repelling a seaborne invasion, now it must keep watch over new regions and functional areas. That, in turn, is likely to have ramifications upon all aspects of PLA military planning, including for military operations in space.

Indeed, whether the PRC moves beyond the Taiwan issue through conflict or not, it would appear that space capabilities are likely to be a focus of future PLA development and improvement. That is, it is likely that the PLA would be interested in improving its ability to exploit space regardless of how or whether the Taiwan situation is resolved, simply because space capabilities are likely to be essential to any future PLA operations.

THE EVOLVING PLA VIEW OF SPACE

As of the Jiang Zemin era, space operations were recognized as becoming more of a factor, but were still seen as supportive at best. The 1997 *PLA Military Encyclopedia*'s entry on "space warfare (*tianzhan*; 天战)" explicitly stated that space was not a decisive battlefield — the key to wartime victory would remain in the traditional land, sea, and air realms. "It is impossible for it [space warfare] to be of decisive effect. The key determinant of victory and defeat in war remains the nature of the conflict and the human factor."[5]

Five years later, at the beginning of the Hu Jintao leadership era, the tone had already changed. In the 2002 supplement to the *PLA Encyclopedia*, a very different assessment is made of the importance of space. In a discussion on the "space battlefield (*taikong zhanchang*; 太空战场)," the entry concludes with the observation that the impact of the space battlefield on land, sea, and air battlefields will become ever greater and the space battlefield "will be a major component

213

of future conflict."[6] It is clear that space, in the interval, was perceived as a substantially more important arena for military operations.

Since then, the PRC has further elaborated on the importance of military space operations. Indeed, the Chinese leadership has demonstrated that not only is it prepared to undertake support operations in space, but that it can, if necessary, engage in actual combat in the realm of outer space. As the January 2007 shoot-down of a *Fengyun-1C* weather satellite made clear, not only has the PRC been engaged in the research and development of anti-satellite weapons, but it has reached the point where such systems are being unmistakably tested.

It remains unclear, however, whether the PRC has developed or promulgated a *doctrine* governing military space operations. Even as the PRC deploys a broader array of space assets, it has still not made public any documents indicating how those assets might be used in the event of war. Similarly, it is unclear whether there is a body of theory, or formally accepted guidelines and regulations, regarding the training of military space personnel and the organization of space forces.

In this regard, Chinese development of their space capabilities may be similar to their development of missile capabilities. The PRC apparently fielded a range of short- and medium-range ballistic missiles without explicitly enunciating a doctrine for their use in advance. It would appear that, at present, although China fields a substantial array of space systems and capabilities, there has not yet been enunciated an explicit doctrine for their employment.

In reviewing Chinese writings on space, though, it soon becomes clear that certain concepts enjoy broad support, suggesting a possible consensus among PLA thinkers about military space operations. In particular, the close symbiosis between space systems and information systems appears to be widely accepted. In many Chinese discussions, information dominance, according to PLA analyses, is the foundation for all other forms of battlefield superiority, including air and naval dominance. The need to establish "information dominance (*zhi xinxi quan*; 制信息权)," though, is often linked to the need for achieving space dominance (*zhi tian quan*; 制天权). As an article in the Central Party School paper, *Study Times*, characterized it, space dominance is the "vital foundation and prerequisite for informationalized units, informationalized weapons, and winning informationalized wars."[7]

This follows a similar observation by one of the more prolific Chinese military space analysts. Senior Colonel Li Daguang, of the PLA's National Defense University, observed in an article published simultaneously in *Liberation Army Daily* and *National Defense Daily*, "information dominance cannot be separated from space dominance. We can say that seizing space dominance is the root for winning the informationalized war."[8]

Among PLA writers it seems that there is general acceptance of the idea that only by establishing dominance of space is it possible to fully leverage the capabilities of modern command, control, communications, computers, intelligence, surveillance, and reconnaissance (C4ISR) systems. This, in turn, is necessary if one is to implement the command and control functions necessary to wage Local Wars under Informationalized Conditions. The ability to engage in these kinds of wars is essential, if the PLA is to fulfill its "historic missions."

In this light, one of the PLA's priorities "beyond Taiwan" is likely to entail the development of space capabilities that will allow it to try to establish space dominance. To that end, there has been substantive discussion of possible guiding principles, types of campaigns, and therefore types of operational forms (*zuozhan yangshi*; 作战样式) and techniques (*zuozhan shouduan*; 作战手段) that the PLA should be able to undertake. Insofar as these discussions influence unit organization, training regimens, and acquisition efforts, they will affect both the construction of Chinese military space strength, and the planning for its use.

Space Dominance.

In examining likely Chinese concepts of military space operations beyond Taiwan, it is important to consider what "space dominance" entails. PLA authors note that space dominance is different from more traditional air or naval dominance. Li Daguang, for example, observes that, while space dominance is a prerequisite for air and naval dominance, it is likely to be more expensive and difficult to achieve, because of the uniqueness of the space environment.[9] Moreover, like information dominance, it is more difficult to achieve permanent space dominance. It is likely to be difficult to wholly prevent an opponent from entering space. Therefore, securing and retaining space dominance throughout the course of a conflict is likely to require sustained effort; the alternative is to accept that space dominance will probably be a more temporary condition.

Guiding Thoughts for Space Operations.

For the PLA, "campaign basic guiding concepts (*zhanyi jiben zhidao sixiang*; 战役基本指导思想)" are a touchstone for thinking through key issues associated with the planning, organization, and prosecution of military operations. Such concepts indicate to the PLA reader that certain tenets are deemed by higher authorities, after extensive study and research, so fundamental that they must be adhered to. If properly derived, they should reflect the laws governing the course of military campaigns, and are therefore the core of military campaign theories.[10]

There is no evidence that the enunciation of the "historic missions" has signaled a shift of the PLA's "campaign basic guiding concept" from "integrated operations, key point strikes." It is therefore likely that the PLA continues to emphasize the importance of "integrated operations (*zhengti zuozhan*; 整体作战)," meaning the integrating of all its forces, integrating operations in all the battlespaces (including land, sea, and air, as well as outer space and the electromagnetic spectrum), and integrating all the methods of warfare (e.g., positional warfare, mobile warfare, guerrilla warfare), across all phases of the war. Similarly, it is likely that the concept of "key point strikes," i.e., concentrating forces at the key strategic direction, at the critical junctures and moments, against essential enemy targets, so as to cripple and paralyze enemy forces, remains in effect.[11]

It is not clear whether there is a "guiding concept" specifically for military space operations. Chang Xianqi, however, in the PLA textbook *Military Astronautics*, proposes a "guiding concept for space operations (*kongjian zuozhan de zhidao sixiang*; 空间作战的指导思

217

想)." Interestingly, it would seem to be modeled on the broader "campaign basic guiding concept": "Unified operations, key point is space dominance."[12]

UNIFIED OPERATIONS (*YITI ZUOZHAN*; 一体作战)[13]

According to Chang and other PLA analysts, the establishment of space dominance will involve disparate forces, both space- and nonspace-based, engaging across a broad arena in complex maneuvers and activities. It will include not only operations in space, but also operations on the ground, in the air, and at sea, as forces act not only against space platforms, but terrestrial support facilities and the data-links that tie the two together.[14] The pursuit of space dominance will therefore require space operations being integrated and unified with other services' operations; the integration and unification of space offensive and defensive operations; and the unified, integrated application of various types of space operations.

Unified Use of Available Strength.

The unified use of all available strength entails two aspects. One is the integration of civilian and military space systems, both in terms of pre-war planning and in wartime use. This integration is important because of the expense of developing and producing space systems. Given their high cost, there are likely to be few reserves or spares. Losses will therefore not be easily replaced.[15] Moreover, few nations can afford the duplication involved in developing discrete civilian and military systems. Therefore, civilian systems are an essential augmentation to military ones. Indeed, it may even be necessary to rely on *international* commercial satellite systems.[16] In this regard, Chinese space analysts have observed that the United States has already had to turn to civilian systems to take up some of the communications and imaging loads in its recent wars.[17] Successful civil-military integration does not simply happen, though. Rather, it requires extensive planning to ensure that civilian systems would be interoperable with military ones.[18]

Another aspect of unified application of available strength is the combination of space capabilities (*kongjian liliang;* 空间力量) with those of land, sea, and air forces. The aim is to fulfill overall operational missions (more on operational missions below), in an efficient manner, regardless of the service or branch origin of the forces involved. Thus, Chinese Air Force officers have noted that both air and space forces engage in reconnaissance and surveillance missions, each complementing the other by compensating for the other's weaknesses.[19]

In combination, space and nonspace forces can generate significant synergies. Ground, naval, air, and missile forces, for example, can suppress enemy terrestrial space facilities, such as launch sites, and interfere with, disrupt, and deceive enemy space forces and data links. In so doing, they can help secure space dominance, by preventing an opponent's space forces from properly operating, and by defending one's own space capabilities.

At the same time, space forces can enhance the operation of ground, air, and naval forces by providing information support and even engaging in space-to-ground attacks.[20] This helps achieve air and naval domination. Just as important, by coordinating land, sea, and air operations, space systems facilitate joint operations, which are a key method of fighting future Local Wars under Informationalized Conditions.[21]

The unified application of space and nonspace forces thus offers the potential opportunity to rapidly overwhelm an opponent.

Unified Application of All Techniques.

In pursuing information dominance and space dominance, the PLA seems to have the view that disruption of an opponent's space infrastructure can be as useful as its destruction.[22] Both hard-kill systems that destroy, as well as soft-kill systems that disrupt, have a potential role in the effort to secure space dominance. As with the unified application of all available forces, part of the reasoning seems to be that applying both sets of techniques can generate synergies, with each measure remedying shortcomings in the other.

According to PLA writings, since soft-kill systems cannot permanently destroy physical facilities, one must rely on hard-kill systems for the important task of inflicting a long-lasting impact on enemy space capabilities.[23] This includes the use of kinetic kill vehicles (e.g., the anti-satellite weapon tested in 2007) or directed energy systems such as lasers, microwaves, or particle beams to damage or destroy satellites.[24] It also includes the application of various ground, air, and naval weapons against terrestrial space-support facilities, such as launch centers and tracking, telemetry, and control (TT&C) facilities. In the latter case, the aim is to damage or destroy high-value targets and kill skilled personnel in order to decrease an opponent's ability to sustain space operations.

Hard-kill systems, however, can create significant political problems. Efforts to destroy terrestrial space-related targets may expand the scale of a conflict. Attacks against an opponent's homeland, for example, may be seen as escalatory. Attacks against space support facilities (e.g., TT&C sites) located in third countries may draw those states into the conflict. Similarly, hard-kill methods used against space-based platforms can also introduce political and diplomatic repercussions. If they generate debris, then they endanger all satellites in orbit, which, again, can lead to diplomatic complications. [25] At a more practical level, space debris may also result in damage to one's own satellite systems.

For this reason, some PLA analyses conclude that one should emphasize *soft-kill* techniques for obtaining space control, especially when trying to affect space-based assets.[26] Whereas hard-kill techniques seek to permanently destroy an opponent's space systems or support facilities, the aim of soft-kill methods are:

- First, to interfere with satellite and missile control systems so that they leave orbit or change direction;
- Second, to interfere with the control and information transmission signals beamed to and from the satellites;
- Third, to interfere with the attitude and control signals governing the satellite's launch, the global positioning system signals, etc.[27]

To these ends, such soft-kill measures as electronic interference, network attacks, and low-energy lasers can dazzle or otherwise degrade systems, thereby producing a "mission-kill" effect without generating debris or other collateral damage. Moreover, such methods as jamming have a certain degree of plausible deniability. This may be important in situations such as targeting international or commercial satellites, where temporary disruption of signals may be preferred to outright destruction of systems.[28] Some of the soft-kill methods that might be applied include electromagnetic attacks and informational or cyber attacks.

Electromagnetic attacks: According to Chinese writings, this category of attack involves the use of electronic signals and jamming to interfere with an opponent's sensors or on-board systems programming. One method is to jam a wide range of signals (in effect, barrage jamming), interfering with a space platform's normal operations. Alternatively, one might engage in careful collection of an opponent's communications and telemetry procedures and signals. Using that information, one might then transmit false and deceptive information, either to the opponent's ground stations (effectively overriding the space platform's signals) or else sending false instructions to the satellite itself (e.g., to point in the wrong direction at key moments).[29]

Information attacks: As Chinese analyses note, the core essence of space systems is their informational nature. Therefore, the ability to interfere, block, and deceive an opponent's space information systems is integral to space information warfare.[30] This suggests that, while one facet of information attacks is the injection of computer viruses into the satellites, the ground facilities, and the data streams, the ability to reconnoiter and infiltrate an opponent's space information networks, even if no damage is perpetrated, is also a useful element of space information warfare.

Unified Coordination of All Operational Activities.

It is important to recognize that, in Chinese analyses, "hard-kill" and "soft-kill" methods are *not* synonymous with "offensive" and "defensive" operations. The objective of both sets of techniques is to reduce an opponent's advantage in space in order to secure information dominance. Thus, even as Chinese authors note the value of soft-kill methods, it is in pursuit of offensive ends. This is essential, according to several PLA analyses, because it allows the attacking side to assume the initiative and thereby allows the weak to defeat the strong. Indeed, one PLA analyst notes that, to seize the initiative, it is important to strike at the enemy's space-related targets at the earliest possible moment.[31]

Defensive operations, though, also have their role. Such measures prevent the enemy from establishing space dominance by limiting the effectiveness of enemy efforts to interfere with, seize, destroy, or disrupt one's own space systems.[32] Defensive measures include efforts at camouflage, concealment, and deception, as well as redundancy and mobility. In particular, some analysts note the need to improve camouflage and concealment measures for terrestrial space-related facilities, including launch and support bases.[33] TT&C facilities, for example, should be camouflaged or otherwise hidden, as much as possible, from enemy reconnaissance systems. Mobile TT&C stations should be developed and deployed to concealed locations, ready to replace fixed sites should the latter be attacked.[34]

Key Point Is Space Dominance (*Zhongdian Zhitian*; 重点制天).

The focus of unified operations, in the context of space, is establishing space dominance. This means being able to exploit space for one's purposes, at times and places of one's choosing, while denying an opponent that same freedom of action. To obtain space dominance, one needs to sustain the smooth operation of space information collection and transmission systems. The key space platforms include:

- Reconnaissance satellites, to conduct comprehensive, timely, accurate intelligence gathering on enemy forces.
- Communications satellites, to provide global, all-weather, unbroken, secure, reliable communications and data relay.
- Navigation and positioning satellites, to allow one's own forces to engage in rapid, precise mobile operations, and engage in precision warfare against an opponent.
- Weather satellites, to collect global weather information.
- Survey and earth-observation satellites, to precisely map various terrestrial terrain features, including potential enemy targets.[35]

Nor are satellites alone sufficient. To be useful, orbiting systems must be backed by a complete supporting infrastructure, including space launch facilities, TT&C systems, and the attendant data-links that bind the space and terrestrial components together. Successful efforts at establishing space dominance entail the sustainment of this entire structure of terrestrial and space systems and associated data and communications links, while striving to degrade or destroy an opponent's.[36]

To this latter end, one needs to conduct unified operations against an opponent's most important space targets. These are the key information and space assets which will most affect the enemy's capabilities, located in the main strategic direction. They should be attacked by one's best forces, at the crucial moments of the campaign, with the aim of degrading the enemy's ability to field unified space power.

TYPES OF SPACE OPERATIONS

Within this guiding operational concept of "unified operations, key point is space dominance," how would the PLA likely seek to establish space dominance in future Local Wars under Informationalized Conditions? PLA writers discuss several different types of space operations that are integral to establishing space dominance. These focus on provision of space information support, space offensive operations, space defensive operations, and space deterrence. These operations are described in terms that resemble those used to describe campaigns.

Space Information Support Operations.

PLA writings make clear that information support from space-based platforms is seen as essential for fighting future Local Wars under High-Tech Conditions or Local Wars under Informationalized Conditions. Key tasks within this mission area of space information support "(*kongjian xinxi zhiyuan*; 空间信息支援)" to the ground, air, and naval forces include:[37]

- Space reconnaissance and surveillance.
- Communications and data relay.
- Navigation and positioning.
- Early warning of missile launches.
- Earth observation, including geodesy, hydro-graphics, and meteorology.

Key tasks within this mission area include:

Providing space reconnaissance and surveillance. This is perhaps the most basic form of operational space activity. The importance of such support has been part of PLA analyses of the first Gulf War.[38] By exploiting the ability to overfly the globe, space-based reconnaissance and surveillance systems can conduct constant electro-optical and electronic surveillance of large areas, unconstrained by terrestrial borders, terrain, or weather.

The PRC currently fields several platforms suitable for space reconnaissance and surveillance purposes. These include the *Ziyuan* (Resource) satellite series, co-developed with Brazil as the China-Brazil Earth Resources Satellite (CBERS), which provides near-real-time electro-optical observation, and the *Fanhui Shi Weixing* (Retrievable Satellite), which drops canisters of film.

Relaying communications and data. Space-based communications and data relay systems can provide global connectivity for large numbers of users, providing instantaneous communications and data transmission among far-flung units. Space communications and data relay systems are an essential counterpart to satellite reconnaissance systems, as they are the main means by which intelligence information may be rapidly and securely transmitted across long distances.[39] Thus, in order to meld forces across service or geographic divides into an organic, integrated whole (*yige youji de zhengti*; 一个有机的整体) and foster the creation of integrated combat capabilities (*zhengti zuozhan xiaoneng*; 整体作战效能), one is forced to rely on satellite communications and data relay systems.[40]

The PRC has deployed *Dongfanghong* (East Is Red)-3 series satellites, and has also developed the DFH-4 communications satellite, although it is unclear whether any of the latter have been deployed at this time. In addition, China can access a variety of commercial communications satellites, such as the Asiasat series. Finally, in April 2008, China launched its first data relay satellite, the *Tianlian* (Sky Link)-1.

Providing Early Warning of Missile Attacks.

Space systems, by virtue of their location, provide unrivaled early detection and tracking of ballistic missiles throughout their flight. At a minimum, then, they can provide prompt warning of enemy ballistic missile attacks. With sufficient refinement, they can also assist missile defense forces by predicting both missile flight paths and impact points.[41]

At this time, however, according to available open source data, there is no evidence of a Chinese missile early warning satellite, nor an active Chinese missile defense program. Just as articles emphasizing the need for data relay satellites predated the actual deployment of such a Chinese system, however, calls for a Chinese missile early warning system may indicate that such a system will be deployed in the future.

Providing Navigation and Positioning Information.

Space navigation systems enable forces to undertake rapid, mobile operations with high precision, and also are the basis for implementing long-range, precision-strike capability, which will reduce friendly casualties as well as damage an opponent.[42]

The PRC's *Beidou* (Big Dipper) navigation satellite system began deployment in 2000. This is an active, regional system, unlike the American global positioning system (GPS) or Russian/Soviet GLONASS, which are global and do not require any transmission by the user.

Observing the Earth and Atmosphere.

This is not so much reconnaissance and surveillance, but geodesy, hydrological, and meteorological observation. The focus is not on finding enemy forces or targets, but understanding the state of the earth, including its magnetic field, gravitational field, terrain, and weather. Such data not only are used to produce maps and weather forecasts, but also can help with weapons selection and guidance.

China has launched the *Fengyun* (Wind-Cloud) series of sun-synchronous and geosynchronous weather satellites and the *Haiyang* (Ocean) maritime surveillance satellites and can employ some of the FSW and *Shijian* (Practice) satellites for geodesy purposes.

As one Chinese analysis notes, such space information support systems, taken together, provide three key benefits.[43] In the first place, they make battlefields much more transparent. Combat forces can therefore be much more effective. They also serve to make command and control much more precise and capable. Forces can respond in real-time or near-real-time to enemy actions, and widely separated units drawn from a variety of services can act in a highly integrated manner. Finally, such systems enable noncontact, nonlinear warfare by enabling long-range, precision strikes.

Thus, taken in combination, the PRC's current array of satellite systems can provide potentially decisive support. As a PLA analysis observes, "Seizing the space information advantage as a high ground is the first decisive condition for seizing information dominance, space dominance, air dominance, naval dominance, land dominance, and therefore the initiative in wartime."[44]

SPACE OFFENSIVE OPERATIONS

In addition to traditional space information support operations, several Chinese analysts seem to believe that future military space activities will include space offensive operations. As one article observed, both the U.S. and Soviet/Russian militaries have steadily shifted their stance away from using space for support functions towards preparing for actual combat in space.[45] Thus, some PLA analyses suggest that it should prepare for space offensive and defensive operations. Assessing the PLA's capabilities relative to these mission areas, however, is much more difficult since, unlike the provision of information support, it is much less clear the extent to which the PLA currently integrates such military space efforts into its operational planning.

The general tenor of PLA writings suggests that space offensive operations involve attacking both space-related targets in orbit *and on the ground*. Essential targets for securing space dominance include not only satellites and other objects in orbit, but also the ground components of space systems, including space launch vehicles, and the attendant data and communications systems that link them together. Attacking an opponent's terrestrial space support functions is an essential means, in this view, of securing an advantage, comparable to traditional attacks against enemy command nodes or military bases.[46] Such attacks carry the additional advantage of retarding an opponent's ability to reinforce or replace damaged or destroyed orbiting systems. As one analysis notes, striking at both space and terrestrial targets is necessary to establish local space superiority.[47]

Attacks against terrestrial targets, especially those based in the enemy's home territory, are likely to have significant strategic implications and potential repercussions. Therefore, attacks against strategic space targets require the direction of the highest level political authorities.[48]

Such attacks should be supplemented by efforts aimed at crippling enemy combat forces. These should be conducted in coordination with land, sea, and air strikes. Such attacks would focus on:

- Command and control facilities and associated elements to paralyze an opponent;
- Logistics and reinforcement centers, as well as power infrastructure and other targets that help sustain the enemy's forces;
- Key missile, air, and naval bases, and combat information facilities, to blunt an opponent's ability to conduct offensive campaigns or seek to establish information, air, or naval dominance;
- Transportation choke points, including railways, highways, vital bridges, and harbors, so as to disrupt an opponent's mobility and isolate their forces.[49]

Such attacks, in the view of PLA analyses, are more operational in nature, and should be undertaken after coordination with the war zone commander. The main methods of undertaking "space strike operations" are to undertake sustained strikes against an opponent, while fending off enemy counterattacks. The conduct of sustained, continuous attacks against the enemy's key targets is intended to deny an opponent any chance to recover. Thus, after an initial phase that strikes key nodes of combat systems, there need to be subsequent attacks throughout the course of the conflict, preventing an opponent from reorganizing its forces or repairing damage inflicted earlier. Such attacks may involve a number of different means, including both hard- and soft-kill methods, aimed at both orbiting and terrestrial systems.

At the same time, commanders should expect an opponent to undertake similar attacks against themselves, and therefore must be prepared to fend off the enemy's counterattacks. In particular, an opponent, upon discovering its own side has organized and prepared space strike operations, may well seek to preempt. Concealing one's own preparations and defending key space facilities and systems are therefore essential to space offensive operations.

Interestingly, PLA writings also raise the prospect of eventual employment of space-based weapons against *terrestrial* targets. According to some PLA writings, future space offensive operations would not only entail efforts that would affect space systems and their supporting capabilities, but might also be undertaken *by* space-based assets. Indeed, several Chinese articles discuss the prospect of space-based weapons attacking terrestrial targets as part of space offensive operations.[50] One article, for example, notes, "Directly striking terrestrial targets from space will become a vital operational technique (*zhongyao de zuozhan shouduan*; 重要的作战手段)."[51]

SPACE DEFENSIVE OPERATIONS

In counterpoint to space offensive operations, there are also "space defensive operations (*kongjian fangyu zuozhan*; 空间防御作战)."[52] Such operations seek to defend one's own space systems from attacks by enemy space or terrestrial weapons, and also to protect national strategic targets from attacks from space systems or ballistic missiles. This latter aspect is echoed in other PLA analyses, which note the importance of ballistic missile defense as part of space operations.[53]

Defensively oriented operations, as one article notes, need not mean solely passive or reactive measures. As one PLA article notes, one can, and should, also employ offensive means and seek the initiative in the course of space defensive operations. Both offensive and defensive means, moreover, should be undertaken by not only space forces, but also by land, sea, and air forces.[54] In the PLA's view, a combination of electronic and physical measures, including firepower strikes, may disrupt and suppress enemy space systems, especially terrestrial support components such as the TT&C facilities, thereby allowing one's own side to achieve space dominance.

The assumption of an offensive stance, even in defensive operations, is likely to be accelerated by advances in technology, which will make space strike weapons more powerful and accurate. As another analysis observes,

> Only by using space attack strength and long-range strike weapons (such as long-range bombers) of other [military] services and branches, at the appropriate time, and using actively offensive activities for concentrated attacks against enemy space launch bases, ballistic missile launch bases, space command and control centers, and aerospace production bases, etc., destroying or reducing the enemy's offensive capacity, can one effectively block and disrupt the enemy's undertaking of space attacks against us.[55]

It is unclear, from the available context, whether such measures should be undertaken early in a conflict, implying preemption, or whether they might arise over the course of the war. What is generally observed in PLA writings, however, is that the struggle for space dominance, as with information dominance, is likely to continue throughout the conflict. Therefore, no matter when such measures commence, they are likely to be sustained.

Supplementing counterattacks and active defenses should be passive measures. Chinese writings suggest that space systems should, as much as possible, incorporate camouflage and stealthy measures, so as to hide the nature and functions of the spacecraft from opposing observation and probes.[56] In addition, they should be hardened or otherwise shielded from enemy efforts at dazzling and interference. Another option is the deployment of small- and micro-satellites in networks and constellations, rather than single large systems. Larger satellites should be capable of altering their orbits to evade enemy attacks and should be capable of functioning autonomously, so that even if their ground-links are severed, they would nonetheless be able to continue operations.[57] Other measures include deploying satellites into orbits designed to avoid enemy detection; employing political, diplomatic, and other channels to mislead opponents of real operational intentions or otherwise influence enemy decisionmaking; and deploying false targets and decoys, to overload opponents' tracking capacities.

Another essential element of a successful defense is provision of proper intelligence support. This is the primary means of detecting enemy offensive preparations in advance of actual attacks. Consequently, one Chinese analysis calls for familiarity with not only the physical aspects of opposing enemy space forces, including numbers, deployment patterns, and weapons capabilities, but also the less concrete aspects. This includes assessing the enemy's likely plans, scale of operations, main direction, and likely uses of technology, tactics, and techniques.[58] This also requires the proper training of a cadre of officers familiar with aerospace operations.[59]

SPACE DETERRENCE OPERATIONS

In the PLA textbook *Science of Strategy (Zhanlue Xue)*, published by the PLA's Academy of Military Science, there is an extensive discussion about the requirements for strategic deterrence. Deterrence, it is noted, may be based upon nuclear, conventional, or information strength. It may also be based upon space-based strength.[60] In each case, the intent is the same: to dissuade an opponent from pursuing certain policies, while persuading an opponent to pursue other policies. As the volume notes, both persuasion and dissuasion "demand the opponent to submit to the deterrer's volition."[61]

Other articles echo *Science of Strategy* in noting the importance of deterrence, both space-based and otherwise. Deterrence is seen as providing the means to achieve one's own strategic goals and defeating an opponent without having to resort to the actual use of force.[62] Instead, by displaying force and indicating a willingness to use one's capabilities, one might compel an opponent to back down.[63]

Space capabilities have several characteristics that make space deterrence especially powerful. In the first place, they offer the potential capacity to neutralize an opponent's nuclear deterrent while expanding one's own integrated deterrent capability. By pairing space defense with nuclear forces, one can attack or defend at will, retaining the initiative while confronting an opponent with an unpalatable set of choices.[64] By enhancing conventional forces' lethality and range, space systems enable "noncontact warfare," and make an opponent less likely to be willing to engage in conventional warfare as well.[65] Space, in essence, enhances both nuclear and conventional deterrence.

Moreover, space systems may intimidate an opponent on their own. Space systems, as noted previously, are very expensive. It is possible, then, to hold an opponent's space infrastructure hostage. Much like nuclear deterrence, space deterrence, becomes a question of cost-benefit analysis: is the focus of deterrence worth the likely cost of repairing or replacing a badly damaged or even destroyed space infrastructure?[66]

Furthermore, because space systems affect not only military but economic, political, and diplomatic spheres, damage to space systems will have wide-ranging repercussions.[67] There may be created financial paralysis, communications breakdowns, transportation snarls, and clear reductions in military capacity.[68] All of these consequences may persuade an opponent that they cannot attain victory at an acceptable price.

In light of the potential import of space deterrence, it appears that there is an implicit "escalation ladder" of PLA measures that one might employ to effect space deterrence. These involve testing space weapons, exercising space forces, reinforcing space capabilities, and actually employing space forces.

Testing Space Weapons.

Several Chinese articles suggest that testing space weapons, especially in peacetime, can influence an opponent's psychological perceptions. By undertaking such tests, one's own overall national level of science and technology are made clear, reinforcing concepts of comprehensive national power, and feeding political and technological deterrent capacities.[69] In some cases, maximum publicity can enhance the deterrent effect of such tests. Any potential opponent is therefore effectively notified that its space assets are likely to be placed in jeopardy in event of crisis. Not only might this dissuade an opponent from pursuing aggression, but it might also undercut its political and diplomatic standing. At the same time, by sometimes engaging in obfuscation, it is possible to generate uncertainty as to one's own capabilities, and thereby manipulate an opponent's perceptions.[70]

Exercising Space Forces.

The next level of deterrence involves exercising one's space forces. These exercises can include such elements as space offense and defense operations, anti-missile exercises, space strategic strike rehearsals, and displays of joint military operations involving both space and nonspace forces. Each such type of exercise has its own intended meaning. Space offense and defense operations, for example, indicate the ability to seize space dominance, whereas anti-missile exercises reflect one's strategic defensive capacity, even in the face of nuclear weapons. Space strike exercises implicitly threaten the entire strategic depth of an opponent, whereas joint exercises with other forces serve as a reminder that a full range of capabilities is potentially at play, and not simply space capabilities.[71]

Whereas tests of space weapons might occur in peacetime, PLA authors suggest that exercises should be undertaken in the context of an ongoing crisis. By holding such exercises, according to one analysis, a nation is helping to mold other's perceptions. Exercises may be seen as an expression of will or commitment, signaling an opponent of one's readiness for war. To this end, one might seek to hold such exercises in sensitive space areas, specifically in order to underscore the seriousness of one's resolve.[72]

As an added benefit, such exercises not only display the space deterrent capabilities of the forces involved, but they also provide valuable unit training.[73] This additional training, in and of itself, can also enhance deterrent effects. Well-trained forces are better able to implement operational plans. Thus, in the opinion of Second Artillery officers Sun Haiyang and Chang Jing-an, U.S. military space exercises have improved America's space deterrent capacity.

Deployment of Additional Space Forces.

In the event of an ongoing, escalating crisis, where space exercises may not have proven sufficient to constrain the crisis, the next step would be to reinforce available space forces. This includes both deploying additional systems, and maneuvering those already in orbit towards "sensitive areas of space (*mingan de kongjian quyu*; 敏感的空间区域)," so as to create a local advantage over an opponent.[74]

Not only does reinforcement of available space forces signal an opponent of one's resolve, but increased reconnaissance and surveillance assets will also complicate an opponent's efforts at maintaining secrecy. The likelihood of discovery, in turn, may dissuade an opponent from commencing hostilities, as the element of surprise is jeopardized. Moreover, should an opponent nonetheless refuse to take steps to de-escalate, increased deployments will also provide greater redundancy in the event of war.[75]

Actual Use of Space Forces.

The actual use of space forces is seen as the ultimate form of deterrence. Different PLA analyses, however, seem to have different definitions of what this means. One article, for example, seems to suggest that *prior* use of space forces lends credibility for subsequent deterrent efforts. Thus, the employment of space forces in previous local wars provide an unmistakable statement of one's own capabilities, as well as one's willingness to take losses and inflict punishment. In this view, "actual capabilities, displayed in real wars, are the foundation of space deterrence."[76]

Other analyses, however, suggest that the deterrence involved in actual attacks is not based on prior experience, but on the effective implementation of actual attacks in an *ongoing* crisis. One author describes such operations as reprimand or punishment strikes (*chengjie daji*; 惩戒打击). The actual employment of space forces, in this view, constitutes the strongest kind of deterrent (*zuigao qiangdu de weishe*; 最高强度的威慑).[77] The aim is to undertake point strikes to "cow the enemy with small battles (*yi xiaozhan er quren zhibing*; 以小战而屈人之兵)."[78]

One type of punishment strike would be to interfere with, suppress, or otherwise disrupt enemy space systems, such as by jamming communications and data links or damaging their command system through computer network attacks.[79] By inflicting confusion and disruption on their space systems, one may cause an opponent to decide to cease hostilities. If they do not, then one's own military activities will operate from a more advantageous position.

The other option is to undertake sudden, short-duration strikes against enemy space systems. In light of the previous option, this would imply that such strikes would involve kinetic means. The types of targets would reinforce this implication: space information systems, command and control centers, communications nodes, guided missile launch bases, energy storage sites and other strategic targets. As noted elsewhere, such targets are likely to receive hard-kill, rather than soft-kill, attacks to disable them for a prolonged period. Strikes against such targets, it is suggested, will inflict a psychological blow upon the enemy, since the destruction of such targets will not be easily repaired. Moreover, such attacks will likely produce cascading effects throughout the enemy's space system, due to their linked nature.[80] That is, by destroying such targets, other elements of the opponent's space infrastructure will likely be affected, whether they are themselves targeted or not. It would likely require extensive efforts and delays, for example, before orbiting satellites could have their orbits shifted, or new systems could be launched, in the wake of such attacks.

This sort of deterrence logic would seem to be rooted in the idea that the ability to inflict punishment is the greatest deterrent. Thus, in one Chinese author's view, "the foundation of space deterrence must be preparation for real war (*bixu yi shizhan zhunbei zuowei kongjian weishe de jichu*; 必须以实战准备作为空间威慑的基础)."[81]

The divergence of views on how to emplace a policy of space deterrence, however, raises questions about the extent to which the PLA necessarily governs larger Chinese space policy. For example, the description of reinforcing available space forces would seem to imply a very slowly developing crisis. It is open to question whether such measured steps would be possible, or whether they would be interpreted in the manner presented, in the event of a rapidly escalating situation.

Similarly, there is a significant discrepancy between how PLA authors describe the utility of testing space weapons, and how the PRC actually behaved at the time of the January 2007 anti-satellite missile (ASAT) test. Not only was there no prior publicity, but the PRC Foreign Ministry seemed to handle the aftermath in a singularly hesitant fashion. Consequently, one must wonder whether the Chinese leadership necessarily subscribes to the same view of deterrence as that laid out by Chinese military space analysts.

It is therefore unclear the extent to which the broader Chinese leadership necessarily subscribes to the concepts of space deterrence, as laid out by PLA authors. Indeed, given the opacity of the Chinese space program, as well as Chinese decisionmaking in general, it is difficult to state with any certainty how the Chinese would undertake military space operations in situations beyond Taiwan.

PROSPECTS FOR THE FUTURE

The difficulty of predicting PLA actions in space is exacerbated by the fact that its actual experience with military space operations is extremely limited. In the first place, the PLA has not actually gone to war in over 25 years (since the 1979 Sino-Vietnam War and the subsequent border clashes). Consequently, there is very little information available on how the PLA would use space systems in time of war, as the PLA itself simply has no recent experience with actual wartime application of space systems.

Furthermore, it is not clear the extent to which the PLA currently relies upon space-based assets for its operations. Preparing for operations against Taiwan, an island off its coast that the PLA has had nearly 60 years to reconnoiter, likely involves less need for space-based reconnaissance or communications. Moreover, while it is likely that the PLA can access national space systems, such as meteorological data, how that information is incorporated into PLA planning and operations is unclear. The Chinese space program is one of the more opaque systems, and how the PLA uses data derived from space systems is similarly nontransparent.

As the PLA increasingly operates farther afield, however, it is likely that it will exhibit a corresponding increase in its reliance on space-based systems for information collection and exploitation. Moreover, PLA writings indicate that the increasing emphasis on joint operations is likely to entail greater reliance on space systems in order to both coordinate the disparate forces, and to provide common situational awareness.

Given the opacity of both the Chinese space program and the PLA, however, it is unclear how obvious any increasing dependence would be. It is likely, for example, that greater exploitation of space systems to coordinate forces would be reflected in their integration into PLA exercises. How one would detect and observe this increase, however, is unclear, especially in the unclassified literature.

An expanding PLA reliance on space systems may be reflected in an expansion of militarily useful systems. These might include higher resolution imaging satellites, military communications satellites that are resistant to jamming, as well as the new *Beidou/Compass* satellite navigation system, which will have global, rather than just regional, capacity. The deployment of the *Tianlian-1* data relay satellite similarly indicates Chinese interest in more global, rather than regional, space coverage (although this system was ostensibly deployed to support the Chinese manned space program).

Given that the growth of the Chinese space program has not paralleled the American or Soviet/ Russian space programs, though, it is important to recognize that the PLA's employment of space systems may well follow a very different path from that of the United States or the former Soviet Union. Indeed, given Chinese analyses of American dependence on space assets, the PLA may specifically seek to avoid creating comparable vulnerabilities as they develop their own military space capabilities. Moreover, so long as the PLA is focused on regional, rather than global, contingencies, it will be operating under different conditions from U.S. forces, which must maintain a more global forward presence. Consequently, the PLA may well not need to rely as heavily on space assets for certain key mission areas (e.g., communications, photo, and electronic reconnaissance).

For the United States, an increasing Chinese presence in space, especially a military one, is therefore likely to complicate its planning and operations. At the most immediate level, in the wake of the 2007 Chinese anti-satellite test, it is clear that the PRC has the ability to attack low-earth orbit U.S. satellites. While the extent of this threat may be unclear, it nonetheless imposes additional considerations on U.S. military planners.

Unlike previous conflicts, in the event of Sino-U.S. tensions, the United States cannot expect to have unconstrained access to space.

In addition, though, it presents the United States with substantial complications even outside the context of a Sino-U.S. military confrontation. In the event of a conflict involving the United States and a third party, the PRC would have the capacity to provide information from its space-based assets to America's opponents. The provision of such information would make operational security much more problematic than was the case during U.S. intervention in the Balkans or during the war in Kuwait or Iraq.

Nor would the PRC necessarily have to actively provide space information to an opponent. The PRC's willingness and ability to sell entire satellite systems to foreign states, such as the Simon Bolivar satellite to Venezuela, means that even poorer nations may be able to simply acquire their own space capabilities. If the PRC becomes a major purveyor of turn-key satellite systems, it is not clear that the United States will be able to prevent a future Saddam Hussein or Slobodan Milosevic from accessing information derived from space—with direct implications for U.S. military operations.

CONCLUSION

The requirement of preparing for Local Wars Under Modern High-Tech Conditions in the 1990s and early 2000s led the PLA to shift towards a more "joint" approach to future wars and campaigns. With the growing importance of information technology, as acknowledged by the need to prepare for Local Wars under Informationalized Conditions, the emphasis has shifted towards unified operations, incorporating the ability to secure information dominance in order to create a common situational awareness among the disparate forces. In the views of PLA analysts, space dominance is essential. This, in turn, suggests that any future conflict involving the PRC is likely to entail military operations that affect space systems.

What the nature of such operations is likely to entail, however, is far from obvious. It is not at all certain, for example, whether there is currently a PLA space doctrine. Nor is it clear that the PLA has formally enunciated a space mission. A survey of Chinese military literature, however, suggests that the above elements are at least under discussion. PLA thinking about its missions beyond Taiwan is therefore likely to incorporate a space component.

Space is not simply essential as an enabler for joint operations, however, or even for securing information dominance. Instead, it is part and parcel of the wider range of expected PLA capabilities, necessary for fulfilling the "historic missions" that are arising even before the PRC is "beyond Taiwan." This suggests that, beyond the purely operational considerations, space capabilities are likely to assume an increasing strategic role as well.

The "historic missions" of the PLA are of growing importance in light of the expanding PRC worldview and heightened global engagement. Where once the PLA could focus primarily on local defense of the homeland, it must now consider how to secure Chinese interests regionally, and eventually even globally. Where once the PLA could focus on protracted wars of annihilation, relying on mass and attrition, now it must be capable of fighting much more abbreviated wars of paralysis that rely on technology and rapid reaction.

As the PLA thinks about fulfilling its historic missions "beyond Taiwan," then, it must consider the requirements that arise for winning new kinds of conflicts. The future PLA is one that will have to be able to fight and win wars through technological sophistication and internally generated synergies. As important, however, given the increasingly global nature of China's interests, it must be capable of preventing the outbreak of conflict in the first place, especially insofar as the PLA itself does not yet have the power projection capacity to assert itself in distant lands.

In this context, then, the PRC's ability to secure space dominance will affect its broader ability to obtain security for itself. The impact of military space operations is not simply, then, the ability to engage a given satellite or deploy a constellation, but increasingly relates to the larger issue of sustaining and supporting the greater national interest. This suggests that PRC and PLA activities in space must be analyzed with an eye not only towards warfighting capabilities, but also in the context of deterrence.

Thinking "beyond Taiwan" means thinking beyond the prospect of a military confrontation over the island, but also clearly encompasses thinking beyond the military component of security. China's burgeoning space power not only provides the PLA with additional capabilities, but also provides the PRC with additional means of influencing its security environment. It affects not only the PRC's military strength, but also its diplomatic, political, and economic capacities as well. Space, then, is not only a factor in assessing the PLA, but is likely to be a key component of future Chinese "comprehensive national power" and national security planning, especially in the world beyond Taiwan.

CHAPTER 7 - ENDNOTES

1. There has been a limited discussion of China's space program in English. It has been discussed in many U.S. Department of Defense (DoD) annual reports to Congress on the military power of the PRC (whose analysis has been critiqued by the Union of Concerned Scientists). There are currently three volumes published on the subject: Joan Johnson-Freese's *The Chinese Space Program* (1998), Brian Harvey's *China's Space Program* (2nd Ed., 2004), and Roger Handberg and Zhen Li's *Chinese Space Policy* (2007), as well as Kevin Pollpeter's SSI monograph, *Building for the Future: China's Progress in Space Technology During the Tenth Five-Year Plan and the U.S. Response*, and Larry Wortzel's American Enterprise Institute (AEI) monograph, *The Chinese People's Liberation Army and Space Warfare*. There have also been several journal articles that discuss the Chinese space program, including Ashley Tellis' "China's Military Space Strategy" (2007 *Survival*) and Joan Johnson-Freese's "Space Wei Qi" (2004 *Naval War College Review*). Finally, two PLA conference anthologies include chapters on China's space program: *A Poverty of Riches* (2003) and *China's Revolution in Doctrinal Affairs* (2005). This chapter draws primarily upon Chinese open-source discussions of military space operations, including the two Chinese space white papers (2000 and 2006), and especially the volume *Military Astronautics* by Chang Xianqi, and articles published in *China Military Science*.

2. Jiang Zemin, "Discussing the RMA with Chinese Characteristics" in *Jiang Zemin Wenzhai* (*Selected Works of Jiang Zemin*), Beijing, China: People's Publishing House, 2006, pp. 576-583.

3. This section is heavily indebted to my CNA colleague Dan Hartnett, who has done pathbreaking work on "China's Historic Missions."

4. This section draws from Daniel Hartnett, "Towards a Globally Focused Chinese Military," draft document (2008).

5. PLA Encyclopedia Committee, *Chinese Military Encyclopedia*, Vol. III, Beijing, China: Academy of Military Science Publishing House, July 1997, p. 602.

6. PLA Encyclopedia Committee, *Chinese Military Encyclopedia*, Supplemental Volume (Beijing, China: Military Science Publishing House, 2002, p. 455.

7. Han Jinqiang, "Space Dominance: Improving Assurance of Fighting and Winning," *Study Times*, November 29, 2006.

8. Li Daguang, "Space Dominance: The Basis for Victory in Information War," *National Defense Daily*, January 6, 2004; and *Liberation Army Daily*, January 6, 2004.

9. Li Daguang, "On Space Supremacy," *Chinese Military Science*, No. 2, 2003; and Li Daguang, "Discussion on Control of the Sky."

10. David M. Finkelstein, *Evolving Operational Concepts of the Chinese People's Liberation Army and Navy: A Preliminary Exploration*, Alexandria, VA: CNA, 2002, p. 52.

11. For further discussion of "integrated operations, key point strikes," see David Finkelstein, *Evolving Operational Concepts*, pp. 52-65.

12. Chang Xianqi, *Military Astronautics*, 2nd Ed., Beijing, China: Defense Industries Press, 2005, pp. 273-279.

13. Note that "*yiti*" may be translated as either "integrated" or "unified." While the former translation is common, in the context here, the latter would seem to be more appropriate. For that reason, as well as to avoid confusion with the term "*zhengti*," we will use the translation "unified" in the body of the chapter.

14. See, for example, Hong Bin and Liang Xiaoqiu, "The Basics of Space Strategic Theory" *China Military Science*, No. 1, 2002; Li Dong, Zhao Xinguo, Huang Chenglin, "Research on Concepts of Space Operations and Its Command," *Journal of the Academy of Equipment Command and Technology*, Vol. XIV, No. 5, 2003.

15. Shen Shilu, Feng Shuxing, Wang Jia, Li Yadong, "Initial Research into Military Aerospace Mission Command Decision-making," *Journal of the Academy of Equipment Command and Technology*, Vol. XVIII, No. 1, February 2007.

16. Chang Xianqi, *Military Astronautics*, pp. 274-275.

17. "Space Information Warfare—Strategic High Ground for Modern Warfare Mobilization," *China Aerospace Newspaper*, June 2, 2004.

18. Xu Gangliang, Luo Yong, "Several Relationships That Our Nation Must Establish as China Develops Its Space power," *Journal of the Academy of Equipment Command and Technology*, Vol. XVII, No. 2, 2006.

19. Wang Yao, "The Theory of Integrated Air and Space Operations," *China Air Force*, No. 5, 2005.

20. Chang Xianqi, *Military Astronautics*, p. 275.

21. Zhang Jiali, Min Zengfu, "On Extending Regional War into the Air and Space," *China Military Science*, No. 1, 2005; and Chang Xianqi, *Military Astronautics*, 2nd Ed., p. 276.

22. Chang Xianqi, "Space Strategy and National Security," *China Military Science*, No. 1, 2002.

23. Chang Xianqi, *Military Astronautics*, p. 275.

24. Wang Xiaohai, "Current State of Development of Space Information Conflict Technologies," *China Aerospace*, September 2007.

25. Chang Xianqi, *Military Astronautics*, p. 290.

26. *Ibid.*, pp. 290-291.

27. Fan Xuejun, "Militarily Strong Nations Are Steadily Developing 'Space Information Warfare'," *Liberation Army Daily*, April 13, 2005.

28. Yang Leping, An Xueying, Zhao Yong, "Concepts, Missions, and Implications of Space Control," *Journal of the Academy of Equipment Command and Technology*, Vol. XIV, No. 4, August 2003.

29. Wang Xiaohai.

30. *Ibid.*

31. Li Daguang, "The Characteristics and Rules of Law of Space Strategy," *China Military Science*, No. 1, 2002.

32. Fan Xuejun.

33. Chang Xianqi, *Military Astronautics*, p. 320.

34. Guan Weiqiang, Qin Daguo, Xiao Lianggang, "Research on Requirements for Aerospace TT&C Systems for Integrated-Style Joint Operations," *Journal of the Academy of Equipment Command and Technology*, Vol. XVII, No. 6, 2006.

35. Chang Xianqi, *Military Astronautics*, pp. 276-277.

36. *Ibid.*, pp. 278-279.

37. Li Dong *et al.*, "Research on Concepts of Space Operations and Its Command."

38. Gao Yubiao, Chief Editor, *Joint Campaign Course Materials*, Beijing, China: Academy of Military Science Publishing House, August 2001, p. 54; and Chang Xianqi, *Military Astronautics*, pp. 247-249.

39. Gao Qingjun, "Aerospace Reconnaissance Characteristics and Limits in High-tech Local Wars," *Journal of the Academy of Equipment Command and Technology*, Vol. XVI, No. 1, 2005.

40. *Ibid.*; and Chang Xianqi, *Military Astronautics*, p. 308.

41. Chang Xianqi, *Military Astronautics*, pp. 134, 146-147.

42. *Ibid.*, p. 147.

43. Lanzhou Military Region Headquarters Communications Department, "Space Information Support and Its Influence on Future Terrestrial Operations," *Military Art*, No. 10, 2003.

44. *Ibid.*

45. Zhang Qinghai and Li Xiaohai, "Space Warfare: From Vision to Reality," *China Military Science*, No. 1, 2005.

46. Hong Bin, Liang Xiaoqiu, "The Basics of Space Strategic Theory," *China Military Science*, No. 1, 2002.

47. Li Dong *et al.*, "Research on Concepts of Space Operations and Its Command."

48. The precise nature of such strategic targets, however, is not defined. Chang Xianqi, *Military Astronautics*, p. 314.

49. *Ibid.*; and Li Dong *et al.*, "Research on Concepts of Space Operations and Its Command."

50. Chang Xianqi, *Military Astronautics*, p. 314; Xiong Xiaolong *et al.*, "Seizing Space Dominance," *Winged Missiles Journal*, October 2005; and Li Dong *et al.*, "Research on Concepts of Space Operations and Its Command."

51. Zhang Qinghai and Li Xiaohai.

52. Chang Xianqi, *Military Astronautics*, pp. 317-321.

53. Zhang Qinghai and Li Xiaohai.

54. Hong Bin and Liang Xiaoqiu.

55. Chang Xianqi, *Military Astronautics*, p. 321.

56. *Ibid.*, p. 316.

57. *Ibid.*, p. 320.

58. *Ibid.*, p. 319.

59. Chang Xianqi, "Developing Military Space to Meet the Challenge of New Military Revolutions," *Journal of the Academy of Command Equipment and Technology*, Vol. X, No. 5, 1999.

60. Zhou Peng and Wen Enbing, "Developing the Theory of Strategic Deterrence with Chinese Characteristics," *China Military Science*, No. 3, 2004.

61. Peng Guangqian and Yao Youzhi, ed., *The Science of Military Strategy*, Beijing, China: Military Science Publishing House, 2005, p. 215.

62. Zhou Peng and Wen Enbing.

63. Wang Xiaohai.

64. Hong Bin and Liang Xiaoqiu.

65. Chang Xianqi, *Military Astronautics*, p. 300.

66. Wang Xiaohai.

67. Li Jingjun and Dan Yuquan, "The Strategy of Space Deterrence," *China Military Science*, No. 1, 2002.

68. Chang Xianqi, *Military Astronautics*, pp. 299-300.

69. Li Jingjun and Dan Yuquan.

70. Li Jingjun and Dan Yuquan; Chang Xianqi, *Military Astronautics*, p. 303.

71. Chang Xianqi, *Military Astronautics*, p. 303.

72. *Ibid.*, p. 303.

73. Sun Haiyang and Chang Jing-an, "The New Form of Deterrence—Space Deterrence," *Military Art*, No. 10, 2003.

74. Chang Xianqi, *Military Astronautics*, pp. 303-304.

75. *Ibid.*

76. Sun Haiyang and Chang Jing-an.

77. Chang Xianqi, *Military Astronautics*, p. 304.

78. *Ibid.*, p. 302.

79. *Ibid.*, p. 304.

80. *Ibid.*

81. *Ibid.*, p. 302.

CHAPTER 8

PLA COMPUTER NETWORK OPERATIONS: SCENARIOS, DOCTRINE, ORGANIZATIONS, AND CAPABILITY

James Mulvenon

INTRODUCTION

Theorists in the Chinese military have long been at the forefront of doctrinal thinking about cyber conflict, arguing that computer network attack offers Beijing some important asymmetric advantages against adversaries with superior technology. Yet the actual manifestations of this theorizing have been heretofore restricted to interesting but relatively minor hacking by Chinese patriotic hacker groups during crises or the alleged, large-scale cyber espionage against unclassified Department of Defense (DoD) computer systems. The well-publicized cyber attacks against Estonia in April 2007 and Georgia in July 2008, however, raise the specter of the use of cyberspace for state-level conflict, particularly as globalization raises the stakes by compelling greater electronic dependencies and interdependencies. This chapter examines computer network operations (CNO) as a tool of Chinese state power, outlining the possible scenarios, doctrinal concepts, organizations, and capabilities being developed by the People's Liberation Army (PLA). Specifically, the chapter explores the use of computer network exploit and computer network attack as *missions* designed to coerce Taiwan toward reunification on China's terms, while deterring or disrupting U.S. military intervention on Taiwan's behalf. In terms of assumptions, therefore, this chapter begins from the premise that we live in the "A" quadrant of Dr. Andrew Scobell's matrix (Chapter 2), since cyber operations often simmer beneath the surface of a cross-strait conflict that can neither be fully resolved or permitted to break out into all-out war between China, Taiwan, and the United States.

Definitional Issues.

The Chinese military did not invent the term "computer network operations" but instead borrowed it from its U.S. counterparts, much as they have done with previous related concepts. Indeed, if one tracks Chinese military terminology over time, it is possible to discern a short lag between the adoption of new cyber concepts in the United States and their eventual adoption in China. This process was aided by the fact that some of the most important first generation PLA cyber theorists, like Wang Baocun, were experts on the American military and not doctrinal thinkers by trade. Thus, one can see the PLA making the same progression from the term "information warfare" (IW) [信息战争] in early writings, moving to "information operations" [信息作战], and then to more specific concepts like "network warfare" [网络战]. As the limited Western literature on the subject shows, the content of these concepts evolved from simple description of foreign ideas in the information warfare literature to increasingly sophisticated adaptions and modifications of the concepts of information operations and computer network operations to the PLA's specific strategic goals, technology levels, doctrinal landscape and even the tortured syntax of Marxist-Leninist-Mao Zedong thought, the strategic wisdom of the Chinese ancients, and dialectical materialism.[1] For example, the common use of the term "countermeasures" [对抗] in core PLA Information Operations (IO) terms like "electronic countermeasures" [电子对抗], "communications countermeasures" [通信对抗], and network countermeasures [网络对抗], is embedded with Beijing's self-perception of itself as the aggrieved party forced to counterattack against hegemonistic forces, even though the text of the concepts contains clear references to preemptive first strikes to gain advantage. For the purposes of this chapter, however, we adopt the clearer PLA definition of computer network warfare:

> The general term for all sorts of information offense and defense actions in which computers and computer networks are the main targets, in which advanced information technology is a basic means, and which take place throughout the space occupied by networks. The core of computer network warfare is to disrupt the layers in which information is processed, with the objective of seizing and maintaining control of the network space.

CYBER: AN EMERGING TOOL OF CHINESE STATE POWER

As demonstrated by the "hacker wars" that followed former Taiwan President Lee Teng-hui's announcement of "special state-to-state relations," the U.S. bombing of the Chinese Embassy in Yugoslavia in 1999, and the EP-3 crisis in 2001, cyber attacks against foreign countries by so-called Chinese "patriotic hacker" groups have become a permanent feature of Chinese foreign and security policy crises since the mid- to late-1990s. Patriotic hacking has arguably been a mixed blessing for China. On the one hand, the emergence of this trend presents the People's Republic of China (PRC) military and political leadership with serious command and control problems. Specifically, uncontrolled hacking by irregulars against the United States and Taiwan could potentially undermine a PRC political-military coercive diplomacy strategy vis-à-vis Taiwan and the United States during a crisis. Unlike traditional military instruments such as missiles, many of the levers of computer network operations by "unofficial means" are beyond the control of the Chinese government. This could negate the intended impact of strategic pausing and other political signals during a crisis. Yet at the same time patriotic hacking offers several new opportunities for the PRC. First, it increases plausible deniability for official Chinese computer network attack and exploit activities. Second, it has the potential to create a large, if unsophisticated set of operators who could engage in disruption activities against U.S. and Taiwan networks.

Yet the overall strategic impact of these patriotic hacker wars has been relatively minor, more correctly described as a nuisance than a threat to other nation-states. More recent phenomena in this arena, such as the Russia-Estonia clash in 2007, the Russia-Georgia crisis in 2008, and especially the widespread allegations of Chinese cyber espionage against the DoD, however, have raised the stakes for cyber conflict as a legitimate tool of state power, portending future and perhaps more damaging uses of the technologies and methods. The crossing of this threshold has been largely facilitated by the increasingly networked nature of the global system, permitting nation states to threaten each other's national power through cyberspace. While the Beijing authorities continue to petulantly insist that China would never engage in cyber conflict, asserting that the idea is "totally groundless and a reflection of Cold War mentality,"[2] recent events strongly suggest that both Beijing and Moscow see cyber conflict as a legitimate, if plausibly deniable, form of 21st century statecraft.

THE PLA AND COMPUTER NETWORK OPERATIONS

In order to explore the full range of the PLA's interest in computer network operations, this section is divided into four broad areas: CNO-related doctrinal concepts, scenarios, organizations, and capabilities.

PLA Doctrinal Framework for Information Operations and Computer Network Operations.

While no official doctrine has been identified, Chinese military strategists describe IO and CNO as useful supplements to conventional warfighting capability, and powerful asymmetric options for "overcoming the superior with the inferior." According to one PRC author, "Computer network attack is one of the most effective means for a weak military to fight a strong one."[3] Yet another important theme in Chinese writings on CNO is the use of computer network attack as the spearpoint of deterrence. Emphasizing the potential role of computer network attack (CNA) in this type of signaling, a PRC strategist writes that "We must send a message to the enemy through computer network attack, forcing the enemy to give up without fighting."[4] Computer network attack is particularly attractive to the PLA, since it has a longer range than their conventional power projection assets. This allows the PLA to "reach out and touch" the

United States, even in the continental United States. "Thanks to computers," one strategist writes," long-distance surveillance and accurate, powerful, and long-distance attacks are now available to our military."[5] Yet computer network attack is also believed to enjoy a high degree of "plausible deniability," rendering it a possible tool of strategic denial and deception. As one source notes, "An information war is inexpensive, as the enemy country can receive a paralyzing blow through the Internet, and the party on the receiving end will not be able to tell whether it is a child's prank or an attack from an enemy."[6]

It is important to note that Chinese CNA doctrine focuses on disruption and paralysis, not destruction. Philosophically and historically, the evolving doctrine draws inspiration from Mao Zedong's theory of "protracted war," in which he argued that "We must as far as possible seal up the enemies' eyes and ears, and make them become blind and deaf, and we must as far as possible confuse the minds of their commanders and turn them into madmen, using this to achieve our own victory."[7] In the modem age, one authoritative source states: "Computer warfare targets computers — the core of weapons systems and command, control, communications, computers and intelligence (C4I) systems—in order to paralyze the enemy."[8] The goal of this paralyzing attack is to inflict a "mortal blow" [zhiming daji], though this does not necessarily refer to defeat. Instead, Chinese analysts often speak of using these attacks to deter the enemy, or to raise the costs of conflict to an unacceptable level. Specifically, computer network attacks on nonmilitary targets are designed to ". . . shake war resoluteness, destroy war potential and win the upper hand in war," thus undermining the political will of the population for participation in military conflict.[9]

At an operational level, the emerging Chinese CNO strategy has five key features. First, Chinese authors emphasize defense as the top priority, and chastise American theorists for their "fetish of the offensive." In interviews, analysts assert their belief that the United States is already carrying out extensive computer network exploitation (CNE) activities against Chinese servers. As a result, computer network defense (CND) must be the highest priority in peacetime, and only after that problem is solved can they consider "tactical counteroffensives." Second, CNA is viewed as an unconventional warfare weapon to be used in the opening phase of the conflict, not a battlefield force multiplier that can be employed during every phase of the war. PLA analysts believe that a bolt from the blue at the beginning is necessary, because the enemy may simply unplug the network, denying them access to the target set, or patch the relevant vulnerabilities, thus obviating all prior intelligence preparation of the battlefield. Third, CNA is seen as a tool to permit China to fight and win an information campaign, precluding the need for conventional military action. Fourth, China's enemies, in particular the United States, are seen as "information dependent," while China is not. This latter point is an interesting misperception, given that the current Chinese C4I modernization is paradoxically making them more vulnerable to U.S. counter-C4I methods. Perhaps most significant, computer network attack is characterized as a preemption weapon to be used under the rubric of the rising Chinese strategy of *xianfa zhiren* [先发制人], or "gaining mastery before the enemy has struck." Preemption is a core concept of emerging Chinese military doctrine. One author recommends that an effective strategy by which the weaker party can overcome its more powerful enemy is "to take advantage of serious gaps in the deployment of forces by the enemy with a high-tech edge by launching a preemptive strike during the early phase of the war or in the preparations leading to the offensive."[10] Confirming earlier analysis of Chinese views of U.S. operational vulnerabilities in the deployment phase, the reason for striking is that the "enemy is most vulnerable during the early phase of the war."[11] In terms of specific targets, the author asserts that "we should zero in on the hubs and other crucial links in the system that moves enemy troops as well as the war-making machine, such as harbors, airports, means of transportation, battlefield installations, and the communications, command and control and information systems."[12] If these targets are not attacked or the attack fails, the "high-tech equipped enemy" will amass troops and deploy hardware swiftly to the war zone, where it will carry out "large-scale air strikes in an attempt to weaken . . . China's combat capability."[13] More recent and authoritative sources expand on this view. "In order to control information power," one source states, "there must also be preemption . . . . information offensives mainly rely on distant battle and stealth in order to be effective, and are best used as a surprise. . . . Therefore, it is clear that whoever strikes first has the advantage."[14] "The best defense is offense," according to the authors of *Information Operations:* "We must launch preemptive attacks to disrupt and destroy enemy computer systems."[15]

Integrated Network Electronic Warfare (INEW). The dominant doctrinal concept encompassing PLA information operations, including computer network operations, is Integrated Network Electronic Warfare [网电一体战], or INEW. As Dai Qingmin explains in his seminal article, INEW is the "organic combination of electronic warfare and computer network warfare."[16] The synthesis of these two realms in Chinese thinking was all the more revolutionary, given long-standing tension among U.S. information warfare experts divided between the electronic warfare (EW) school, which argued that computer network attack fell within the broad definition of the electromagnetic spectrum, and the new CNO school, which insisted that computer network attack was a fundamentally different dynamic than traditional EW missions like jamming. Rather than see them as competing, Dai and the INEW advocates argue that combining them is the essence of "integrated combat operations" against "enemy information systems" with the goal of "seizing battlefield information superiority."[17] Specifically, INEW utilizes both EW and CNO to weaken and disrupt the entire process by which battlefield information systems acquire, foreword, process, and use information. Integrated network-electronic warfare uses electronic warfare to disrupt the opponent's acquisition and forwarding of information. It uses computer network warfare to disrupt the opponent's processing and use of information.[18]

The resulting doctrinal concept "serves as information operations theory with Chinese characteristics," playing "an important guiding role in the construction of our Army's information operations forces and in fighting and winning future high-tech local wars."[19] In particular, INEW provides the doctrinal underpinning for the integration of computer network attack, often treated as an isolated covert action in other militaries, into larger PLA campaigns.

The Key CNO Scenarios.

The Legacy CNO Scenario: Taiwan. It is important to contextualize the PLA's interest in computer network operations within Beijing's larger perceived strategic environment. In the minds of the Chinese leadership, the available evidence suggests that the most important political-military challenge, and the most likely flashpoint for Sino-U.S. conflict is Taiwan. In seeking to reunify the island with the mainland, however, it is important to note that the PRC has a political strategy with a military component, not a military strategy with a political component. The PRC would prefer to win without fighting, since Beijing's worst case outcome is a failed operation that would result in de facto independence for Taiwan. Also, the leadership realizes that attacking Taiwan with kinetic weapons will result in significant international opprobrium and make the native population ungovernable.

Should the situation deteriorate into direct military conflict, the PLA since 1992 has been hard at work bolstering the hedging options of the leadership, developing advanced campaign doctrines, testing the concepts in increasingly complex training and exercises, and integrating new indigenous and imported weapons systems. At the strategic level, the writings of Chinese military authors suggest that there are two main centers of gravity in a Taiwan scenario, both of which can be attacked with computer network operations in concert with other kinetic and nonkinetic capabilities. The first of these is the will of the Taiwanese people, which they hope to undermine through exercises, cyber attacks against critical infrastructure, missile attacks, special operations forces (SOF) operations, and other operations that have a psychological operations (psyops) focus. Based on its own analysis from the 1995-96 exercises, as well as public opinion polling in Taiwan, China appears to have concluded that the Taiwanese people do not have the stomach for conflict and will therefore sue for peace after suffering only a small amount of pain. The second center of gravity is the will and capability of the United States to intervene decisively in a cross-strait conflict. In a strategic sense, China has traditionally believed that its intercontinental ballistic missile (ICBM) inventory, which is capable of striking the continental United States (CONUS), will serve as a deterrent to U.S. intervention or at least a brake on escalation. Closer to Taiwan, the PLA has been engaged in an active program of equipment modernization, purchasing niche anti-access, area-denial capabilities such as long-range cruise missiles and submarines to shape the operational calculus of the American carrier battle group commander on station. At the same time, a key lesson learned from analyzing U.S. military operations since Operation DESERT STORM was the vulnerability of the logistics and deployment system to cyber attack.

Center of Gravity Number One: The Will of the People on Taiwan. Chinese strategies to manipulate the national psychology of the populace and leadership on Taiwan involve the full spectrum of information operations, including psyops, special operations, computer network operations, and intelligence operations. To this end, Beijing can employ all of the social, economic, political, and military tools of Chinese national power, as well as enlist the assistance of private sector players and sympathetic co-conspirators on Taiwan. The goal of these efforts is to shake the widely perceived psychological fragility of the populace, causing the government to prematurely capitulate to political negotiations with the mainland. In a sense, China seeks to use the immaturity of Taiwanese democracy against itself. Analysis of both Beijing's strategies in this arena as well as Taipei's ability to resist such methods confirms Taiwan's high level vulnerability to Chinese soft coercion, and raises major questions about the island's viability in the opening phase of a PRC coercion campaign, their credibility as a source of intelligence information on the mainland and a keeper of U.S. secrets, and their expected ability to interoperate successfully with U.S. forces in a crisis.

Taiwan's vulnerabilities in the critical infrastructure protection arena can be divided into two categories: informational and physical. On the information side, Taiwan is a highly information-dependent society with a relatively low level of information or computer security. Significant disruptions in information systems could have major negative effects on the island, particularly in the economic and financial realms, and increase fear and panic among the population. Past Chinese uses of regional media to send psyops messages have also enjoyed success in affecting popular morale and public opinion. For example, an Internet rumor in 1999 that a Chinese Su-27 had shot down a Taiwan aircraft caused the Taipei stock market to drop more than 2 percent in less than 4 hours.

On the physical side of the equation, Taiwan's current capability and readiness level is much lower than one might expect for a state under such a direct level of threat, especially when compared with other "national security states" like Israel or South Korea. Critical infrastructure protection has been a low priority for the government, and Taiwan is acutely vulnerable to Spetsnaz-like or fifth column operations, aided significantly by ethnic and linguistic homogeneity and significant cross-border flows, which facilitate entry and access to potential targets. In terms of civilian infrastructure, Taiwan's telecommunications, electric power, and transportation infrastructure are all highly susceptible to sabotage. These weaknesses have been indirectly exposed by periodic natural disasters, such as the September 1999 earthquake and the September 2001 typhoon, when the communications infrastructure effectively collapsed. Taiwan's ports, including Su'ao, Jeelung, and Gaoxiong (the third highest volume container port in the world), are attractive targets. Port charts and ship movements are available on the Internet, and Gaoxiong in particular has two narrow mouths that could easily be blocked with scuttled vessels. Taiwan's highways are a vulnerable bottleneck, particularly given the large number of undefended mountain tunnels and bridges that could be destroyed by SOF units. Finally, the power grid is known to be fragile, marked by numerous single-point failure nodes, and no cross-hatching of subgrids to form redundancy. The loss of a single tower in the central mountainous region, thanks to a landslide, knocked out 90 percent of the grid a couple of years ago, and delays in construction of a fourth nuclear plant have constrained capacity.

SOFs and fifth column are also a major threat for disruption of military command and control and decapitation of the national command authority, as well as providing reconnaissance for initial missile and air strikes and battle damage assessments (BDA) for follow-on strikes. Entry into the country for SOF is not a substantial obstacle, thanks to ethnic and linguistic homogeneity and the dramatic increases in cross-strait people flows. Between 1988 and October 2002, for example, more than 828,000 mainlanders visited the island. Moreover, these special forces could also facilitate control of key civilian and military airfields and ports that could be used as points of entry for invading forces. The lack of operational security at key facilities is particularly inexplicable and appalling. Visits to national political and military command centers reveal them to be relatively unguarded, with poor information security practices, including the use of personal cell phones in supposedly secure areas. The Presidential Palace in downtown Taipei, home to the President and his key staff, has no fenceline and no security checkpoints. Building information, including the location of the President's office, is openly available on the Internet. Given the poor performance of President Chen's personal security detail during the 2004 assassination attempt on his life, the possibility of elimination of the top leadership through direct action cannot be discounted.

Finally, there is substantial open source evidence to suggest that China is winning the intelligence war across the strait, raising serious doubts about the purity of Taiwanese intelligence proffered to the United States, the safety of advanced military technologies transferred to the island, and the ability of official Taiwan interlocutors to safeguard shared U.S. secrets about intelligence collection or joint warplanning. In the last 5 years, a steady series of leaked stories have appeared in the Taiwan and other regional media, describing either the rounding up of Taiwanese agent networks on the mainland or the unmasking of high-ranking Taiwanese agents in the military, with similar successes a rarity on the Taiwan side, despite significant political incentive to publicize such discoveries.[21] Reported examples since early 2003 include the arrest of the president of the PLA Air Force Command Academy, Major-General Liu Guangzhi; his former deputy, Major-General Li Suolin, and 10 of their subordinates;[22] the arrest of 24 Taiwanese and 19 mainlanders in late 2003;[23] the arrest of Chang Hsu-min, age 27, and his 24-year-old girlfriend Yu Shi-ping;[24] the arrest of Xu Jianchi;[25] the arrest of Ma Peiming in February 2003;[26] and the arrest and conviction to life imprisonment of Petty Officer First Class Liu Yueh-lung for passing naval communications codes to the PRC.[27] Farther back, high-profile intelligence losses include the discovery, arrest, and execution of General Logistics Department Lieutenant-General Liu Liankun and Senior Colonel Shao Zhengzhong as a result of Taiwanese government intelligence disclosures about the fact that warheads on Chinese missiles fired near the island in 1996 were unarmed,[28] the arrest and sentencing of Hainan Province deputy head Lin Kecheng and nine others in 1999 for providing economic, political, and other kinds of intelligence to the Taiwan Military Intelligence Bureau (MIB),[29] and the arrest and imprisonment of a local official named Wang Ping in Nanchong, Sichuan, for allegedly also working for the MIB.[30] In addition, retired senior Taiwan intelligence officials, including National Security Bureau personnel chief Pan Hsi-hsien and at least one former J-2, continue to travel to and often reside in China despite Taiwan regulations barring such movement for 3 years after retirement.[31] At the same time, Taiwan and international media are regularly filled with leaks about sensitive U.S.-Taiwan military interactions or weapons transfers, sourced to either legislators or standing Taiwan government officials. Examples include disclosures about possible deployment of an Integrated Underwater Surveillance System (IUSS) north and south of the island to detect Chinese submarines,[32] the provision of early warning data on Chinese missile attack from the Defense Support Program (DSP) satellite constellation,[33] and the alleged signals intelligence (SIGINT) cooperation between the National Security Agency and Taiwan on Yangming Mountain.[34] All of these possible compromises raise serious concerns about future technology or information sharing with Taiwan.

Center of Gravity Number Two: U.S. Military Intervention. When Chinese strategists contemplate how to affect U.S. deployments, they confront the limitations of their current conventional force, which does not have range sufficient to interdict U.S. facilities or assets beyond the Japanese home islands. Nuclear options, while theoretically available, are nonetheless far too escalatory to be used so early in the conflict. Theater missile systems, which are possibly moving to a mixture of conventional and nuclear warheads, could be used against Japan or Guam, but uncertainties about the nature of a given warhead would likely generate responses similar to the nuclear scenario.

According to the predictable cadre of "true believers," both of the centers of gravity identified above can be attacked using computer network operations. In the first case, the Chinese IO community believes that CNO will play a useful psychological role in undermining the will of the Taiwanese people by attacking infrastructure and economic vitality. In the second case, the Chinese IO community envisions computer network attacks effectively deterring or delaying U.S. intervention and causing pain sufficient to compel Taipei to capitulate before the United States arrives. The remainder of this section outlines how these IO theorists propose operationalizing such a strategy.

Specific Targeting Analysis of Network Attacks Against Logistics.

There are two macro-level targets for Chinese computer network operations: military network information and military information stored on networks. Computer network attack seeks to use the former to degrade the latter. Like U.S. doctrine, Chinese CNA targeting therefore focuses specifically on "enemy command and control (C2) centers," especially "enemy information systems." Of these information systems, PLA writings and interviews suggest that logistics computer systems are a top military target. According to one PLA source, "we must zero in on the . . . crucial links in the system that move enemy troops . . . such as information systems."[35] Another source writes, "we must attack system information accuracy, timeliness of information, and reliability of information."[36] In addition to logistics computer systems, another key military target for Chinese CNA is military reliance on civilian communications systems.

These concepts, combined with the earlier analysis of the PLA view that the main U.S. weakness is the deployment phase, lead PLA IO theorists to conclude that U.S. dependence on computer systems, particularly logistics systems, is a weak link that could potentially be exploited through computer network attack. Specifically, Chinese authors highlight DoD's need to use the civilian backbone and unclassified computer networks (i.e., NIPRNET) as an "Achilles Heel." There is also recognition that operations in the Pacific are especially reliant on precisely coordinated transportation, communications, and logistics networks, given the "tyranny of distance" in the theater. PLA strategists believe that a disruptive computer network attack against these systems or affiliated civilian systems could potentially delay or degrade U.S. force deployment to the region while allowing the PRC to maintain a degree of plausible deniability.

The Chinese are right to highlight the NIPRNET as an attractive *and* accessible target, unlike its classified counterparts. It is attractive because it contains and transmits critical deployment information in the all-important time-phased force deployment list (TPFDL), which is valuable for both intelligence-gathering about U.S. military operations but also a lucrative target for disruptive attacks. In terms of accessibility, it is relatively easy to gather data about the NIRPNET from open sources, at least before September 11, 2001 (9/11). Moreover, the very nature of the system is the source of its vulnerabilities, since it has to be unclassified and connected to the greater global network, albeit through protected gateways. To migrate all of the NIPRNET to a secure, air-gapped network would likely tax the resources and bandwidth of DoD military networks.

DoD's classified networks are an attractive but less accessible target for the Chinese. On the one hand, these networks would be an intelligence gold mine, and is likely a priority CNE target. On the other, they are less attractive as a computer network attack target, thanks to the difficulty of penetrating their high defenses. Any overall Chinese military strategy predicated on a high degree of success in penetrating these networks during crisis or war is a high-risk venture, and increases the chances of failure of the overall effort to an unacceptable level. Moreover, internal PRC writings on information warfare show no confidence in the PRC's ability to get inside network-centric warfare aboard deployed ships or other self-contained operational units. Instead, the literature is focused on preventing the units from deploying in the first place, and thereafter breaking the C4I linkages between the ships and their headquarters.

Chinese CNE or CNA operations against logistics networks could have a detrimental impact on U.S. logistics support to operations. PRC CNE activities directed against U.S. military logistics networks could reveal force deployment information, such as the names of ships deployed, readiness status of various units, timing and destination of deployments, and rendezvous schedules. This is especially important for the Chinese in times of crisis, since the PRC in peacetime utilizes U.S. military web sites and newspapers as a principal source for deployment information. An article in October 2001 in *People's Daily,* for example, explicitly cited U.S. Navy web sites for information about the origins, destination, and purpose of two carrier battle groups exercising in the South China Sea. Since the quantity and quality of deployment information on open websites has been dramatically reduced after 9/11, the intelligence benefits (necessity?) of exploiting the NIPRNET have become even more paramount.[37] Computer network attack could also delay resupply to the theater by misdirecting stores, fuel, and munitions, corrupting or deleting inventory files, and thereby hindering mission capability.

The advantages to this strategy are numerous: (1) it is available to the PLA in the near-term; (2) it does not require the PLA to be able to attack/invade Taiwan with air/sea assets; (3) it has a reasonable level of deniability, provided that the attack is sophisticated enough to prevent tracing; (4) it exploits perceived U.S. casualty aversion, over-attention to force protection, the tyranny of distance in the Pacific, and U.S. dependence on information systems; and (5) it could achieve the desired operational and psychological effects: deterrence of U.S. response or degrading of deployments.

PLA CNO Organizations.

The PLA's computer network operations organizations can be divided into three broad categories: command organizations, doctrinal and professional military education institutions, and research and development organizations.

PLA CNO Command Organizations. The General Staff Department (GSD) Communications Department versus the GSD 4th Department (Electronic Countermeasures Department). For years, a debate has raged over whether the GSD Communications Department or the GSD 4th Department (Electronic Countermeasures Department) had operational responsibility for computer network operations in the PLA, specifically the CNA mission. While the Communications Department clearly has personnel well-versed in the technical details of the PLA's communications and computer networks, the Electronic Countermeasures Department since its inception has been directly responsible for not only traditional EW jamming, but also "electronic offense," or the use of electronic and information systems to attack the enemy's electronic and information systems. An early, pre-Internet open source description of these differentiated roles can be found in the 1997 *Guidebook for Staff Officer's Professional Work in Wartime*.[38] In 1999, the preface of an important book by the then-head of the PLA Electronic Engineering Academy, Dai Qingmin, revealed that *Introduction to Information Warfare* was published by the PLA Publishing House only after an appraisal by the GSD Electronic Countermeasures Department. When Dai became head of the 4th Department shortly thereafter, a series of articles and books were published under his byline on information operations-related topics including "Pay Close Attention to Airborne Information Operations," *Introduction to Information Warfare* (2001),[39] *Information Warfare Review* (1999),[40] "On Four Abilities for Informationized Warfare,"[41] "Innovating and Developing Views on Information Operations,"[42] *Information War Concepts*,[43] and "On the Development of Army Informationization and Information Warfare."[44] It is also instructive to note that Dai, after he retired from active duty, assumed the directorship of the "All-PLA Informationization Consultation Committee," which is in part responsible for the development of PLA systems for offensive IO missions.

Yet the rise of the Internet and the development of computer network operations appeared to raise new questions about which department would take the lead in this new warfare arena. An important signpost in the PLA debate appeared in the February 2002 issue of *China Military Science*, in which the heads of the GSD Communications Department (Major General Xu Xiaoyan) and GSD 4th Department/Electronic Countermeasures Department (Major General Dai Qingmin) each made their case for operational control of CNO in a pair of dueling articles.[45] Dai Qingmin's article "On Integrating Network Warfare and Electronic Warfare" introduced the concept of INEW (discussed above), and clearly won out over the concepts in Xu's article, "A Concept for a Strategy of Development in which Informationization Drives Mechanization." During his tenure at the GSD/4th Department, Dai also edited a more detailed version of the article's thesis, entitled *Introduction to Integrated Network and Electronic Warfare* [网电一体战概论]. Dai's INEW concept continues to be the dominant doctrinal core for PLA information operations until the present day, very likely consolidating the leadership position of the GSD/4th Department on related CNO issues.

GSD Third Department (SIGINT). Given the known mission profile of the GSD Third Department, it is reasonable to speculate that it may have the lead role in the defensive/information assurance mission (CND) as well as intelligence preparation of the battlefield (CNE).

Joint Campaign Command HQ and the Warzone.[46] While the GSD 4th Department is the locus for CNA planning during peacetime, some wartime responsibilities fall to the Joint Campaign Command HQ under the Warzone. Within the Main Command Post [基本指挥所] of the HQ, various centers direct the IO and CNO-related functions. The most important of these is the Information Countermeasures Center [信息对抗中心]. This unit is composed of relevant service commanders and their staff officers. It is responsible for providing advice on information countermeasure issues, planning and coordinating information systems, and guiding and coordinating the information countermeasures of every level of the operational group. The center is composed of comprehensive planning, electronic countermeasures [电子对抗], *network warfare* [网络战], information system defense, information security and secrecy, weapons and equipment support, and comprehensive support departments. During wartime, this structure strongly suggests that personnel from the GSD/Fourth Department will be the "trigger pullers" at both the national and warzone level.

PLA CNO Doctrinal and Professional Military Education Organizations. Doctrinal Organizations.

1. Academy of Military Sciences (AMS) is the PLA's premier military science research institution, reporting directly to the Central Military Commission (CMC). The academy is the locus of development of PLA strategy and doctrine, and is also responsible for the coordination of various military research bodies, often at the behest of the CMC and the military leadership. While the majority of its work is academic, AMS's Campaign and Tactics Department [战役战术部] also performs a similar function to the U.S. Training and Doctrine Command (TRADOC) in designing, attending, and assessing military exercises in the field. AMS is also the principal institution responsible for exploring the future of military conflict, leading the analysis of the Revolution in Military Affairs (RMA) and cyber warfare. Some of the earliest IO and CNO-related research in the PLA was initiated at AMS, beginning with translation and analysis of foreign IW writings in the Academy's Foreign Military Studies Department. The first generation of AMS scholars included Wang Pufeng and Wang Baocun. Later, as information operations evolved and matured in the PLA, important work was conducted in the AMS Campaign and Tactics Department.

2. The National Defense University (NDU) is the PLA's most senior professional military education institution, training the best and brightest of the PLA for leading command positions. The NDU does conduct some research, though its focus is much more near-term than the AMS. Wang Baocun summarized the difference this way: "The NDU teaches officers, while the AMS writes papers and gives advice to the CMC. NDU must think about the current PLA and

be practical (how to deal with IW now). AMS must think about the future, out 10-20 years."[47] The primary office at NDU responsible for examining information operations issues is the Command Education Research Office [指挥教研室]. Two important NDU scholars on IO issues were Liu Guifang and Wang Jiaohuai.

3. The Wuhan Communications Command Academy (CCA) is the senior professional military education institution in China for PLA communications and electronics personnel.[48] It is responsible for training future communications and electronics unit leaders in doctrine, policy, technology, and leadership.[49] In 1999, CCA hosted the first all-army collective training session for division and brigade chiefs of staff in IW theory, which has continued to this day.[50] It is also the locus of PLA dissemination of doctrinal and teaching materials on information operations, and is the only institution certified to accredit information operations instructors for PLA educational institutions at every level and in every service. The CCA offers 31 command and control related cross-disciplinary courses, with emphasis on IW at the core of undergraduate and graduate training. In December 1998, CCA established the PLA's first IW simulation experiment center. In the same year, the GSD Communication Department endorsed two CCA publications on IW for use as teaching materials, *Command and Control in Information Warfare* and *Technology in Information Warfare*.[51] The textbooks were drafted by a task force of 20 PLA IW theorists and instructors from CCA.

PLA CNO Capability Assessment.

Setting the Bar Too High: A More Realistic Assessment of PLA Cyber Capabilities. In terms of courses of action, interviews and classified writings reveal interest in the full spectrum of computer network attack tools, including hacking, viruses, physical attack, insider sabotage, and electromagnetic attack. One of the most difficult challenges of this type of analysis is measuring China's actual computer network attack capability. In rough terms, a computer network attack capability requires four things, three of which are easy to obtain and one of which is harder. The easy three are a computer, an Internet connection, and hacker tools, thousands of which can be downloaded from enthusiast sites around the globe. The more difficult piece of the puzzle to acquire is the operator himself, the computer hacker. While individuals of this ilk are abundant in China's urban centers, they are also correctly perceived to be a social group unlikely to relish military or governmental service.

PLA CNO Capabilities and the Patriotic Hacker Phenomenon. The issue of PLA CNO capabilities is not easily separated from the rise of "patriotic hacking" by increasingly sophisticated, nationalistic hacker groups. Some Western analysts have been tempted to assert that the patriotic hackers are "controlled" by Beijing, and should therefore be included in PLA CNO capabilities estimates. Among the arguments marshaled to support this thesis is that consistently harsh punishments are meted out to individuals in China committing relatively minor computer crimes, while patriotic hackers appear to suffer no sanction for their brazen contravention of Chinese law. Other analysts begin from the specious premise that since the Chinese government "owns" the Internet in China, therefore patriotic hackers must work for the state. Still others correctly point to the fact that a number of these groups, such as Xfocus and NSFocus, appear to be morphing into "white-hat" hackers (i.e., becoming professional information security professionals), often developing relationships with companies associated with the Ministry of Public Security or the ministry itself. Yet interviews with hackers and officials strongly suggest that the groups truly are independent actors, more correctly labeled "state-tolerated" or "state-encouraged." They are tolerated because are "useful idiots" for the regime, but they are also careful not to pursue domestic hacking activities that might threaten "internal stability" and thereby activate the repression apparatus. Indeed, most of the groups have issued constitutions or other organizing documents that specifically prohibit members from attacking Chinese web sites or networks.

Even if it is true that patriotic hacker groups are not controlled by the state, Beijing is still worried about the possible effect of their behavior in a crisis with the United States and/or Taiwan. Analysis of several recent "hacker wars" over the last 2 years suggests an evolving mechanism for shaping the activities of "patriotic hackers." In August 1999, after the conclusion of the cross-strait hacker skirmish that erupted in the wake of Taiwan President Li Teng-hui's declaration that the island's relationship to the mainland was a "state-to-state relationship," a *Liberation Army Daily* article lauded the "patriotic hackers" and encouraged other hackers to join in during the next crisis with Taiwan. In April 2001, *Guangzhou Daily* reprinted without attribution a Wired article on the impending outbreak of a "hacker war" between Chinese and American hackers, which many hackers saw as a sign of government backing. A media-generated hacker war thereafter ensued, with Chinese and American hackers defacing hundreds, if not thousands, of web sites. In May 2001, however,

278

an authoritative *People's Daily* article rebuked both Western and Chinese hackers, calling activities by both sides "illegal." This signaled to the hackers that the state had withdrawn its sanction of their activities, and hacker activity quickly tapered off in response to the warning.

A year later, patriotic hacker chat rooms were filled with discussion and planning for a "first anniversary" hacker war. In late April 2002 on the eve of the proposed conflict, *People's Daily* published another unsigned editorial on the subject, decrying the loose talk about a hacker war and warning of serious consequences. Participants in the hacker chat rooms quickly recognized the signal, and the plans for a new hacker war were abandoned. In neither case could this dynamic be called control, but instead reflects the population's keen sensitivity to the subtle messages in government propaganda, which continues to create successfully a Leninist climate of self-deterrence and self-censorship that is more powerful than active state repression. As some groups move into "white-hat" positions, however, the relationship might actually transition from a ruler-ruled dynamic to a partnership motivated by reasons ranging from nationalism to naked self-interest.

Script Kiddies vs. New Tool Development. Measuring the PLA's CNO capability also involves the assessment of a group or country's ability to generate new attack tools or exploits. Outside analysts, many of whom are programmers themselves, tend to reify countries like Russia that abound with highly talented programmers, and look down upon countries or individuals that simply use off-the-shelf "script kiddie" tools like distributed denial of service (DDOS) programs. DDOS is admittedly a blunt instrument, but a fixation on

279

finding more sophisticated attacks, which reflects the widely-held but logically tenuous assumption that state-sponsorship correlates with sophistication, may be counterproductive. Instead, analysts should employ a simple "means-ends" test. In the Chinese case, DDOS, despite its relatively simplicity, looks like the right tool for the right mission. From the Chinese point of view, for example, hammering the NIPRNET and forcing it to be taken down for repairs would be considered an operational success, since it could potentially delay or degrade U.S. logistics deployments to Taiwan.

CONCLUSIONS AND IMPLICATIONS

The Chinese military views computer network attack as an attractive asymmetric weapon against high-tech adversaries like the United States, particularly given the latter's dependence on unclassified information systems for global power projection. These vulnerabilities offer enticing opportunities for cyber espionage in peacetime and hold out the prospect of disrupting and even helping to deter U.S. military forces in wartime. Yet the large and growing PLA literature on information operations is also beset by a glaring omission: the refusal of Chinese military analysts to acknowledge that Beijing's own command, control, communications, computers, intelligence, surveillance, and reconnaissance (C4ISR) is paradoxically making China more vulnerable to the very same asymmetric strategies. Indeed, a significant part of the policy answer to the U.S. cybersecurity crisis vis-à-vis China may lay in offense rather than defense. Simply relying on logs of intrusions against unclassified networks is not sufficient to pierce the veil of the attribution problem, but leveraging offensive capabilities in support of defense holds the promise of both better offense and better defense.

CHAPTER 8 - ENDNOTES

1. Key Western writings on the subject of PLA computer network operations include: Timothy L. Thomas, *Cyber Bytes: Chinese Information-War Theory and Practice*, Fort Leavenworth, KS: Foreign Military Studies Office, 2004; Timothy L. Thomas, "Chinese and American Network Warfare," *Joint Force Quarterly*, No. 38, August 2005; *Coping with the Dragon: Essays on PLA Transformation and the U.S. Military*, Washington, DC: Center for Technology and National Security Policy, National Defense University, December 2007; James Mulvenon, "Chinese Information Operations Strategies in a Taiwan Continegency," Testimony before the U.S.-China Economic and Security Review Commission, September 15, 2005; Toshi Yoshihara, *Chinese Information Warfare: A Phantom Menace or Emerging Threat?* Carlisle, PA: Strategic Studies Institute, U.S. Army War College, November 2001; Timothy L. Thomas, *Like Adding Wings to the Tiger: Chinese Information War Theory and Practice*, Fort Leavenworth, KS: Foreign Military Studies Office, November 2000; Major (Ret.) Charles F. Hawkins, "The People's Liberation Army Looks to the Future," *Joint Force Quarterly*, Summer 2000, pp. 12-16; Michael Pillsbury, *Chinese Views of Future Warfare*, Washington, DC: Institute for National Strategic Studies, National Defense University, 2000; Bates Gill and Lonnie Henley, *China and the Revolution in Military Affairs*, Carlisle, PA: Strategic Studies Institute, U.S. Army War College, May 1996.

2. Dai Qingmin, "On Integrating Network Warfare and Electronic Warfare," *Zhongguo junshi kexue*, Vol. 1, February 2002, pp. 112-117.

3. Foreign Ministry Press Conference, September 4, 2007.

4. Wang Houqing, Zhang Xingye, *The Science of Military Campaigns* [战役学], Beijing, NDU Press, 2000, pp. 173-74.

5. Nu Li, Li Jiangzhou, and Xu Dehui, "Strategies in Information Operations: A Preliminary Discussion," *Military Science,* April 2000.

6. *The Science of Military Campaigns,* p. 170.

7. Wei Jincheng, "New Form of People's War," *Jiefangjun bao,* June 25, 1996, p. 6.

8. Mao Zedong, "On Protracted War" (May 1938), in *Selected Works of Mao Zedong,* Vol. II, Beijing, China: Foreign Languages Press, 1961, paragraph 83.

9. Lu Daohai, ed., *Information Operations* [信息作战], Beijing, China: PLA Arts and Literature Press, p. 288.

10. *Information Operations,* p. 296.

11. Lu Linzhi, "Preemptive Strikes Crucial in Limited High-Tech Wars," *Jiefangjun bao,* February 14, 1996.

12. *Ibid.*

13. *Ibid.*

14. *Ibid.*

15. *The Science of Military Campaigns ,* pp. 178-79.

16. *Information Operations,* p. 324.

17. Dai Qingmin, "On Integrating Network Warfare and Electronic Warfare."

18. *Ibid.*

19. *Ibid.*

20. *Ibid.*

21. Among the rare examples, which perversely strengthen the case for significant counterintelligence concerns on Taiwan, are three military officers (Majors Pai Chin-yang, Tseng Chao-wen, and Chen Sui-chiung) arrested for spying and two individuals (Huang Cheng-an and his girlfriend) arrested for

transferring technology from the Chungshan Institute for Science and Technology to the mainland. See William Foreman, "Taiwan Arrests Military Officer On Spy Charges – The Third Such Case In Month," *Associated Press*, December 3, 2003; and "Taiwan Detains Woman Over Alleged Spying," *South China Morning Post*, January 30, 2004. An earlier case also involved Yeh Yu-chen and Chen Shih-liang and technology from the Chungshan Institute. See "Taiwan Attempts Damage-Control After Alleged Chinese Spy Ring," *AFP*, August 7, 2003.

22. "Top PLA Officers Accused of Spying for Taiwan," *Straits Times*, April 16, 2004; "Beijing Arrests Military Officers on Spy Charges," *China Post*, April 17, 2004.

23. The timing and propaganda exploitation of the arrests, which coincided with the Taiwan presidential campaign, suggests that the Chinese already had the individuals under surveillance and chose to arrest them for maximum political effect. See Philip Pan, "China Arrests 43 Alleged Spies; Move Increases Effort to Undermine Taiwanese President," *Washington Post*, December 24, 2003; "Chinese Mainland Smashes Taiwan Spy Ring," *Xinhua*, December 24, 2003; "Espionage, Corruption Cases In China, December 2003-February 2004," *BBC Monitoring International Reports*, February 14, 2004; Joe McDonald, "China Parades Accused Taiwanese Spies In Front Of Cameras Amid Tensions With Island," *Associated Press*, January 16, 2004; and "Taiwan Spies Visited by Families," *Xinhua*, January 20, 2004.

24. "China Detains Two More Taiwanese Suspected of Espionage," *AFP*, February 13, 2004, citing Chinese state media.

25. *Chongqing Ribao*, August 8, 2003, p. 1.

26. *AFP*, September 2, 2003, p. 1.

27. Brian Hsu, "Taiwan Naval Officer Gets Life For Espionage," *Taipei Times*, December 18, 2002.

28. John Pomfret, "Taiwanese Mistake Led To 3 Spies' Executions," *Washington Post*, February 20, 2000.

29. *People's Daily* article in August 1999, cited in Pomfret, "Taiwanese Mistake."

30. Sichuan television report in October 1999, cited in Pomfret, "Taiwanese Mistake."

31. "Former Taiwan Spy Chief Denies Leaking Secrets During His Four Years In China," *Taiwan News*, April 14, 2004.

32. Michael Gordon, "Secret U.S. Study Concludes Taiwan Needs New Arms," *New York Times*, April 1, 2001.

33. "US to Share Early-Warning Missile Data With Taiwan," *AFP*, October 8, 2002.

34. Wendell Minnick, "Taiwan-USA Link Up on SIGINT," *Jane's Defense Review*, January 23, 2001; Wendell Minnick, "Spook Mountain: How US Spies on China," *Asia Times Online*, March 6, 2003; and Wendell Minnick, "Challenge to Update Taiwan's SIGINT," *Jane's Intelligence Review*, February 1, 2004.

35. Lu Linzhi, "Preemptive Strikes."

36. *Information Operations,* p. 293.

37. DoD's revised web site administration guidance, which can be found at *www.defenselink.mil/webmasters/policy/dod_web_policy_12071998_with_amendments_and_corrections.html*, specifically prohibits the following: "3.5.3.2. Reference to unclassified information that would reveal sensitive movements of military assets or the location of units, installations, or personnel where uncertainty regarding location is an element of a military plan or program."

38. Ma Jinsheng, *Canmou junguan zhanshi yewu zhinan* (*Guidebook for Staff Officer's Professional Work in Wartime*), Beijing, China: Academy of Military Sciences, August 1997.

39. Dai Qingmin, Min Zongguang and Chen Kelin, *Introduction to Information Warfare*, Beijing, China: PLA Press, 2001.

40. Dai Qingmin, *Information Warfare Review*, Beijing, China: PLA Press, 1999.

41. Dai Qingmin, "On Four Abilities for Informationized Warfare," *Jiefangjun bao*, July 1 2003, p. 6.

42. Dai Qingmin, "Innovating and Developing Views on Information Operations," *Zhongguo junshi kexue*, August 20, 2000, pp. 72-77.

43. Dai Qingmin, *Xinxizhan gainian* (*Information War Concepts*), Beijing, China: PLA Publishing House, 2001.

44. Dai Qingmin, "On the Development of Army Informationization and Information Warfare," *Zhongguo junshi kexue*, December 20, 2002, pp. 66-70.

45. Dai Qingmin, "On Integrating Network Warfare and Electronic Warfare," pp. 112-117; and Xu Xiaoyan, "A Concept for a Strategy of Development in which Informationization Drives Mechanization," *Zhongguo junshi kexue*, February 1, 2002, pp. 107-111.

46. This section draws heavily from the excellent work of Kevin Pollpeter on command and control in the warzone.

47. Interview, August 10, 2000.

48. A good summary of WCCA can be found at *baike.baidu. com/view/1521221.htm*.

49. Long Zequn, "Using Hi-Tech to Develop 'Hear-All Devices,' the Communications Command Academy Sets Multiple Records," *Hubei ribao*, May 4, 2002.

50. Sun Haicheng, Yang Jie, and Zhang Guoyu, "Let Information Warfare Training Rule the Training Sites:Practice and Reflections from the First All-Army CollectiveTraining Session for Division and Brigade Chiefs of Staff in Information Warfare Theory," *Jiefangjun bao*, July 13, 1999, p. 6.

51. Lei Yuanshen, "New Breakthrough in Study of Information Warfare," *Jiefangjun bao*, July 21, 1998, p. 6.

CHAPTER 9

CHINA'S REGIONAL POWER PROJECTION: PROSPECTS FOR FUTURE MISSIONS IN THE SOUTH AND EAST CHINA SEAS*

Mark Cozad

EXAMINING FUTURE ROLES AND MISSIONS

China's decisionmakers and scholars are engaged in a wide-ranging discussion regarding future roles and missions for the People's Liberation Army (PLA) in light of an evolving national security environment.[1] Due to China's ever expanding role in international affairs, this discussion encompasses a much broader array of national security themes than in the past and is heavily focused on determining critical PLA missions beyond Taiwan. While the resolution of the Taiwan issue would certainly clear the way for an expanding review of the PLA's missions, China's national security community is actively looking at these missions and weighing long-term strategic interests, resources, and modernization against a variety of possible crisis scenarios. These discussions and subsequent policy statements from China's military leaders highlight the challenges confronting a modernizing, economically strong, and globally connected China, many of which are driving PLA modernization and training to address these missions. Much of the current debate is also focused on the level of effort and resources that should be applied to these new missions, a matter which has

---

* This chapter represents the views of the author and does not represent the official position of the Department of Defense or the Defense Intelligence Agency.

yet to be resolved. Protecting access to energy and resources, Chinese citizens abroad, economic lifelines, and strategic lines of communication are at the center of these debates. Geographically, the East and South China Seas are two critical areas in the middle of this debate. While the discussion has been vigorous, it is far from clear how these new issues will impact not only PLA military strategic guidelines, but also the building and development of future force structure. This chapter examines the current debate as discussed by Chinese national security scholars and practitioners and does not address regional perspectives on the direction that China is moving. The author has only identified these discussions in the context of a persistent status quo in which there is no conflict over Taiwan and no resolution of the issue.[2] As a result, this chapter discusses future missions in the East and South China Seas.

For the foreseeable future, Taiwan will remain the primary, underlying factor driving China's military strategy and modernization. Despite this, China's national security thinkers recognize the plethora of issues confronting its emergence as a global power, and, as a result, a number of debates have surfaced about how best to address these future security challenges.[3] The key question is to what extent new missions in the East China Sea and South China Sea, independent of their respective roles in a Taiwan crisis, will shape China's military modernization over the next several years. While many of the capabilities the PLA has developed or acquired over the past 15 years can support a variety of possible strategies, emerging priorities and missions beyond Taiwan will likely have varying impacts on the way the PLA allocates resources, trains its force, and develops supporting infrastructure and technologies.

ARE THESE MISSIONS BEING DONE TODAY?

In short, yes. The PLA, despite its heavy focus on potential Taiwan conflict scenarios, has recognized for some time that its military must be shaped to respond to an array of regional contingencies, ranging from stability on the Korean peninsula to supporting territorial claims in the East and South China Seas.[4] As a result, the PLA today is trained and equipped for missions that could support multiple future scenarios and direction coming from PLA senior leaders will continue this trend.[5] In recent years, the PLA Navy (PLAN) and Air Force (PLAAF) have conducted regular patrols and presence missions in the East and South China Seas, have carried out goodwill visits to countries throughout the region, and regularly present a PLAN and PLAAF presence in disputed areas. Additionally, Beijing is placing significant emphasis on building up the infrastructure to support deployments in contested regions, most notably in the South China Sea.[6]

In addition, in recent years the PLA has placed a great deal of emphasis on developing its power projection and area denial capabilities through the development of long-range bombers and cruise missiles, anti-ship ballistic missiles, and modern destroyers and submarines. Along these lines, the PLAN and PLAAF have also done a limited, but increasing, amount of training focused on developing these power projection capabilities including air-to-air refueling, at-sea replenishment, and long-range submarine patrols.[7]

Presently, these key mission areas remain limited in terms of training and capability; however, the PLA has demonstrated its interest in developing more robust capabilities to protect its interests in these critical regions. The key issue that to this point has limited the

PLA's focus on further developing these capabilities has been Taiwan.[8] While many of the missions described here would logically support varying types of Taiwan contingencies, Taiwan has focused both PLAAF and PLAN development on localized conflict designed to support operations against Taiwan and to counter and delay third party intervention in a crisis. The PLA has not focused on long-range power projection as a mission in itself, particularly as it relates to supporting territorial claims and the development of great power status. The degree to which the PLA has pursued these missions in recent years is largely a factor of how it has aligned its military for a potential conflict with Taiwan.

THE CENTRALITY OF TAIWAN AND THE FUTURE OF POWER PROJECTION

The PLA has been heavily focused on developing capabilities and plans for Taiwan contingencies over the better part of the past 2 decades, following the determination that the threat posed by the Soviet Union had waned. Since then, the core of officer training and force development has centered on Taiwan, particularly the development of amphibious capabilities to invade, subdue, and secure the island. This trend has been especially prevalent since the early 1990s and the promulgation of the New Generation Operational Guidelines and the subsequent series of operational studies designed to define the PLA's most critical operating environments. Since then, the PLA has placed significant emphasis on developing and training its force for this set of missions. Most notably, the PLA has worked to develop capabilities specifically with an eye toward supporting an amphibious invasion of Taiwan. These capabilities include a joint logistics system, improved command and control for multi-service operations, naval capabilities to challenge and delay the U.S. Navy in key areas, and the development of airpower and precision strike capability for localized conflict.[9] While many of the PLA's capabilities can be refocused to address other potential contingencies, their overall capabilities and sustainability for many scenarios remain limited and scoped against specific capability sets vice medium to large-scale conflict with a modern adversary in a number of domains.

Another critical factor shaping the PLA of today is the organizational culture and historical roots of the military. The PLA remains a military dominated by the army, despite recent promotions of the navy, air force, and second artillery corps commanders to the Central Military Commission (CMC). As such, the PLA has traditionally lacked expertise and experience in maritime and air operations, both of which are central to any future conflict with Taiwan, especially with the involvement of the United States. The PLA is now beginning to examine new operational capabilities that increasingly fall outside of the traditional ground force mindset. Along with this broader focus, there have been a number of new ideas about the future roles and missions of the PLAN and PLAAF and their respective strategic roles.[10] As these discussions evolve, new missions in the East and South China Sea will ultimately be addressed.

A central issue over the next decade will be whether or not the PLAN and PLAAF will begin to develop sustainable, broadly-scoped capabilities that will allow them to challenge the major regional powers, particularly to support territorial claims and operations outside of their limited critical role in a Taiwan conflict. For this to occur, senior civilian and military leaders will have to address the issues of developing a force structure, providing resources, and training the military to think of employing these capabilities in a more expansive set of operational scenarios.[11] At this point, it is unclear what direction this decision will take; however, some current developments provide a snapshot into the future development of the force.

Force Structure.

The PLA has yet to abandon its efforts to develop an amphibious capability that will allow it to forcefully unify Taiwan.[12] While the major focus of PLA modernization in recent years has been on naval, air, and missile systems, PLA attempts to modernize its amphibious force are gaining steam with the deployment of new amphibious systems. In addition, the PLAN is now fielding large numbers of *Houbei* guided missile patrol boats, while construction on modern destroyers and diesel submarines has apparently slowed.[13] The PLAAF has fielded an array of modern fighters and surface-to-air missiles; however, it has not developed its aerial refueling or heavy lift capabilities sufficient to enable sustained operations over much of the region.[14] While these investment choices could change in coming years to emphasize capabilities that would enable power projection and sustainment in the South and East China Seas, the PLA to date has only on a limited basis built its force for these missions.

Resources (Budget and Infrastructure).

While there is a great deal we do not know about China's defense spending, there has been an increase in the amount of expenditure in recent years dedicated to infrastructure development, particularly logistics facilities, transportation routes, and naval bases.[15] In addition, the PLA has invested a significant amount of money in modernizing its forces. In the next several years, the PLA will have to continue these investments, particularly the infrastructure buildup in the South China Sea in order to improve its power projection capabilities.

Training.

PLA training over the past 15 years has been heavily focused on amphibious operations with both the PLAN and the PLAAF focused on their respective missions to support Taiwan contingencies. As a result, over the past 4 years the PLA has demonstrated a number of improvements in the complexity and quality of training, the same central theme of Taiwan persists, with emphasis being placed on improved command and control, joint operations, and electronic warfare. To date training has not included key areas such as long-range mobility training, rapid deployment, and long duration sustainability training.

DRIVERS FOR THE DEVELOPMENT OF POWER PROJECTION CAPABILITIES

As the preceding sections describe, the PLA of today is still focusing on Taiwan, which continues to drive its modernization and force structure. There are a number of other factors, however, that could significantly change the PLA's focus over the next decade. This section will examine several key missions critical to China's strategic ambitions; organizational and bureaucratic drivers that will have a major impact on future decisions; and perceived threats, competitors, and partners that will shape China's strategic decisionmaking about future military strategy and investments. Although the PLA today continues to pursue many of the capabilities and objectives that have shaped it over the past 2 decades, there is a growing debate within China about the future role of the military and how it will support China's aspirations to achieve great power status.

Drivers for Future Missions.

Over the past 4 years, and particularly since the release of the 2006 *National Defense White Paper*, there have been a number of discussions within the People's Republic of China (PRC) about future security requirements and the role the PLA would play in supporting these strategic objectives.[16] Other events, such as the tsunami in Southeast Asia, the earthquake in Sichuan, riots in Tibet, and threats to Chinese workers and business people overseas, have all highlighted the need for senior PRC policymakers to broaden their perspective on national security.[17] These discussions and events have sparked considerable debate within Chinese think tanks and the military about the future roles and missions of the PLA. In some respects, these discussions have fallen along the lines of service interests, particularly as discussed by the PLA, PLAN, and PLAAF. Interestingly, many other parts of the discussion have been framed as traditional versus nontraditional missions. In this discussion, there is recognition that the PLA's critical missions must evolve to support a more globally-connected China and move beyond strictly land-oriented concerns to ensure the physical safety of the party and maintenance of internal stability. Although some publications have been explicit about what the potential future missions are, many are implied based on PRC discussion of its most critical interests, its vulnerabilities, and its perceptions of areas where employing the military will have the most utility.

One of the most recent discussions has centered on protecting sea lines of communication (SLOCs) critical to ensuring China's commerce and energy supplies.[18] The most notable part of this discussion has centered on the Malacca Strait and the potential vulnerability of the large portion of China's imported energy that makes its way through the Strait.[19] However, at this time, there has been no clear discussion regarding the specifics of the threat to include who presents the most real threat to this vital SLOC. With SLOC protection as a driver for future missions, the PLA will undoubtedly need to conduct detailed studies of the threat, the environment, and force requirements and ultimately evaluate these studies as part of a broader discussion of PRC military strategy. Subsequently, these studies would drive modernization efforts and basing in such a way that would enable the PLA to protect this vital interest. To date, this discussion has not taken place.

Along with SLOC protection, another key driver that could force the PLA to more readily address the missions of the South and East China Seas include protection of resources, to include off-shore oil and gas fields, important commercial interests, and free flow of strategic materials to China.[20] In many cases, this driver is centered on maintaining and reemphasizing China's territorial claims in both regions and also the recognition of its exclusive economic zone (EEZ). To date, these discussions have surfaced in official PRC or PLA press on a very limited basis, most likely due to concerns of exacerbating already tense situations in both areas. While there have been a number of recent incidents that have increased concern among those in the region, Beijing has largely tried to work cooperatively with other claimants to avoid direct conflict and to demonstrate its good will. Military patrols have increased in both areas, but not in a way that implies permanent presence or an aggressive effort to physically secure these regions. In the coming years, as China's energy requirements continue to increase and China's military becomes more capable and confident, Beijing may decide to become more assertive in settling territorial claims, particularly those that could shore up China's energy needs. At this time, however, it appears that Beijing remains focused on maintaining good relations with the United States and others in the region to promote continued stability and growth.

Another key aspect that may draw China to pursue extended missions beyond Taiwan is an increase in its military-to-military diplomacy efforts in a way that will demonstrate China's new military capabilities. Over the past decade, there has been a steady increase in China's military diplomacy in the region, largely aimed at countries in South and Southeast Asia.[21] Key events have included short combined exercises with foreign navies, port visits, two high profile exercises with Russia, and numerous visits by senior leaders of the PLA. In the coming years, these events will almost certainly continue and are likely to become a key component of China's power projection in both the East and South China Seas. In short, these types of activities allow Beijing to develop relationships with others in the region, maintain an increasingly robust presence in strategically important areas, and demonstrate to those in the region that China's military has become one of the major powers capable of projecting force anywhere in the region. The prime benefit of pursuing this path is that China can demonstrate its military capabilities to the entire region in a manner that is not overtly threatening. While this driver could present an attractive avenue for Beijing to pursue, PLA engagement remains limited, despite the increases in recent years. In addition, it is uncertain how this focus will develop if the PLA is intent on pursuing large-scale amphibious capabilities. In many respects, these missions are not mutually exclusive; however, as PLA senior leadership more aggressively trains for Taiwan-related missions, it may limit the availability of PLAN assets for wider engagement in the region.

The last key driver that could push the PLA to address missions beyond Taiwan is the protection of Chinese interests abroad, particularly as China's global footprint increases.[22] Over the past 2 years, piracy in the Gulf of Aden and attacks on Chinese citizens in the Horn of Africa and Sudan have raised the question among Chinese security specialists about the need to more thoroughly address protecting citizens and assets engaged in business overseas.[23] With respect to the immediate region, the most likely requirement could come in Southeast Asia. While Chinese populations have been present in Southeast Asia for hundreds of years, they have not been Chinese citizens and have not had a major impact on Beijing's national security decisionmaking. As Chinese business interests expand, however, Chinese citizens could become more lucrative targets for kidnappers, terrorists, and organized crime. To date, there has only been a limited discussion about how to address these problems, largely spurred by developments in Africa. This may change in the future as increasing numbers of Chinese citizens go abroad and look to their government for protection. At this point, there is no clear indication of how the current PLAN deployment to the Gulf of Aden will impact future naval strategy and force structure.

Organizational and Bureaucratic Considerations for Future Missions.

Another key factor that will dictate the extent to which Beijing pursues future missions in the East and South China Seas is the set of organizational perspectives driving China's national security decisionmakers, both military and nonmilitary. As mentioned earlier in this chapter, a number of factors over the past decade have forced China's leaders to more broadly examine key issues of national security.[24] While the discussion of new national security challenges continues to evolve, there are a number of bureaucratic perspectives that will continue to shape the future missions and structure of the PLA.

The 2006 Defense White Paper highlighted several key issues that could drive the PLA to develop its capabilities and to train for a more robust presence in the East and South China Seas, particularly the South China Sea. Protecting SLOCs and future energy resources was a critical point highlighted in the White Paper and in multiple other books and studies on China's national security. To date, the PLAN and PLAAF have already ensured that China's presence in these areas is made visible to those in the region; however, it has attempted to refrain from posturing its force in such a manner that it might be provocative to other claimants. In addition, while PLA strategists have highlighted the need to ensure the security of China's energy and economic resources moving through vital SLOCs, there has been little if any discussion about the specific nature of the threat and the military solution required to meet this undefined threat. In the midst of continuing concerns and strategic focus on Taiwan, it remains to be seen how much emphasis the PLA will place on these new missions, given a poorly defined threat and the unknown consequences of the global financial crisis on PLA spending. As a result, Chinese strategists have looked at other means by which they can secure strategic interests to include building diplomatic and economic relationships, military diplomacy, and alternative supply chains for strategic resources.[25]

In his speech to the 17th Party Congress, Chinese President Hu Jintao did mention building China's national defense capabilities in such a manner that they could contribute to an expansive list of evolving security threats, however, he also made a point of explicitly highlighting the need to pursue nonmilitary means to address critical security concerns such as energy security.[26] A recurring theme from China's political and military leadership has been to rely on nonmilitary solutions for many problems because of China's relative weakness and limited resources for the comprehensive military modernization required to fully address China's strategic needs across the region, and ultimately, the globe.[27] Chinese leaders have continually highlighted that while spending on the PLA has increased at double digit rates over the past decade, much of these increases have had to pay for personnel costs and infrastructure development. Additionally, in terms of specific modernization efforts, the majority of China's modernization dollars over the past 2 decades have gone to two key areas, developing capabilities for a potential conflict with Taiwan and defending mainland China.[28] Recognizing the state of China's military following Operation DESERT STORM, the PLA kept its long-term focus on ensuring that capabilities in these two areas kept pace with military modernization trends worldwide. While many PLA capabilities could be employed in a range of contingencies and are not strictly centered on Taiwan, power projection and sustainment in the East and South China Seas is not one of these.

In large part, these priorities are unlikely to change in the next decade unless Beijing believes that sufficient resources have been devoted to ensuring an overwhelming capability to take Taiwan and defend the mainland. Most importantly, it is unclear how resource constraints, or a lack of constraints, will influence the development of the PLAN and PLAAF, particularly in terms of specialized capabilities critical to missions in both areas, but not seen by the PLA as critical to success in a Taiwan contingency. While the PLAN, PLAAF, and Second Artillery Corps were the main beneficiaries of the PLA's increased funding in recent years, the systems and capabilities introduced into their inventories were supportive of PLA planning for Taiwan scenarios, not for power projection.[29] Better understanding of spending and budgeting are critical shortfalls in our ability to predict the future development of the PLA for expanded missions in the East and South China Seas.

Along with overall threat perceptions and prioritization of specific planning scenarios, within the PLA the ground force component has dominated strategic thinking since its inception.[30] The development of a modern PLAAF and PLAN are still relatively new features of this evolving military, and many of the strategic concepts remain aspirational, particularly from the standpoint of force structure, technology, and training. At this point, it is unclear how much influence the PLAAF and PLAN will have in coming years, particularly in relation to the PLA ground component. Recent discussions by thinkers from both services highlight future security threats along with roles and missions; however, it is unclear how much influence these views hold in the broader strategic thinking among CMC members and China's political leadership.[31] Over the next decade, this could lead China's political leaders to dictate changes in military strategy to deal with an expanding set of future security challenges facing the PRC. At present, it does not appear that any major decisions have been made. As a result, many of these new missions will not gain the traction required to develop more robust capabilities to perform them for several years.

PERCEIVED THREATS AND COMPETITORS

China's threat perceptions and the development of military capabilities throughout the region are the most likely catalyst that will force Beijing to rethink its current mission capacity in the East and South China Seas. In addition to new thinking about the PLA's strategic role as an organization, China's expanding role in the world has led to a robust discussion among many circles of China's national security community about China's future geostrategic goals and the key security threats they will face over the coming generations.[32] While the majority of those writing on these issues agree in principle on many of the key themes shaping China's future security, they differ on the extent (or in some cases existence) of threats, the methods for dealing with these threats, and ultimately the military resources required to plan for these threats over the long term.[33]

Several of these recurring themes center on the need to protect energy resources, territorial claims, maritime rights, and key SLOCs. Both the East and South China Seas figure prominently in these discussions on a number of levels. Correspondingly, each of these key issues has led to general discussions about key competitors who are or potentially could challenge China's interests or claims. The main competitor, as these arguments are framed, is the United States, particularly as it relates to future coercion in times of crisis and U.S. relations with other claimants or competitors.[34]

A key theme through these discussions emphasizes the need to develop capabilities commensurate with the problems and tasks at hand. A particular overarching point raised by some authors is that any future capability developments need to be viewed in a limited regional capacity, with the understanding that direct competition with the United States, particularly in the maritime domain, could place a significant resource burden on the PRC with limited payoff and effect.[35] A critical point on this outlook, however, is that this was not viewed as a continual state, rather it was seen as a current reality over the next one or two generations. Conversely, many PRC strategists also have questioned China's traditional strategic orientation inland with the view that great powers required maritime strategies and capabilities that would allow them to protect their long term interests. At present, Chinese security specialists are examining the arenas where they will need to develop critical capabilities. In most respects, these capabilities are specifically focused on and address U.S. strengths.[36]

Other regional players regularly mentioned include Japan as a key competitor for energy resources in the East China Sea and several Southeast Asian countries with competing claims in the South China Sea. While many of the PRC writers recognize that a competition exists, few have talked about these competitions in recent years primarily through a military lens. There appears to be a widespread belief, at least for now, that most of the immediate issues surrounding energy and territorial claims within the East and South China Seas are matters better dealt with through diplomatic and political means.[37] While this understanding does exist, these same thinkers recognize the importance of having a credible military capability and regular presence throughout the region.

While traditional security threats figure prominently in these discussions of future roles and missions for the PLA, there is also a marked increase in the frequency and detail of discussions about nontraditional security roles for the PLA.[38] Although the PLA has been involved in disaster relief and peacekeeping operations for some time now, policymakers in Beijing are beginning to highlight the importance of these missions to China's overall foreign policy objectives.[39] While missions such as peacekeeping and humanitarian relief do not factor prominently in force structure development and the development of future missions in the East China Sea, events in the South China Sea following the tsunami of 2004 have highlighted the importance of military roles for these types of missions. Based on current planning and developments, it appears that China's civilian and military forces are committed to supporting the development of these capabilities and increasing their participation as a means of bolstering China's foreign policy objectives in the region.[40]

As discussed earlier, military diplomacy is also playing an increasingly important role in how China defines roles and missions within the region. PLA interaction with regional militaries has increased steadily over the past decade and is now seen as a critical part of China's strategic approach to gaining influence in the region.[41] Combined exercises with regional partners, visits by high-ranking PLA officers, and educational exchanges are seen as a central part of the PLA's mission. In particular, military diplomacy is seen as a critical tool in dealing with regional tensions.

THE INFLUENCE OF FUTURE SECURITY DEVELOPMENTS ON THE PLA

There are a number of factors that could force the PLA to fundamentally alter its Taiwan-centric focus and posture. Many of these discussions are underway now. To determine the potential scope of these changes, it is important to examine the factors that would foster change and then examine the factors that could prevent it. Many of these cleavages are apparent today.

Factors Driving Change.

Several factors could eventually drive China's leaders to reorient the PLA in a manner that would better address the range of future security challenges that China is now facing. While many of these factors are apparent to some extent, any major changes would take time to fully implement. The debates about how to deal with them are well on their way, however.

The first and most obvious factor that would reorient the PLA's focus would be the resolution of the Taiwan issue. While the manner in which this issue may be resolved is beyond the scope of this chapter, removing this issue as a key political driver and the primary planning scenario for the PLA would undoubtedly drive the PLA to reconsider its posture and focus in the region. It would also likely have a major impact on the organizational approach the PLA has taken to strategic planning for at least the past 20 years. Of particular importance, resolution of the Taiwan issue may lead China's leaders to move on to the last remaining territorial disputes in the East and South China Seas. While there has been little, if any, discussion on this to date, the prominent role that territorial integrity and sovereignty play in China's grand strategy are clear. This would also be compounded by the potential to develop and exploit the energy resources held by these claims.[42]

The second issue, short of resolution, would be a fundamental leadership reevaluation of PRC's Taiwan strategy and supporting policies.[43] As China-Taiwan relations continue to improve following the 2008 Taiwan legislative and presidential elections, China's leaders are likely to address what policies worked and which did not in dealing with cross-Strait relations in the run up to the election. In future years, Chinese strategists and policymakers may determine that PLA capabilities have reached a point where they can effectively coerce and deter Taiwan and present a credible deterrent to the United States. At that point, an analysis of the future cost of developing the PLA for large-scale amphibious operations versus the payoff for providing a more regionally, and potentially globally, projected PLA may lead China's leaders to alter the relative priority Taiwan has held over the past 2 decades. China's leaders eventually may conclude that the PLA's capabilities are sufficient when viewed in concert with the diplomatic, economic, political, and informational components of Beijing's Taiwan strategy.

A third alternative, most likely tied to a reevaluation of Taiwan policy, would be a reexamination of China's strategic priorities that drive military strategy and planning.[44] Over the past decade, a number of security challenges already highlighted here have surfaced. In light of China's goals to become a major regional and global power, the PLA may be forced to reorient its strategy in such a way as to support these broader national objectives. Many of the discussions of these issues have yet to highlight a concrete threat for which to plan, but recognize that a variety of factors could require different capability sets.

Lastly, a major bureaucratic shift in which the PLAAF, PLAN, and Second Artillery were given more prominent roles in the CMC and upper levels of military leadership may drive PLA roles and missions in new directions. A major component of the ongoing debates about future security issues is centered on whether the PLA is a land power, maritime power, or both.[45] In addition, these debates have also focused on the types of capabilities required for these missions, particularly maritime, air, and space capabilities.

Factors Inhibiting Change.

While there are a number of factors that could drive change, there are also a number of factors that may work against any sort of change in strategic focus for the PLA. In many cases, these factors would keep the PLA focused on its current missions and, without the resolution of the Taiwan issue, predominantly focused on Taiwan scenarios.

Bureaucratic entrenchment and the continued prominence of the army is the most likely factor that will prevent major changes. In terms of current missions, Taiwan is a central point around which the army organizes and trains and maintains influence over the development of the other components of the PLA. While service commanders have been included on the CMC in recent years, the key military leadership roles are filled by army generals. While there are scenarios and compelling reasons for developing the PLA in other directions, the strategic orientation of the military has been that of a land power and over the past 2 decades the main organizing issue has been Taiwan.[46] Without a major shift in the military bureaucracy and a reorientation of PLA organizational culture, any major changes in mission focus will likely slow down or cease altogether.

Resource tradeoffs and constraints are another issue that could slow the sourcing and development of other mission capabilities. Again, the mission focus on Taiwan is a central component of the resource discussion. As China's leaders are confronted with competing issues requiring government budgets and focus, the PLA competes for a share of those resources. In recent years, military spending has increased dramatically and enabled the PLA to buy or develop a broad array of sophisticated, modern weapons.[47] Two factors have made this possible. The first is the backward state of the PLA through most of the 1990s. This backwardness allowed the PLA to focus on purchasing new weapons across the board and served as a very open reminder of the extent of these modernization efforts. The second issue is the primary focus on missions supporting the broader Taiwan scenario. All of the services purchased capabilities that were part of a broader operation, and, while not all were specifically tailored to a Taiwan contingency, those capabilities that were clearly beyond Taiwan were pursued on a limited basis. In the next several years, the PLA will be confronted with new requirements and taskings that could demonstrate or create resource constraints on the PLA.[48] While modernization has progressed rapidly, the PLA's push to develop a professional force will undoubtedly place increased constraints on all services. Additionally, most of the modernization resources in recent years went to fund purchases for the PLAN, PLAAF, and Second Artillery Corps. With the continued emphasis on Taiwan contingencies, the next several years will require significant spending on amphibious and ground force capabilities. It is unclear how these will all be funded. Finally, with the discussion of future missions, the services are now in competition to fund their critical requirements, all of which are not focused on Taiwan, and many of which are expensive to develop and maintain. For any major shift in the roles and missions of the PLA, there will need to be a conscious effort to address the resource aspects of organizing, training, and equipping the PLA to perform those missions.

Another key issue that could hinder a major shift in focus toward the East and South China Seas is using other approaches, beyond the development of military capabilities, to address core security concerns.[49] In many discussions about the need to develop capabilities to protect SLOCs, energy, and territorial claims, many authors mention the military component as supporting the overall strategy, but much less prominently than other diplomatic, economic, and cooperative approaches.[50] There is also a general effort to further understand the exact nature of the threat.[51] Currently, there is recognition that diplomatic efforts are the key to dealing with these territorial disputes in the region. Beijing has made great effort to engage actively with Japan and, outside of a few cases, has not been overly aggressive in pushing its claims in the East China Sea. In the South China Sea, many see engagement with the Association of Southeast Asian Nations (ASEAN) as well as with the individual claimants as critical to any future solution to these territorial disputes.

For any future change to come about based on a redefinition of the key threats facing Chinese interests in the region, there must be a concrete understanding of what the threat is, where it resides, and what role the military can play in solving or alleviating the threat.[52] In the case of energy security and the protection of SLOCs, there is a wide recognition that potential threats exist, but there is also an assertion in some circles that these threats may not be as significant as frequently portrayed.[53] For any future strategy to take hold, especially if it has to compete with a well-entrenched, nationally vital priority like Taiwan, the threat will have to be defined in a manner that forces all senior military leaders to recognize the importance of shifting resources to deal with it. With the recent trend in Taiwan relations, coupled with a growing recognition of the need to develop capabilities to combat nontraditional threats, the groundwork for a future shift is already in place.

PLA REQUIREMENTS FOR EXPANDED MISSIONS IN THE SOUTH AND EAST CHINA SEAS

The PLA has yet to decide or be directed to shift its strategic focus to expanded missions. Based on the factors outlined earlier in this chapter, if the PLA were to expand its roles and missions in these two strategically important areas, there would have to be a number of actions taken in terms of strategic and operational objectives, force modernization, and deployment patterns. In addition, current missions, such as access denial and sea control, which are now largely shaped by Taiwan scenarios, would have to evolve to accommodate a different set of realities and objectives.

The first key shift that would have to take place would be for some overarching decision that an improved military posture would improve China's strategic interests and claims in the East and South China Seas. In particular, some type of guideline would likely be promulgated outlining China's broad intent, a specific threat for which to plan, and then in-depth research and analysis to determine the best operational solutions for particular problems.[54]

In the East China Sea, new strategic guidance could address perceptions about increasing Japanese capabilities, Japanese operations expanding beyond traditional self-defense roles, a perceived threat or need for the energy resources in the region, and finally a perception that diplomatic efforts are not sufficient to address PRC claims in the region. Many of these same issues would also surface for a shift in guidance in the South China Sea, but would focus on regional competitors. In addition, other key shifts in the South China Sea could come about due to PRC insecurity about energy supplies, key SLOCs necessary to support strategic materials and commerce, and, finally, piracy. Any combination of these factors could push senior Chinese political and military leaders to have to address military readiness to combat these problems. In addition, clearly defining the threats will be a critical part of determining how military forces can best support future operations.

As a corollary to defining the threats that will drive future missions, PLA leaders will also likely outline other military missions that will be critical to supporting China's regional objectives. These factors will figure most prominently in the South China Sea and will potentially place the PLA in the same areas as U.S. military engagement efforts. Military diplomacy, disaster relief, and humanitarian/peacekeeping support will all continue to be major themes PLA seniors will emphasize in the coming years.[55]

Once the specific threats and operating environments are defined, PLA researchers would most likely perform large amounts of research to examine new operational roles for the specific services; new equipment and weapons requirements; and new requirements for infrastructure, logistics, and sustainment efforts.[56] This type of research has been underway for Taiwan scenarios for several years and continues today. While discussions of new roles and missions have evolved for the East and South China Seas, there has been little concrete research of these scenarios outside of the role they would play in a Taiwan contingency.[57]

FORCE REQUIREMENTS FOR VARIOUS MISSIONS

While the PLA today has a regular presence in both the East and South China Seas, for sustained operations in these areas future missions will dictate new modernization requirements. Although the PLA has pursued many of these systems and capabilities in the past, they have yet to attain the capabilities.

Access Denial.

Due to the emphasis the PLA has placed on countering key U.S. capabilities, many of the access denial capabilities required by the PLAN and PLAAF are either fielded, in late stages of testing, or being developed today. The focus of this mission area is largely the same in both Taiwan and non-Taiwan scenarios: keeping third parties out as long as possible in order to accomplish China's objectives.[58] Key capabilities in this arena include anti-ship ballistic missiles, advanced naval air defense systems, long-range cruise missiles, and medium-range ballistic missiles. While this listing of capabilities is by no means exhaustive, it does highlight the growing capability of the PLA to target both U.S. ships and bases throughout the region. While this capability is expanding, by its nature it is only designed for a short-term effect. It does not give the PLA a sustained, power projection capability critical to address many of the problems they may face outside of a Taiwan scenario.

SLOC Protection.

Many Chinese writers recognize the potential vulnerability of China's SLOCs and fear that in future crises, the United States has the potential to use its maritime power to coerce China by cutting off the flow of energy, trade, or strategic resources.[59] As the piracy issue in the Gulf of Aden led to the PLAN's first anti-piracy deployment, it is unclear how this will impact future military development, particularly as regional security efforts in Southeast Asia to combat piracy are under way and appear to have a positive effect cutting the number of annual cases of piracy.[60]

Currently, the PLA has only a limited capability to perform this mission on a large-scale on a sustained basis. Due to the limited number of modern ships, at-sea replenishment capabilities, and corresponding infrastructure, if confronted with a viable threat to its SLOCs, the PRC is faced with a significant threat. To build this capability, the PLAN would require more modern destroyers equipped with advanced air defense capabilities, nuclear submarines for increased time at sea, replenishment ships and oilers, and bases in the region with the capacity to support this force and its logistic requirements.[61] The PLAAF and PLAN Air Force (PLANAF) would require a much improved aerial refueling capability. Developing the capabilities to expand its capability to protect SLOCS will be a major investment that could divert resources from other priorities. Using the U.S. Navy as the main threat will require significant buildup in the PLAN at-sea capability due to the limited utility of and short duration effects achieved by the PLA's current access denial capability. In addition, in most scenarios, this mission will arise out of a broader crisis involving other parts of the PLA. At current force levels, the PLA would be hard pressed to counter these threats.

Presence and Support to Territorial Claims.

Many of the resource requirements needed to build SLOC protection capabilities will be required to develop this capability. The main difference is the primary threat. In the East China Sea, sustaining presence to enforce or demonstrate territorial claims will force the PLAN and PLAAF to confront the Japanese Maritime Self-Defense Force (JMSDF) and the Japanese Air Self-Defense Force (JASDF). While Japan's military is very capable, the amount of resources needed by the PLA to adequately sustain this presence and deal with crisis situations is much less than countering a sustained effort to prevent the United States from interdicting PRC SLOCs. In the South China Sea, there is no competitor for the Chinese navy among the regional players. Additional resources would not be required to support sustained PLAN and PLAAF presence around PRC territorial claims.

Crisis Support and Disaster Relief.

This mission area will require vastly fewer resources, but will require some investment over time. The PLA is already doing this, suggesting that lessons learned from the U.S. response to the 2004 tsunami have taken hold and senior military leaders see much utility in developing these types of capabilities to further China's interests in the region. In particular, completion of an amphibious transport dock (LPD) and new hospital ship indicate the PLA intends to take this mission seriously in the coming years. At this time, there is not a great deal of information that would indicate the extent to which this mission area will be resourced.

Military Diplomacy.

Military engagement will remain a relatively low cost mission area for the PLA that will allow it to use the limited resources it has to great effect in the region. In recent years, there have been a large number of military diplomacy efforts, which have increased from year to year. To continue to support this mission area will require no additional resources.[62]

The last consideration, which does not fall into a particular mission area, is the extent to which the PRC desires to counter U.S. presence in the region. While the PLA has greatly enhanced its capability in recent years to counter key U.S. strengths, many of these advances are for relatively short-term effects and do not directly counter the United States for sustained periods of time.[63] Many Chinese security experts believe that this type of competition is not sustainable at the present time and that PLA development should be focused on addressing the most critical maritime threats in a scoped, disciplined fashion by developing a navy that has some capability to project power across the region while defending the mainland. Undoubtedly, this formulation will change in coming years as China continues to build its power and modernize.

WHAT THE FUTURE HOLDS

China's future modernization choices should not be cast as "either-or" decisions. Future roles and missions and the corresponding equipment and capabilities to satisfy will eventually come. As China has demonstrated over the past 2 decades, it has the capability to develop military capabilities rapidly. The case for future missions beyond Taiwan is more influenced by the timing of these decisions and the resources available to pursue this vast array of capabilities. In the coming decades, Beijing will be confronted with a host of budgetary constraints that may impact the PLA's ability to develop all of the capabilities it wants to pursue in the short term. The PLA recognizes this tradeoff, however, and has set its sights on a long-term modernization program that will continue over the next several decades. There should be little question that the PLA will ultimately meet these modernization objectives, the question is when it will do so.

The current debates underway in China's national security community are not a question of which path the PLA will pursue. This has already been dictated by China's growing role in the global economy, its strategic resource requirements, and its desire to be a great power. The current debates have definitely framed the future of the PLA and its presence in the East and South China Seas will undoubtedly grow. The key issue remains at what point these missions and capabilities will be developed and fielded. As a result of the various factors highlighted in this chapter, to include the organizational perspectives in the PLA and available resources and future threat assessments, most of the PLA's future missions in the East and South China Sea will continue to be supportive of Taiwan crisis scenarios. They will center on countering third party intervention by focusing modernization on an adversary's key vulnerabilities and limited duration effects. Over the next decade, these missions are likely to evolve, however, as the PLA fields the capabilities it feels are necessary for Taiwan contingencies. At that point, a wider scope of PLA modernization will truly begin to develop, enabling China to have military capabilities to address its various security concerns, while maintaining its focus on the core missions that have been central to Chinese military planning over the past two decades.

As China continues to grapple with the future security threats that will ultimately dictate the PLA's strategy and structure, its choices will present numerous policy considerations. Most notably, China's decisions will be based on the factors outlined in this chapter, many of which, are outside of U.S. control. This will make it extremely difficult, at best, to influence China's decisions on military strategy and modernization.

It will be critical for U.S. policymakers to determine what type of Chinese military they would most like to see and equally important for them to understand the PLA they will most likely encounter. While this chapter outlines many near term considerations, and in many cases constraints, driving which roles and missions China pursues in the East and South China Seas, over time, new technologies; years of comprehensive, focused modernization efforts; and resources will allow the PLA to broaden its scope and widen its range of choices and capabilities.

CHAPTER 9 - ENDNOTES

1. For an expanded discussion on China's national military strategy, see David M. Finkelstein, "China's National Military Strategy: An Overview of the 'Military Strategic Guidelines,'" in Roy Kamphausen and Andrew Scobell, eds., *Right-sizing the People's Liberation Army: Exploring the Contours of China's Military,* Carlisle, PA: Strategic Studies Institute, U.S. Army War College, September 2007, pp. 109-115. Other articles in that volume also provide an expanded discussion of PLA modernization and force structure. For additional work on the impact that energy will have on China's future military strategy and force structure, see Gabriel B. Collins, Andrew S. Erickson, Lyle J. Goldstein, and William S. Murray, eds., *China's Energy Strategy: The Impact on Beijing's Maritime Policies,* Annapolis, MD:, Naval Institute Press, 2008.

2. Reference Chapter 1, Figure 1, "How China Manages Taiwan." Based on available sources, this chapter examines the issue of future roles and missions through the prism of quadrant A of this reference graphic.

3. The major missions and drivers outlining the international security environment can be found in the following sources:: *China's National Defense in 2006,* Beijing, China: Information Office of the State Council, December 29, 2006; Liu Yuejin, ed., *The Science of National Security,* Beijing, China: Academy of Military Science Press, 2001. More detailed discussions of the specific security and

force structure implications of these missions will be provided later in the chapter.

4. Wang Houqing, Zhang Xingye, *The Science of Campaigns,* Beijing, China: National Defense University (NDU) Press, 2000. Key discussions are provided on multiple campaigns that are not uniquely structured for supporting Taiwan contingencies such as blockade campaigns, border counterattack campaigns, and the small-scale campaigns outlined under the chapter on Joint Island Landing Campaigns.

5. Cao Zhi, "CMC's Guo Boxiong Urges Improving PLA Capabilities to 'Fulfill Historic Missions'," Beijing, *Xinhua, September* 27, 2005, in CPP20050927320021; and Zhang Qingsheng, "China's Military Diplomacy," Beijing *Xuexi Shibao,* May 14, 2007, in OSC CPP20070517332001.

6. Richard Fisher, Jr., "Secret Sanya—China's New Nuclear Naval Base Revealed," *Jane's Intelligence Review*, April 15, 2008.

7. Trefor Moss, "Power to the People: China's Military Modernisation, Part One," *Jane's Defense Weekly*, July 21, 2008; and Bernard D. Cole, "Beijing's Strategy of Sea Denial," in Jamestown Foundation *China Brief*, Vol. 6, Issue 23, November 22, 2006.

8. Cole, "Beijing's Strategy of Sea Denial"; Jeff Cheng, "China's Military Expansion Against Taiwan in the Next 8 Years," in *Kanwa News*, June 20, 2008.

9. Nan Li, Eric McVadon, and Qinhong Wang, "China's Evolving Military Doctrine," *Issues and Insights,* Pacific Forum, Center for Strategic and International Studies (CSIS), Vol. 6, No. 20, December 2006, p. 13. In addition, see the 2006 China's National Defense for discussion about Taiwan as the primary threat to China's national's Defense; and David M. Finkelstein, "China's National Military Strategy: An Overview of the 'Military Strategic Guidelines'," in Kamphausen and Scobell, eds., *Right-sizing the People's Liberation Army: Exploring the Contours of China's Military,* Carlisle, PA: Strategic Studies Institute, U.S. Army War College, September 2007, pp. 109-115.

10. Shi Chunlun, ""A Commentary on Studies of the last Ten Years Concerning China's Sea Power," Beijing, *Xindai Guoji Guanxi*, in OSC CPP20080603590001, April 20, 2008; and Liu Jiangping and Zhui Yue, "Management of the Sea in the 21st Century. Whither the Chinese Navy," Beijing, Dangdai Haijun, in OSC CPP20070628436012. For a comprehensive discussion of PLAAF doctrinal developments and new operational concepts, see Kevin M. Lanzit and Kenneth Allen, "Right-Sizing the PLA Air Force: New Operational Concepts Define a Smaller, More Capable Force," in Kamphausen and Scobell, eds., *Right-sizing the People's Liberation Army: Exploring the Contours of China's Military*, Carlisle, PA: Strategic Studies Institute, U.S. Army War College, September 2007, pp. 448-458.

11. Tao Shelan, "PLA Admiral States Need for Offensive as well as Defense Capabilities," Beijing, China, *Zhongguo Xinwen She*, in OSC CPP200701097008003, January 9, 2007; and Zhou Yawen, Li Gencheng, and Tang Zhongping, "South Sea Fleet Base Enhances Ship-Borne Weaponry Support Capabilities," Beijing, China, *Jiefangjun Bao*, in OSC cpp 20080325710013, March 25, 2008; and Ju Hailong, "Can the South China Sea Issue Be Resolved Peacefully?" Beijing, China, *Shijie Zhishi*, in OSC CPP 20070223329001, February 1, 2007.

12. Cole, p. 2; and Li, McVadon, and Wang, pp. 13-15.

13. Unattributed, *www.globalsecurity.org/military/world/china/navy.htm* and *www.sinodefence.com/navy/surface/default.asp.*

14. Andrei Chang, "Combat Missions of the PLAAF's Five Key Fighter-Bomber Regiments," *Kanwa News*, June 30, 2008; and Andrei Chang and Yuri Baskov, "Fourth J-10 Fighter Regiment Established at PLAAF No. 1 Division," *Kanwa News*, March 30, 2008.

15. Dennis J. Blasko, Chas W. Freeman, Jr., Stanley Horowitz, Evan S. Medeiros, and James C. Mulvenon, *Defense-related Spending in China: A Preliminary Analysis and Comparison with American Equivalents*, Washington, DC: United States-China Policy Foundation, 2007, pp. 1-3; and Quan Xiaoshu and Li Xuanliang,

"'China Focus': China's Defense Budget To Grow 17.6 percent in 2008," Beijing, China, *Xinhua* in OSC CPP20080304968220, March 4, 2008. See also Michael S. Chase, "Balancing China's Budgetary Priorities: Defense Spending and Domestic Challenges," in *Jamestown Foundation China Brief,* Vol. 7, Issue 20, October 31, 2007.

16. Yuejin Liu, ed., *Science of National Security,* Beijing, China: China University of Political Science and Law Publishing House, 2004. This volume contains a comprehensive discussion of the current themes in the realm of national security research. See also Shou Xiaosong, "Views on the Innovative Development of the Party's National Security Strategic Theory," Beijing, *Zhongguo Junshi Kexue,* in OSC CPP20080623436002, August 20, 2007; and Zhang Ce, Shi Yansheng, and Yang Jianjun, "Being Reinforcements for Responding to Nontraditional Security Threats: Deliberation on PLA's Completion of Diverse Military Tasks," Beijing, *Zhongguo Guofang Bao,* in OSC CPP20080701436003, June 26, 2008.

17. Zhang Ce, Shi Yansheng, and Yang Jianjun, pp. 3-4.

18. For a comprehensive treatment of this subject, see Gabriel B. Collins, Andrew S. Erickson, Lyle J. Goldstein, and William S. Murray, eds., *China's Energy Strategy: The Impact on Beijing's Maritime Policies,* Annapolis, MD: Naval Institute Press, 2008, pp. 1-12, 252-299, and 336-351.

19. Zhao Hongtu, ""Reconsidering the Malacca Dilemma and China's Energy Security," Beijing, *Xindai Guoji Guanxi,* in OSC CPP20070724455004, June 20, 2007; Ju Hailong, "Can the South China Sea Issue Be Resolved Peacefully?" Beijing, China, Shijie Zhishi in OSC CPP20070223329001, February 11, 2008.

20. *Ibid.*

21. Liang Guanglie, "Chinese Military Foreign Diplomacy Is In Step With the Times," Beijing, *Jeifangjun Bao,* in CPP 20081223702009, December 23, 2008. Also see Zhang Qingsheng, "China's Military Diplomacy, Beijing, *Xuexi Shibao* in OSC cpp20070517332001, May 14, 2007.

22. Liu Yuejin, ed. Many of the same aspects and components of national security are also described in Shou Xiaosong's article.

23. Shi Hua and Zhang Beixin, "Chinese Navy Will Protect Ships Free of Charge," Beijing, China, *Huanqiu Wang Online*, in OSC CPP20081229671001, December 24, 2008; Mark McDonald, "China considers Naval Mission Against Pirates in Gulf of Aden," *New York Times*, December 18, 2008, p. 6; Johnathan Adams, "China Projects Naval Power in Pirate Fight," *Christian Science Monitor*, December 30, 2008, p. 1. While this chapter discusses anti-piracy in the context of future missions in Southeast Asia, the recent PLAN deployment to the Gulf of Aden has been a significant indicator of those missions Beijing feels compelled to pursue. At this point, it is not clear how this will impact the PLAN over the long-term.

24. Wang Yizhou, "National Security in the Stage of Peaceful Development," Beijing, *Shijie Zhishi* in OSC CPP20061220329003, December 1, 2006; and Li Limin, "Some Points for Consideration in China's Asia-Pacific Geostrategy," Beijing, *Xiandai Guoji Guanxi* in OSC CPP20080723508002, May 20, 2008. In addition, publications such as the Defense White Paper, *The Science of National Security*, and *The Science of Military Strategy* provide broader discussions of China's major national security challenges.

25. Kristen Gunness, "China's Military Diplomacy in an Era of Change," paper prepared for the National Defense University Symposium on China's Global Activism: Implications for U.S. Security Interests, Washington DC, Jun 20, 2006; Dr. Xuecheng Liu, "China's Energy Security and It's Grand Strategy," Muscatine, IO: The Stanley Foundation Policy Analysis Brief, September 2006, pp. 3-8. The second article provides a broad overview of Beijing's current energy strategy and the multifaceted approach China is taking to secure resources.

26. Hu Jintao, "Hold High the Great Banner of Socialism with Chinese Characteristics and Strive for New Victories in Building a Moderately Prosperous Society: Report to the 17th National Congress of the Community Party of China," Beijing, *Xinhua*, October 25, 2007.

27. Kristen Gunness and Joshua Kurlantzick, "China's Charm Offensive in Southeast Asia," *Current History*, July 2006, pp. 271-274.

28. Cole, p. 2; and Li, McVadon, and Wang, pp. 13-15.

29. As discussed in the DoD *Annual Report on China's Military Modernization*, PLA investment and development of power projection capabilities remains limited, but is slowly increasing. While the report in recent years has highlighted potential new missions, it highlights China's continued focus on Taiwan.

30. Finkelstein, pp. 109-115.

31. Jeifangjun Bao, "Make Ceaseless Efforts to Strengthen Core Military Capacity Building; Important Experience from 30 Years of Reform, Opening Up," Beijing, *Jeifangjun Bao* in OSC CPP20081203710007. This article provides an editorial view of the range of missions the PLA is being directed to support. While insightful, this article, and others, do not provide in-depth insight on programmatic and resource decisions as they align with missions.

32. Yuejin, Liu ed, and Shou Xiaosong; and Zhange Ce, Shi Yansheng, and Yang Jianjun.

33. One component of this debate is centered on whether China should remain a landpower, evolve into a seapower or achieve some balance. This discussion is covered in Li Yihu, "Sea and Land Power: From Dichotomy to Overall Planning: A Review of the Relationship Between Sea and Land Power," Beijing, *Xindai Guoji Guanxi* in OSC CPP20070712455001, August 20, 2007; Sun Peisong, "Where Exactly is the focus of China's Interests," Beijing, *Huanqiu Shibao* in OSC CPP20071226325001 December 7, 2007.

34. *Jeifangjun Bao* editorial. This article lays out common themes in PLA writing on major threats, in particular third party intervention by a strong adversary, which refers to the United States.

35. Shou Xiaosong.

36. Roger Cliff, Mark Burles, Michael S. Chase, Derek Eaton, and Kevin L. Pollpeter, *Entering the Dragon's Lair: Chinese Antiaccess Strategies and Their Implications for the United States*, Santa Monica, CA: Rand, 2007, pp. 51-79.

37. Liang Guanglie, "Chinese Military Foreign Diplomacy Is In Step With the Times," Beijing, *Jeifangjun Bao* in CPP 20081223702009, December 23, 2008. See also Gunness and Kurlantzick.

38. Shou Xiaosong. Nontraditional threats are also outlined in a number of other publications to include the Science of National Security and the recent *Jeifangjun Bao* editorial on strengthening core military capabilities, which outlines the necessary balance between preparing for traditional and nontraditional threats.

39. Information Office of the State Council, *China's National Defense in 2006*.

40. Li Keshuang and Zhao Debin, "Firmly Improve Capability to Carry Out Military Operations Other Than War," Beijing, *Jeifangjun Bao* in OSC CPP 20081125710010 November 25, 2008. Also see Zhao Jianwei, "Promoting the Formation of Logistical Support for Capabilities for Non-combat Military Maneuvers," Beijing, *Jeifangjun Bao* in OSC CPP20081114705008.

41. Liang Guanglie.

42. Information Office of the State Council, *China's National Defense in 2006*. See also Shou Xiaosong and the *Jeifangjun Bao* editorial on core capabilities.

43. Hu Jintao, "Join Hands to promote Peaceful Development of Cross-Strait Relations; Stive with Unity of Pupose for the Great Rejuvenation of the Chinese Nation," Beijing, *Xinhua* in OSC CPP20081231005002, December 31, 2008.

44. While there is no specific discussion of reexamining strategic priorities, the previous modifications to the China's strategic guidelines are outlined in Finkelstein's paper and also the *Jeifangjun Bao* editorial on core capabilities.

45. Li Yihu and Sun Peisong.

46. Information Office of the State Council, *China's National Defense in 2006*.

47. Kamphausen and Scobbell, eds, *Right-sizing the People's Liberation Army*. This volume describes many of the major trends in PLA modernization in much greater depth and examines future directions for military modernization.

48. Chase.

49. Liang Guanglie.

50. Unattributed, "Deputy Li Tiemin: Ensure Safety of Strategic Seaways for China," Beijing, *Jiefangjun Bao* in OSC CPP20070315721004, March 14, 2007; Zhou Hongtu, "Reconsidering the 'Malacca Dilemma' and China's Energy Security," Beijing, *Xiandai Guoji Guanxi*, June 20, 2007; and Ju Hailong, "Can the South China Sea Issue Be Resolved Peacefully?" Beijing, *Shijie Zhishi* in OSC CPP20070223329001, February 1, 2007.

51. Shou Xiaosong and Zhou Hongtu.

52. *Ibid.*

53. For a detailed discussion of this nature, see Zhou Hongtu. This issue is also discussed at length in Collins, Erickson, Goldstein, and Murray.

54. Finkelstein, pp. 81-93. This publication outlines the process by which strategic guildelines are issued. While the groundwork for a future decision was laid in 2004 by Hu Jintao's discussion of the PLA's historical missions, no following guidance of the nature outlined in Finkelstein's study has been observed.

55. Liang Guanglie, Li Keshuang, and Zhao Debin; and Zhao Jianwei.

56. Finkelstein, pp. 81-93.

57. The author has not identified any documents or studies that appear to be institutional research supporting this effort. This may be a limitation in research materials; however, information of this type would likely not be available to the general public.

58. Cliff, Burles, Chase, Eaton, and Pollpeter, pp. 51-79.

59. Collins, Erickson, Goldstein, and Murray.

60. China's deployment of naval forces to the Gulf of Aden to support anti-piracy missions is a significant indicator of the level of concern among China's civilian and military leaders. At this point, however, it is unclear how this will influence future force structure and missions in the South China Sea.

61. Lessons learned from the PLAN antipiracy deployment will give China's leaders much more insight into the operational requirements necessary for expanding this capability in the future.

62. Liang Guanglie and Zhang Qinsheng.

63. Liu Yijian, "Theory of the Command of the Sea and Its Trend of Development," *Zhongguo Junshi Kexue* in OSC CPP20050427000217, January 1, 2005; and Dai Xu, "Rise of World Powers Cannot Do Without Military Transformation," Beijing, *Huanqui Shiba*o in OSC CPP20070326455002, March 15, 2007.

CHAPTER 10

PLA "JOINT" OPERATIONAL CONTINGENCIES IN SOUTH ASIA, CENTRAL ASIA, AND KOREA

Larry M. Wortzel

Introduction.

The underlying assumption of this chapter is that within the limitations of technology and resources, a nation's military capacity will grow to secure vital national interests. This chapter addresses how the Chinese People's Liberation Army (PLA) is poised and exploring ways to secure and defend China's interests, with specific reference to the Korean Peninsula, Central Asia, and South Asia.[1] A second important assumption implicit in the chapter is that China's armed forces will not face a major, protracted conflict with or over Taiwan in an attempt to unify that island with the mainland. That is, the Chinese military can "get beyond Taiwan as its primary mission" relatively undamaged.

Maintaining a generally peaceful environment gives the PLA time to adapt to a wider range of missions to "foster a security environment conducive to China's peaceful development" while also "ensuring the interests of national development."[2] In fact, the general "line" from Communist Party Chairman Hu Jintao emphasizes the need to maintain a peaceful external environment so that China's economy and military can develop.

Whether some form of the status quo continues, whether an armed standoff between Taiwan and China goes on, or if some resolution that achieves a *modus vivendi* across the Taiwan Strait is attained, the PLA can continue to develop at a moderate pace to carry out the goals set for it by the leaders of the Chinese Communist Party (CCP). The general trends examined are also valid if there is some resolution to the cross-Strait military and political standoff on terms Beijing can accept that involve a modest conflict, so long as that conflict does not involve the United States and seriously weaken the PLA. Of course, the reaction of other countries to how the PLA "gets beyond Taiwan" may change the diplomatic and security environment facing China's leaders, but it allows the CCP and the PLA to pursue their nation's interests without major interruption. One thing is certain: the PLA has missions and plans well beyond Taiwan, and if the PLA is not forced to maintain a strong force for Taiwan contingencies it will be able to concentrate on other missions designed to secure and defend China's national interests.

Within the general context of China's national security, defense preparedness and military strength are critical issues. They are related to maintaining a strong economy and pursuing national interests. The general approach taken by security experts in China today is that the core of security in the defense arena is a "strong, capable military."[3] Preventing Taiwan from moving toward independence is a high priority, as is gaining control of Taiwan at some future time.[4] Strategy texts also identify the United States as a major threat to China's national security ("美国对我构成军事威胁").[5]

Writing for the U.S. Government's Open Source Center, Daniel Hartnett of the CNA Corporation has assessed the broad definition of Chinese security and what the Central Military Commission (CMC) calls "the historic missions of the Armed Forces [the PLA]."[6] Hartnett attributes this mission to a speech by CMC

328

and CCP Chairman Hu Jintao on December 24, 2004. CMC vice chairman Guo Boxiong, in a week-long meeting at the National Defense University for the PLA in September 2005, reinforced these as the synthesis of the military theories of Deng Xiaoping and Jiang Zemin by Hu Jintao.[7] The "historic missions" are:

- To reinforce the armed forces' loyalty to the CCP;
- To help ensure China's sovereignty, territorial integrity, and domestic security in order to continue its national development; and,
- To help safeguard China's expanding national interests.[8]

These are important to us in the context of future PLA contingency missions because they establish a formal framework and ideological justification for using the military in a regional and global context. PLA national security thinkers increasingly make reference to expanded contingency and force presence missions for the PLA. In one text for the PLA National Defense University, Senior Colonel Wang Lidong expressed the view that as the PLA strengthens to carry out its external missions, it will need to develop a stronger maritime capacity as part of China's "comprehensive national security."[9] The third point in particular, "safeguarding China's expanding national interests," is a responsibility that requires the PLA to develop the capacity to operate and have a presence at longer distances away from continental China.[10]

The "historic missions" provide broad guidance and justification for security thinkers in China to explore approaches to military theory, roles, and missions for forces, and new equipment and technology to increase China's capacity to operate as the military force of a nation with global interests. In terms of missions "beyond Taiwan," PLA Academy of Military Science theorist Jiang Yamin reminds China's students of warfare that Hu Jintao's charge to the PLA to provide a firm national defense for China "in the 21st century" means that the PLA must have a strong capability to counter attacks at long distances and defend distant lines of communication.[11]

Another theme that will recur throughout this chapter is the emphasis Chinese security thinkers are placing on maritime security and the security of the sea lines of communication. From the standpoint of joint military contingency missions, this theme affects how the PLA defines its missions in the South China Sea, the Indian Ocean, the East China Sea, and the Korean Sea. Concepts of maritime security and sovereignty affect how the Navy and Air Force develop or improve their weapons and systems as well as command, control, communication, computers, and intelligence surveillance and reconnaissance (C4ISR) systems. Granted, some in the PLA place primary emphasis on military strength to ensure territorial integrity and Taiwan unification as the key national security issue,[12] but many other security thinkers are expanding the concept of national security to include economic security and energy security as major factors among China's national interests.[13]

In his National Defense University text, Wang Lidong notes that the oceans are critical to the global economy and increasingly becoming "a strategic point" (literally, "a place contested by all strategists" 海洋越来越成为兵家必争之地).[14] This change in orientation from a nation primarily focused on its littoral waters and territorial sovereignty leads Chinese strategists to conclude that "China must develop the capacity to project power and protect its interests in distant seas."[15] At the Academy of Military Science, Jiang Yamin makes essentially the same point, calling for capabilities to pursue and protect China's interests, support economic development, defend its distant lines of communication, and prevent a distant attack.[16] Military analysts in India, and at the *Kanwa Defense Review* based in Canada, believe that to achieve this goal of being able to protect sea lines of communication at distances away from the Chinese littoral, the PLA will have aircraft carriers in the future.[17] In Beijing, however, despite stories from India and Canada, Li Jie, a PLA officer at the Academy of Military Science, denied such rumors.[18] Li opined that although he believed china was "entitled" to aircraft carriers, the PLA may pursue them on its own schedule. To carry out some of the missions set for the PLA by the CCP, however, aircraft carriers and long-range aerial refueling capabilities are exceedingly useful. The PLA is now examining a couple of former Russian aircraft carriers and most likely will attempt to experiment with carrier operations at some time in the next decade.

All this illustrates that China's security thinkers, whether in the PLA or at academic institutions, see it as natural that their nation builds a military capacity to protect and defend its global interests far beyond its borders. They advocate the need to be able to respond to contingencies. They see the economic and energy components of national security as a key Chinese national interest. These security thinkers are unabashed in their discussion of these matters, and they advocate developing future weapon systems and doctrines to carry out such missions. At the same time, they argue that developing this military capacity to carry out external missions is not an act of belligerence and will contribute to world peace and stability.[19]

General Zhang Shenxia, writing from his position as commandant of the Academy of Military Science, argues that "China has chosen a course to ensure a peaceful rise. China needs a peaceful rise for itself and at the same time is working to safeguard world stability and overall development."[20] The "Peaceful Rise" policy was subject to some debate inside the party, with some in the PLA arguing that the formulation limited the PLA from taking on "out-of-area missions" beyond Taiwan.

In a meeting of senior PLA Air Force officers in May 2004, Jiang Zemin suggested that perhaps the formulation should be set aside, since the thesis potentially limited China's military development and modernization. This objection was both a manifestation of friction between Jiang and Hu Jintao and a demonstration of genuine concern within the PLA that it could continue to modernize and strengthen.[21] In the end, after some period of debate, the CCP arrived at the position that "there is no contradiction between military modernization or military strength and China's peaceful rise."[22] China's policymakers today see military development as complementing China's peaceful rise.[23]

In the areas covered in this chapter, the Korean Peninsula, South Asia, and Central Asia, Beijing has backed up its fundamental interests with diplomacy and invested billions of dollars of infrastructure projects, some to open better trade routes and others to ensure access to ports and resources.[24] The PLA has also been a part of this broader approach to national interest and security, with exercises, arms sales, aid to defense industries, and military assistance to nations in the region.[25] The bottom line up front is that as these regions and the countries in them are increasingly important national interests for China and are part of a broader national strategy, the military will necessarily develop capabilities to secure the country's interests.

South Asia.

U.S. relations with India are among the foremost future security concerns of the PLA and China's security thinkers. In a PLA Academy of Military Science book on China's national security strategy and national interests, Ba Zhongtan and his co-authors charge that the United States is "interfering in South Asia affairs" with the goal of "immobilizing China."[26] PLA officers remain deeply suspicious of India's long-term military objectives. One article in the *China Military Science* quotes Indian strategists as suggesting that to guarantee India's fate, Indian forces must control the maritime domain surrounding India (in characterizing the Indian view the Chinese authors use 完全控制我国周边海域).[27]

Naturally, this is a matter of concern for the PLA, which sees the potential for interdiction of its own strategic lines of communication. Indeed, much of what China is doing in Bangladesh and Myanmar must be assessed in the context of concerns over India's future military development. Although Myanmar is a member of the Association of Southeast Asian Nations (ASEAN), it sits in a transition zone. It has trade, historical, and cultural ties to ancient India. China is clearly developing its own military and economic interests with Myanmar not simply to provide an outlet for trade from southwest China, but also to cement security relations with Rangoon.

From the Indian perspective, there are a number of concerns about China's future decisions (see

Appendix I, Chinese Foreign Infrastructure Projects). At a January 15, 2008, speech at the Chinese Academy of Social Sciences, Indian Prime Minister Manmohan Singh expressed concerns about the Sino-Indian border dispute and other issues (see Appendix II, Chinese Arms Deals and Military Assistance). According to Singh,

> India is deeply concerned about the border issue mainly because of two reasons. First, India's most abundant iron ore mines are in the disputed border region of the Himalayas. Second, the border region is closely related to the fight for water resources as all of India's great rivers trace their sources in the melted ice and snow of the Himalayas.[28]

Singh went on to say that, "it goes without saying that water, as a strategic resource, has made the disputed border areas more significant. Currently, India's water resources are in an acute shortage. Water is often delivered by wagons even in areas of New Delhi inhabited by wealthy people because of water shortages that last from winter to summer." He minimized security problems in this speech, concentrating on economic and development issues.

Nonetheless, in the security and defense community, observers are quite concerned about PLA activities and China's developing naval, air, and air defense capabilities opposite India.[29] One complaint this author has heard from India's defense attachés in Washington and Beijing has been picked up in a defense-related publication from Canada—that the Second Artillery Corps has upgraded its *Dong Feng* 21 intermediate-range missile forces, replacing the old *Dong Feng* 3s.[30] This is probably a reference to changes in the PLA Second Artillery Corps force structure in western

China, not deployments in Tibet, which are highly doubtful.[31] India is also reopening old airfields close to the Karakorum Pass and outfitting new mountain divisions as New Delhi watches the infrastructure developments by China in Tibet near the disputed areas.[32] In the maritime arena, Indian concerns have placed Myanmar in the spotlight, where India and China are competing for port projects.[33] India plans to have a fleet of aircraft carriers and new submarines in the next decade and has modernized its own nuclear forces.[34]

Further, Indian defense personnel see their services as lagging behind China in developing data exchange and network centric warfare capabilities.[35] To correct this, India will get three airborne warning and control system (AWACS) aircraft from Israel, Russian Il-76s, and ensure that missiles, air, and sea platforms have the data exchange systems to use the information. Also, some of India's Air Force will deploy closer to the Sino-Indian border with new SU-30MKI fighters and air-to-ground supersonic missiles.[36]

Beijing and New Delhi are finding ways to work together militarily, despite mutual wariness. In 2007, after two rounds of bilateral meetings to decide a scenario, the PLA and Indian ground forces held a 1-week, joint antiterrorism exercise designed to respond to the "current regional and international antiterrorism situation."[37] During training at the company level, the two armies exchanged platoon leaders for part of the exercise, embedding a foreign platoon commander into a rifle company from the other side. Thus both nations are taking advantage of opportunities to reduce potential tension and engage in security and confidence building measures.

335

While in India, observers keep their eyes on the defense imbalance, Chinese analysts concentrate on the economic side of Sino-Indian relations.[38] Indeed, Chinese publications are mostly silent on any security problems between the two countries.[39] In one *Wen Wei Pao* assessment from Hong Kong, Wang Wei sticks to documenting advances in bilateral trade, noting the possibility of a "China-India Free Trade Zone," while minimizing the likelihood of any conflict between the two nations.[40] In India, meanwhile, newspapers catalogue cross-border skirmishes.[41] Still, China is engaged in a series of trade and infrastructure projects, military assistance, and diplomatic moves that, for all practical purposes, flank India in the Persian Gulf region as well as the Indian Ocean, and cement alliances and relations in other areas of South Asia.

In Afghanistan, to exploit mining rights in a copper field south of Kabul, Beijing will construct a freight railroad, investing $2.8 billion in the project.[42] Directly flanking India, with New Delhi's traditional rival, Pakistan, China is building a deep sea port in Gwadar.[43] The two countries are also planning rail links between northwest Pakistan and Xinjiang.[44] China will construct a series of electric power stations in Pakistan, including nuclear and conventional power generation plants.[45] In the Mianwali district of the Punjab, China will work with India to set up a 600-megawatt nuclear power plant.[46]

On India's eastern flank in South Asia, China's National Machinery Import and Export Corporation signed a contract to manage coal production of the Barapukuria mine in Bangladesh.[47] Also with Bangladesh, the two countries signed an agreement on "nuclear cooperation to look for nuclear raw materials and construct a 600-megawatt nuclear power plant.[48]

Myanmar is a special case. Like Afghanistan, it is in a regional transition zone. Although an ASEAN member, Myanmar is on the Indian Ocean and has traditional cultural and historical links to India. Also, India has security, economic, and population interests in Myanmar. Therefore, it is important to consider China's interests, military relationship, and investments in Myanmar when discussing the PLA's potential regional contingency missions.

The opening of an expanded "Myanmar Road" on what was the track of the World War II supply route is over a decade old. This was a project designed to improve trade opportunities for western China, linking Yunnan with ports on the Bay of Bengal and the Andaman Sea.[49] The road will also be expanded to include east-west links to Thailand and Cambodia, a rail link is planned from Kunming to Singapore, and the old route the PLA worked on from Kunming to Bangkok while the United States was in Vietnam will be linked to sections of the Myanmar Road. Beijing has signed a series of oil and gas deals with the Myanmar government to explore on-shore and offshore resource opportunities.[50] There is also some discussion of building an oil pipeline between Myanmar and the city of Chongqing, with a refinery to be built to handle the imports.[51] This is expected to move 6.5 trillion feet of natural gas over a 30-year period from a gas field in the Bay of Bengal.[52] Thus, it is clear that two growing, energy-starved economies, those of China and India, are in a competition for influence and resources in and around Myanmar. Given the guidance that the PLA must be in a position to defend China's economic interests, Chinese military planners certainly must be thinking about the implications of these extensive investments.

The PLA and Defense Ministry planners in China also have been active in advancing Beijing's interests in South Asia. Bangladesh, one of the main purchasers of Chinese defense equipment, has ordered surface-to-air missiles from China for a frigate, PL-7 and PL-9 air-to-air missiles, as well as C-801/C-802 anti-ship missiles.[53] The Bangladesh armed forces have bought 65 type 96 D-30, 122 millimeter towed gun systems from China, as well as 16 F-7MG fighter aircraft.

Myanmar has bought a number of fire control radars for their domestically produced patrol boats, as well as anti-ship missiles. There are common reports of "Chinese troops running around Myanmar in Chinese trucks." These reports are probably explained by Myanmar's purchase of 2,500 2 1/2 ton trucks from China. Myanmar's military leaders have also ordered training aircraft for their air force and engines for a frigate to be built in Myanmar. Beijing has assisted with the expansion of the naval base in the Coco Islands, which is only 30 miles from the Andaman Islands, claimed by India. Finally, most of the tanks, armored personnel carriers, artillery systems, anti-aircraft guns, and a number of missile patrol boats in Myanmar's inventory were bought from China.[54]

The reaction of the PLA to riots in Tibet in March/April 2008 and the reaction to the earthquake in Mianyang, north of Chengdu are examples of how the military would respond to joint contingencies involving India, Bhutan, or Nepal. Generally speaking, the PLA moved quickly to get forces to the region. In the case of Tibet, the way the military reacted to the Sino-Indian War and to the buildup around Tiananmen and Beijing in 1989 is a reasonable model for how the PLA reinforces and supplements local units with out of area forces.

There are three all-weather highways available for reinforcement of Tibet. In the west, should the PLA need to reinforce the Aksai Chin in the far western sector or the middle sector of the border opposite Simla, Himachal Pradesh and Uttar Pradesh, the PLA can rely on forces from Lanzhou Military Region (MR).[55] Of course, there are other units that could react quickly to contingencies against India or opposite South Asia, including elements of the 15th Airborne Army and special operations *daduis* of the PLA.

An article in an Indian defense journal acknowledges that India has to divide its military focus between threats from Pakistan and a potential border conflict with China.[56] According to this article, the PLA has prepared for contingency operations in Tibet and on the Sino-Indian border by putting five or six logistics brigades in Tibet, preparing rapid reaction units in the 13th and 21st Group Armies, developing and improving remote airfields along the border, and developing contingency plans to move the 15th Airborne Group Army into the region.[57] The same article laments that the PLA has low-yield tactical nuclear weapons available if needed on the battlefield, while Indian forces lack such a capability.

The PLA has had a long, fruitful arms sales and security assistance relationship with Pakistan, as have Chinese defense industries. China has provided anti-ship missiles and fire control radars for Pakistan's missile boats, helped to establish air surveillance systems, and sold anti-aircraft missiles to Pakistan.[58] Beijing has also sold frigates, combat aircraft, training aircraft, and helicopters to Pakistan, all of which explain why Indian military thinkers place Pakistan and China at the top of their threat lists.

You Ji, a lecturer in politics at the University of New South Wales, Australia, suggested that China will focus on the security of its energy supplies, expanding its maritime strategy to include contingency operations to secure the Indian Ocean.[59] It looks as though China may need these maritime capabilities. General G. D. Bakshi, a senior research fellow at the United Service Institution in New Delhi, recently pointed out that "India sits like an unsinkable aircraft carrier across the ocean and astride their key shipping lanes."[60] According to the UK Telegraph, Bakshi added that China's rising influence in Asia "must be at our expense," and India could not afford to send a "message of weakness."[61]

You Ji also believes that Beijing will seek to work with the countries around the Straits of Hormuz and Malacca to prevent maritime terrorism and piracy. He predicts that China will seek shorter routes across land, with ports and pipelines in Pakistan (Gwadar), Myanmar, and Thailand. Further, You predicted that the PLA Navy will expand its ability to operate regionally and work to achieve "freedom of movement" in regional waters.[62] Finally, he believes that for at least a decade, the PLA Navy will have to depend on the U.S. naval presence and on cooperation with regional navies to keep sea lines of communication open because it will not have the capability to conduct routine maritime patrols or to protect its own surface action groups with submarines.[63]

Sri Lanka, Nepal, and Bhutan are areas that are not likely to trigger any sort of contingency operations by the PLA. China has largely stayed out of the insurgency in Sri Lanka. Bhutan is a small and generally pliant neighbor. Nepal may be an area where Beijing increases its diplomatic pressure and arms sales (depending on how much influence the Maoist party gets in government). Prachanda (Pushpa Kamal Dahal), the

Prime Minister of Nepal, visited China for the close of the Olympics. This was a departure from the normal practice of making India the first foreign visit. He made the normal obligatory remarks about supporting China on the Tibet issue. Other Nepali officials were split on the issue. Nepalese Foreign Minister Upendra Yadav said to the press that Nepal intends to maintain equal ties between China and India, while Congress Leader Bimalendra Nidhi argued that the timing of the visit shows that Prachanda is pro-China.[64]

Central Asia.

The reaction by China's security, foreign policy, and military establishment to the geo-strategic landscape in Central Asia differs from that in South Asia. Whereas in South Asia much of China's military planning and diplomacy is designed to isolate, contain, or flank India, with which Beijing fought a war in 1962, in Central Asia China's leaders have been careful to consider the interests of their primary potential rival—Russia. Also, there is pressure on the Central Asian countries to "diversify pipeline routes," through which they supply natural resources so as to avoid being subject to monopoly prices to get the only major export these countries enjoy out to purchasers.[65]

It is important to remember that there are about 9 million ethnic Uighurs in China. Some 300,000 more of this Turkic minority group are in Kazakhstan, and 50,000 in Kyrgyzstan. Some of these Uighurs seek an independent "East Turkestan." In Kyrgyzstan the Uighurs apparently murdered a Chinese diplomat in 2002 and bombed a bus, killing 19 Chinese visitors in 2003.[66] During the time I served as an attaché in Beijing in the mid-1990s, I got regular reports from contacts about Uighur minority groups tied to the East Turkistan independence movement killing PLA troops and their families on roads from PLA farms into town. Moreover, illegal Chinese immigrants are moving into neighboring Central Asian countries, creating security and economic problems.[67]

Russia formed the Commonwealth of Independent States (CIS) in 1991 which included Kazakhstan, Kyrgyzstan, Tajikistan, Uzbekistan, and Turkmenistan (Turkmenistan withdrew from full membership in 2005, becoming an associate member). Moscow also formed the Collective Security Treaty Organization (CSTO), as a means to prevent CIS members from "aligning with NATO [the North Atlantic Treaty Organization]," and in 2003, Russian Defense Minister Sergei Ivanov "claimed the right to intervene in these countries."[68] Later, in Shanghai in 1996 and Moscow in 1997, the five Central Asian Republics, China, and Russia agreed to a series of military confidence-building measures, which were later summarized in Alma-Ata in 1998, Bishkek in 1999, and Dushanbe in 2000.[69] Indeed, Moscow has established a CIS-wide joint air defense system that includes the air defense forces of all five Central Asian nations.[70]

When the Shanghai Cooperation Organization (SCO) was created in 2001,[71] after those 5 years of formative meetings, it was done to promote Chinese and Russian interests as much as to counter American interests.[72] The ethnic Uighur problems mentioned above, however, were also a factor that motivated China. As it framed relations with the countries in Central Asia, Beijing has been careful to ensure that military and security issues were not points of division and that its relations in the region did not create tension with Moscow, which still has strong security interests in Central Asia. Moscow still has space-launch and recovery facilities in Kazakhstan and some of its military industrial complex remains distributed in these former parts of the Soviet Union. Counterterrorism and regional security are still central issues for the SCO.[73] At the time this chapter was written, five other countries sought membership in the SCO (Mongolia, Iran, India, Pakistan, and Turkmenistan, but various member states have not been able to agree on expanding the organization).[74] This potential expansion is opposed by Beijing for several reasons: Chinese officials want to ensure that the SCO serves its purposes in balancing against Moscow in Central Asia; they do not want to antagonize the United States; and they get some benefit from the anti-terrorist and anti-separatist stance of the SCO.

China has conducted anti-terrorist exercises with the SCO in 2003, in the territories of Kazakhstan and China. In August 2005, the PLA held "Peace Mission 2005," with Russia; and in 2006, conducted "Cooperation 2006" with the armed forces of Tajikistan. Perhaps the largest of the confidence building measures in which the PLA has been involved, however, was "Peace Mission 2007."[75] This exercise involved all six SCO members in a "combined operations" (合同作战) exercise that brought the heads of state and defense ministers from all the countries together as observers.

After the close of the 2008 Olympics in Beijing, Hu Jintao visited Dushanbe for the 2008 SCO meeting, working out exchanges on anti-terrorism, regional energy issues, and military confidence-building measures.[76] The SCO, therefore, remains a cornerstone of Beijing's approach in Central Asia.

Beijing is building a great deal of infrastructure to support oil and gas imports from Central Asia, however, and needs political stability in the region to ensure China's energy security (see Appendix I).[77] Beijing's regional experts recognize that a number of countries are competing for influence and resources in the region, but see China itself as having a "unique geographical advantage" in gaining access to the resources in Central Asia.[78] Moreover, leaders in both Russia and China want to avoid confrontation and prevent the United States from dominating Central Asia, using NATO as one tool to do so.[79] Even so, Chinese scholars emphasize that along with the "going west" strategy to expand the economy of western China and take advantage of the infrastructure-building in Central Asia, Beijing should avoid military conflict, emphasize the "Five Principles of Peaceful Coexistence," work on fighting terrorism in the region, and concentrate on "military confidence-building measures."[80] The program with the SCO is to "fight the 'three evils' of extremism, terrorism, and separatism," a program designed to keep Xinjiang intact and ensure cooperation with neighboring states (see Appendix II).[81]

China is one contributing source to the Central Asia Regional Cooperation Program (CAREC). This 10-year, $18.7 billion project will build five transportation corridors connecting Kazakhstan to Xinjiang; Turkmenistan to Tajikistan, Kyrgyzstan to Xinjiang, and Siberia to China through Mongolia; Siberia to Central Asia and Afghanistan; and Pakistan to China and Tajikistan.[82] Also, China will fund the China-Kyrgyzstan-Uzbekistan railroad, with a terminus in Kashgar, Xinjiang.[83] Another rail link will connect the China-Kazakh border city, Korgas, to the Chinese rail system.[84] In other rail projects in Central Asia, Beijing will help with 11 infrastructure projects, including a highway and rail connection for a cost of $11 billion.[85]

The China National Petroleum Corporation bought PetroKazakhstan from a Canadian company and will build a series of oil and gas pipelines from Xinjiang to Kazakhstan with links to Turkmenistan.[86] To assist Kyrgyzstan, as a goodwill gesture, China is discussing building a series of electric power stations, including hydropower sites.[87] With Turkmenistan, China is now working on a gas pipeline that will end in Guangzhou, stretching all across Xinjiang and central-south China.[88] To secure access to oil and gas in Uzbekistan, the China National Petroleum Corporation will invest $210 million in exploration and will build a high capacity pipeline back to China.[89]

In Xinjiang, the PLA has made improvements that supplement internal security forces and can also be used for contingency operations in Central Asia. The PLA's helicopter aviation regiments are equipped to carry out electronic warfare operations in addition to conducting raids, precision attacks, and air assault missions.[90] When gauging the PLA's ability to react to contingencies in Central Asia, it is critical to consider how Beijing reacts to domestic security problems. It is likely that the same, or similar, PLA forces would be involved. Units from Nanjing and Lanzhou MRs have deployed there in the past.[91]

Korean Peninsula.

That the PLA would develop contingency missions for North Korea makes a lot of sense; it is there that the PLA confronted its most serious military threat after the founding of the PRC. China's own records show it lost 114,000 soldiers killed in action during the Korean War; 34,000 noncombat deaths from wounds, in hospitals, or from illness; 380,000 soldiers wounded; and 29,000 missing in action.[92] These losses underscore just how seriously the leadership of China takes security on the 38th Parallel, which it sees as the buffer between China and Japan as well as the United States.[93] Indeed, observers in South Korea believe that "China conceives itself to have the right" to make decisions on intervention.[94] Shen Dingli, of the Institute for International Studies at Fudan University, has told observers that policymakers in the PRC prefer a buffer in North Korea between South Korea and the U.S. forces there.[95] He also told this author that rather than let North Korea collapse, China will provide basic subsistence.[96]

However, for this writer, conversations with senior officers of the PLA in 1995 and 1996 frame the approach the PLA takes on the Korean Peninsula. I have been told by a defense minister, a chief of the General Staff Department (GSD), and a deputy chief of the GSD that "China will not let North Korea collapse." With respect to contingency missions on the Korean Peninsula, one of these senior leaders said in 1996 that "if the leaders in the United States think the U.S. military or its ally, South Korea, can simply march north in the event of a collapse in North Korea without some consultation with the PLA, it will look like 1950 all over again." These are critical points because they affect how far the United States and its allies can go in pursuing sanctions related to the "Six Party Talks," as well as how to craft any response to crises on the Korean peninsula. On the other hand, given the statements from these senior leaders, there seems to be some room for bilateral military security consultations discussing potential responses to instability on the Korean Peninsula.

There are other parallels in thinking on approaches toward North Korea's nuclear weapons program and maintaining the regime in Pyongyang in China's security community between 1995-96 and today. As early as 1995, PLA officers knowledgeable of North Korea opined that Pyongyang had 4-5 nuclear weapons at that time. They reasoned that these were of deterrent value. More recently, in 2006, scholars in Shanghai opined that "North Korean nuclear weapons were 'safeguarding' China's side door."[97] After a series of conferences in Brussels and Seoul, in 2006, participants concluded that, among other things, "avoiding the economic costs of an explosion on the Korean Peninsula was a priority for China, as was sustaining the two-Korea status quo."[98] One scholar in Shanghai said that "China had a formal commitment in its bilateral Treaty with North Korea that it must observe in the event of a conflict on the Peninsula."[99] Even at the Academy of Military Science, in a meeting in 2007, PLA officers opined that Northeast Asia has lived with a nuclear-armed North Korea for over a decade. They advised patience in negotiations. And Chinese security thinkers, a decade ago and last year, were comfortable that U.S. extended deterrence was sufficient to maintain stability, keep Japan from developing nuclear weapons, and deter Pyongyang from aggressive acts.[100] Formally, the line from China's government, from official and proprietary think tanks, and from mainstream Chinese scholars is that "China supports a non-nuclear Korean Peninsula (中国主张朝鲜半岛 无核化)."[101]

The historical ties with North Korea as a communist ally and a natural buffer state against Japanese, South Korean, and U.S. forces keep Pyongyang central to Chinese interests in Northeast Asia.[102] However, the central leadership of China and the senior leaders of the PLA still pay attention to South Korea. Indeed, just 1 day after the 2008 Olympics closed in Beijing, Hu Jintao traveled to Seoul, South Korea, to discuss trade, economic relations, and issues related to North Korea.[103] This attention is reciprocated by Seoul. China is now South Korea's largest trade partner. Two-way trade between the two countries is $145 billion a year. Also, South Korean investments in China were at $22.54 billion in 2007.[104]

All that said, most observers acknowledge that "China is North Korea's most important ally," and Beijing has sustained the Kim Jong-Il regime (see Appendix I).[105] The official line in Beijing is that "China has played a constructive role in easing the tension and resolving the [North Korean] nuclear crisis."[106] Among the most serious contingencies that China must consider is that if the Kim regime in North Korea collapses or cannot control the population, Beijing could face a massive influx of refugees along the shared 800-mile border.[107] Moreover, as the PLA leaders with whom I had contact feared, any such collapse would certainly bring South Korean and U.S. intervention. Thus the PLA must be prepared to move supplies into North Korea and move forces in to restore order and to secure the Sino-North Korean border.

Beijing has been the donor of last resort that kept North Korea in food and fuel through famine and energy crises for decades.[108] At one point when the United States, South Korea, and the European Union (EU) cut support for Pyongyang, China increased its crude oil exports to North Korea by 45 percent and its grain exports by 96 percent.[109] The Chinese leadership also has made decisions that create potential problems with Japan and could lead to territorial conflict. Pyongyang has a strong indigenous arms industry, and it is rare that China supplies weapons to North Korea (see Appendix II).

Japan and both Koreas, the Democratic People's Republic of Korea (North Korea or DPRK) and the Republic of Korea (South Korea or ROK), are in a dispute over the area formerly known as Liancourt Rocks. Japan annexed the islands in 1905, its first annexation of territory from Korea after the Sino-Japanese War. Both Koreas call the islands Tok-do (or Dokdo), and Japan claims them as the Takeshima Islands.[110] The islands are about 216 kilometers from the Korean Peninsula and 87 kilometers from South Korea's Ullung Island. They sit 115 kilometers from Japan's Oki Island. The original challenges were over fishing grounds, but today some South Korean officials believe that there may be exploitable oil or gas deposits around the island.[111] Since 1954, the ROK coast guard has stationed a battalion on the islands permanently.[112] The Chinese foreign ministry supports the position held by both North and South Korea; that the islands belong to Korea. This puts Beijing in good graces with both Pyongyang and Seoul, but means that in the event of a confrontation between the Japanese forces and either Korea, the CMC, and the Politburo Standing Committee (PBSC) must wrestle with whether to involve the PLA. Beijing has also signed a deal with North Korea to jointly develop offshore oil reserves at unspecified locations, another action that could affect contingencies with Japan.[113]

Beijing has its own problems with North Korea's regime. In official statements, books, and state-controlled media, the PRC leadership provides support for the DPRK and takes no position advocating regime change.[114] PLA officials reiterate the official Chinese call for a "denuclearized Korean Peninsula."[115] The 2006 national defense white paper describes the situation on the Korean Peninsula as "complex and challenging," but advocates no change in policy.[116]

Even in closed forums, there is almost a taboo on discussing "regime change" in North Korea. In a 2006, closed-door meeting with officials from the China Institute for International Strategic Studies and the China Institute for Contemporary International Relations, representatives from these organizations expressed frustration with the slow pace of progress on the nuclear issue with the DPRK.[117] However, the Chinese officials attending also expressed concerns about the implications for China of a collapse in North Korea. At the Central Party School's China Reform Forum, also in 2006, senior leaders took a similar position, arguing for patience on the part of the United States.

In the same year, in Shanghai, specialists of Korean affairs at the Shanghai Institute for International Studies (SIIS) assessed that Pyongyang sought to gain the initiative in any negotiations, and therefore engaged in provocative behavior, but wanted a nuclear deal.[118] They expressed no serious concerns about U.S. or Japanese action to intercept any missiles the DPRK might test, if the intercepts took place outside DPRK territory. However, they counseled against any strikes inside North Korea. The "fundamental objective of Beijing's policy with the DPRK is the maintenance of stability and peace on the Korean Peninsula," according to the most senior Korea scholar participating in the Shanghai discussions.

During meetings with scholars from Fudan University who get involved in national level security policy discussions in Beijing, scholars who had traveled to North Korea counseled patience and advised against any preemptive strike by the United States.

At Fudan and at SIIS, Chinese scholars cautioned that China has a bilateral commitment and security treaty with North Korea "that China must observe." They advised that any military action against North Korea would inevitably involve China. However, they did not suggest that "regime change" was a preferred Chinese policy. Rather, stability on the peninsula was their objective. In fact, the Shanghai-based scholars reacted strongly to the term "regime change" and suggested that it had connotations of the U.S. attack on Iraq to remove Saddam Hussein and a policy of preemption. One scholar revealed that there is a commitment in the PRC-DPRK security agreement that would commit China to assisting the DPRK in the case of a U.S. attack.

In a series of meetings in 2007, representatives of the Ministry of Foreign Affairs, the Academy of Military Science, the China Institute for Contemporary International Research, and the China Institute for International Studies also were willing to comment on North Korea, noting that Pyongyang was unstable, difficult to negotiate with, and required patience.[119] No participant on the Chinese side, however, in private conversation or in plenary meetings, departed from the official position counseling patience with the DPRK. Although a couple of Chinese participants, with whom this writer had decades of contact, expressed frustration with North Korea's actions, none suggested that the PRC leadership sought regime change.

A former PLA intelligence officer that still writes on North Korea and has regular contacts with the PLA Second Department and the Ministry of State Security counseled only caution and patience.[120] He said that dealing with North Korea was frustrating, but that Kim Jong-Il did not seek a war. He did not suggest that regime change or change in Beijing's policy was a good idea. Indeed, like the scholars in Shanghai, he said that when an American used the term "regime change," the term had connotations of an armed attack on Pyongyang. He advised against such an action as well as using that term to describe approaches to North Korea.

To highlight the sensitivity of the CCP to any open criticism of the DPRK, remember that in 2002, the Beijing journal *Zhanlue yu Guanli (Strategy and Management)* published an article by Wang Zhongwen of the Tianjin Academy of Social Sciences that was critical of North Korea.[121] Wang suggested that China's interests were in stability on the Korean Peninsula and that North Korea's actions did not help stability. In a short time, that issue of *Strategy and Management* was recalled from the shelves, and the postal service of China took them back. The electronic version of the article disappeared from the journal's web site, and even web log discussion about the article disappeared. Still, some scholars are publishing in Hong Kong on the subject, complaining that North Korea is a drag on China, and a buffer on the Korean Peninsula may no longer be needed.[122]

In summary, although many in China's security community and senior military leaders may be frustrated with North Korea's behavior, the critical importance of stability in the region dictates a policy of patience and support for the North.

Summing up the Chances of Joint Contingency Operations.

The PLA is slowly adapting to joint concepts and operations. Like most of the force, equipment, and doctrinal changes in the PLA, these things move slowly, with halting steps, and a lot of experimentation. The PLA today certainly understands the concepts.[123] Application, however, seems to be moving slowly.[124] It helps if observers keep their expectations low; after all, when it got its Su-27s it took more than a decade to move from introduction into the force structure to operational readiness for the PLA Air Force to use these aircraft with any proficiency.

Integrating the *Sovremenny* destroyers into the Navy took about the same period. However, fitting new weapon systems to older platforms sometimes goes exceedingly quickly. Once the PLA got the *Sunburn* hypersonic anti-ship missile, China's defense industry managed to reverse engineer it quickly and adapt it to other ships. We can expect to see similar improvements on air-launched anti-ship missiles, just as the PLA lost no time in developing air-launched land attack cruise missiles. All of these are things that will give the PLA capabilities to operate jointly outside China beyond Taiwan contingencies. Also, the PLA has done reasonably well with data links and cooperative targeting, integrating some airborne and special operations forces with the ground forces, and Navy-Second Artillery Corps integration.[125]

While joint concepts as they are approached in the western context may be new for the PLA, the Chinese armed forces and their civilian and military leaders are used to contingency planning. They were good at reacting to contingencies in the Korean War; they moved quickly and flexibly to respond opposite India in 1962; the CMC got forces moved quickly prior to the Tiananmen Massacre in 1989; they respond reasonably quickly to floods and earthquakes; and the force response to the race riots in Tibet in 2008 were fast and proportional.

Chinese military thinkers have sketched out for themselves a road map over an extended period of time to achieve joint contingency capabilities.[126] David Finkelstein emphasizes that the PLA seeks to "field credible operational capabilities to deter aggression against . . . its [China's] interests (political or economic)," as well as to "support the diplomatic element of national power with real 'teeth'."[127] He seems to have called it right. Inside the CCP and the PLA, this "road map" is anchored in the military legacies of Deng Xiaoping and Jiang Zemin.[128] The PLA depends on observations of U.S.-led coalition operations in Kosovo, Afghanistan, and Iraq as models for how to employ precision weapons, sensors, and communications in joint operations.[129]

CMC and PLA leadership have set out a patient pathway of three phases or "three steps" (The Three-step Development Strategy, or 三步走的发展战略)[130] to greater military strength and operational effectiveness for the PLA stretching from the late 20th century to the mid-21st century.[131] The first phase is about over. This first phase was to take from 10-20 years and build a firm base of military technology and modernization. The second phase is to use another decade and, "according to China's national economic power," increase budgets and build a stronger military. Third, after "30 years or so of work," toward the middle of the 21st century, the PLA is to "complete the process of building a modern, strong military."[132]

In his report to the 17th CCP national congress, Hu underwrote the basic goal to "attain the strategic objective of building computerized armed forces and building and winning IT [information technology]-

based warfare."[133] Hu's speech reinforced the emphasis on methodically building a strong, modern armed force capable of defending China and its interests with technology and tactics supported by China's economy and level of economic development.

More recently, this "three-step approach" as the basic CCP line in military modernization was reaffirmed by Chen Zhou, a PLA strategist, in the Central Party School publication *Xuexi Shibao*. Chen characterized the steps as "laying a solid foundation by 2010, making major progress by 2020, and basically reaching the strategic goal of building an informatized army and becoming capable of winning informatized wars by the mid-21st century."[134]

This should tell us that we cannot expect to see dramatic changes in either the posture or the capabilities of the PLA to conduct joint contingency operations out of area, even in contiguous states, over the near term (say 5-10 years). Instead, observers will probably see an evolution of new operational doctrine and the equipment and forces to implement them over time. The challenge for U.S. policy makers will be to monitor these changes and improvements in capabilities while measuring the likely intent of Chinese decision-makers.

The basic "line" set by the CCP leadership is also important to understand. The PLA has been told to adopt a basically defensive military posture in the near term (10 years or so) while it develops a new range of capabilities in response to new missions. There is always an "internal line" and an "external line" in CCP guidance, but the external line is the one we see, and for now, the diplomacy and military actions are consistent with maintaining a "peaceful environment." What we do not see is how the highest levels of the CCP conceive

China and the PLA's posture later in the 21st century. In any case, this "defensive posture" has some active elements to it, and the PLA can be very prickly over some sensitive issues relating to sovereignty and air or naval activities.

Based on the texts in this chapter, the PLA seems to be aiming at a military force capable of:

- responding to domestic problems,
- securing China's sovereign territory,
- defending China's economic and political interests at long distances,
- patrolling vital sea lines of communication,
- denying potential adversaries the freedom to coerce China with impunity, and
- limiting proximity to the coast, from which potential adversaries can conduct strike operations against the Chinese mainland.

In one text exploring future operational concepts, Jiang Yamin, writing for the Academy of Military Science, argues that 600 years ago China had the strongest economy with the most powerful military in the world capable of conducting long-distance operations.[135] He laments that this capability deteriorated to the point that in 1840, "with only a few thousand troops," a successful invasion of China was mounted, illustrates the effectiveness of such operations.[136] Even though the general trend in the world is toward "peace and development," he argues, "the threat of warfare still exists" and China needs a strong military capable of operations across long distances as a means to deter others (literally, 止戈为武).[137]

There is one contingency area, however, that could lead to a PLA reaction in the maritime arena by naval forces, naval air, or long range air. The PLA (and probably the CMC and Foreign Ministry) are now allergic to attempts to stop and search or detain ships at sea. Although there has been considerable improvement in China's behavior with respect to actions to stop the proliferation of weapons of mass destruction (WMD), their technologies, and their delivery systems, Beijing has kept its distance from the Proliferation Security Initiative (PSI). The reluctance of China's foreign affairs and defense community to take an active role in the PSI may relate to China's experience with the U.S. Navy and Department of State during the Yinhe Incident in 1993.[138]

In a text written for the PLA National Defense University, *Guojia Haishang Liyi Lun (On Maritime National Interest)*, a PLA senior colonel complains bitterly about China's "embarrassment at the hands of the United States" during the Yinhe Incident.[139] According to Wang Lidong, the fact that a Chinese ship had to submit to boarding and search by the U.S. Navy, even after the PRC Foreign Ministry denied to the U.S. State Department that the Yinhe carried WMD chemical precursors, is "an example of [American] imperialism and power politics" (霸权主义和强权政治 的表现), the exact language used in the PRC Ministry of Foreign Affairs press statement on the incident in 1993.[140] Wang, writing in a text used to train senior PLA officers about to achieve (and of) flag rank, opines that U.S. actions demonstrate that China did not have the capacity to protect its own maritime interests at that time. In response, he advocates a stronger navy able to protect Chinese maritime interests at sea. If Wang Lidong's attitude represents the prevailing sentiment in the PLA and the CMC, it is unrealistic to expect China's cooperation in the PSI, which involves stopping ships of sovereign states for inspection.

With respect to Central Asia, the ground forces, air forces, and special operations forces that might respond to domestic contingencies in Xinjiang and Gansu are roughly the same ones that might be called on for any problems in the region. Of course, the CMC and the PBSC will have to weigh carefully Russian interests, and any Chinese joint contingency operations in Central Asia will be constrained by estimates of a Russian response. To handicap the likelihood of events:

- The PLA is more likely to be used with the cooperation and assent of the government of a Central Asian country to stabilize an area around an oil or gas field or pipeline;
- It is not likely that the PLA would be used to respond to cross-border terrorist camps without some assent from the other nation;
- If Chinese workers or diplomats were killed or kidnapped, PLA or Chinese security forces would probably seek to cooperate with the forces of the nation in which the event occurred; and,
- In the event of a complete collapse of order in a Central Asian nation that threatened Chinese economic or political interests, any response probably would be calibrated and carefully coordinated with Russia and the rest of the SCO.

In other words, while the PLA can bring a lot of operational capabilities to bear on events in Central Asia, the political climate in which it would have to operate seriously constrains its action.

In South Asia, the likelihood of joint contingency operations is higher and probably would involve ground forces, the People's Armed Police (PAP), the

PLA Air Force, the PLA Navy, and to some extent the Second Artillery Corps. Also, it is likely that the PLA Navy will be more active in the sea lines of communications from the Strait of Malacca through the Indian Ocean and to Pakistan, where Beijing has deep and historic interests. Certainly the possibility of contingency operations will increase with more port operations in Gwadar and the rail links being built. India here can be both an exacerbating factor and a constraint on any PLA reactions.

The Sino-Indian border is stable, but there is always some possibility, however low, of confrontation there. Such an event would probably involve the ground forces, the air forces, including long-range aviation, and the Second Artillery Corps.

Myanmar is becoming increasingly important from a diplomatic and economic standpoint to China. It will likely be one of the way points for PLA Navy task forces when they eventually venture out of the South China Sea and the Pacific if the PLA begins regular maritime patrols along sea lines of communication. The radar sites and listening posts in the bay off Myanmar are going to be areas of irritation for India. Thus any contingencies there would probably mean all the arms and services of the PLA would be involved.

To handicap the likelihood of contingency operations in South Asia:

- The PLA is more likely to be used in case of serious problems in Myanmar. China's port complex, its radar posts, and its road and rail links will increase in importance relative to China's national interests in the future.
- As the PLA Navy becomes more active and evolves into a regular presence in the Indian Ocean, the likelihood is higher that it could be used in disaster relief in Bangladesh.

- Over the course of the next decade, the PLA Navy will likely seek a presence in the Indian Ocean and the Bay of Bengal that will involve combined operations with other countries in South Asia.
- Renewed border conflict with India is less likely, but if such a conflict occurs, the PLA would use all its arms and services.[141]
- A serious collapse in Pakistan or a conflict between Pakistan and India would trigger a Chinese contingency reaction, even if China did not intervene.

In Northeast Asia, any contingencies involving North Korea will involve all the arms and services of the PLA. Also, here there are constraints from South Korea, Japan, and the United States, if not also Russia. Perhaps the most volatile issue, although limited in scope, will be competing maritime claims and how they sort out.

To handicap the likelihood of PLA contingency operations in Northeast Asia:
- The CMC, the GSD, and the PBSC would likely try to avoid involvement in a territorial dispute among North Korea, South Korea, and Japan; but the PLA might be used in a maritime or air presence role as well as for reconnaissance.
- The likelihood is high that in the event of a collapse in North Korea, the PLA would be used to stabilize the situation and even to restore control.
- The likelihood is high that the PLA would be used in the vicinity of the North Korea-China border in the event of instability in North Korea.

- There is a high likelihood that China would at least consult with, if not coordinate its actions with the United States and other countries in the region.[142]

Finally, over the next decade, it is likely that the PLA Navy will begin more regular maritime patrols. These will probably be of small scale, self-supporting, and they will probably use refueling and resupply points in places friendly to Beijing. But such operations will elicit a reaction from India, which in the same time frame may well begin its own regular maritime presence patrols. Such activities are not volatile, but they can add to the tensions in a region and create contingencies for the PLA Air Force and the Second Artillery Corps. Also, Japan may react to an increased Chinese maritime or air presence in the region.

There are policy implications for the United States from these possible outcomes. In Central Asia, U.S. military engagement, foreign assistance, and diplomacy are important to maintain influence. Also, it may be useful for the United States to become more involved in the SCO as a means of maintaining influence in the region.

In South Asia, relations with India and Pakistan are important means to remain engaged in the region. Military cooperation and arms sales should be part of any engagement program. Also, the rapid response by U.S. forces to the inevitable natural disasters and calamities that strike many of the countries in the region are an excellent way of keeping up good relations without forcing those countries to make "zero-sum" decisions on how they relate to China. Myanmar is a difficult situation, but here the United States can work through other allies such as Thailand or Japan to help balance Chinese influence.

In the case of North Korea, it is probably useful to continue bilateral discussions in addition to the six-party talks. China has influence, but American, Japanese, and South Korean actions must be designed against the backdrop of North Korea's ally that "will not allow" the country to collapse. Also, at the highest levels of security consultation, senior defense officials from the United States and China should at least make it clear that each side sees itself as having military stakes in resolving conflict on the Korean Peninsula. As for attempting to raise such issues as bilateral contingency planning, this writer believes such moves are premature and that, in any case, PLA leaders would resist such attempts if there is no burning need for them.

CHAPTER 10 - ENDNOTES

1. China's interests and approaches to the Korean peninsula are identified in Scott Snyder, *North Korea's Decline and China's Strategic Dilemmas,* USIP Special Report #27, Washington, DC: U.S. Institute for Peace, October 1997, *www.usip.org/pubs/specialreports/ealy/snyder/China-nk-pt1.html.* Snyder points out that Chinese scholars accept that the system in North Korea needs reform, that the PRC takes a pragmatic approach to the Peninsula, and that China's main goal is regional stability on the Peninsula. He makes much the same points in 2006 in a USIP publication, *www.usip.org/pubs/usipeace_briefings/2006/0517_six_party_talks.html.* On Central Asia and China's interests, see Nicklas Norling and Niklas Swanström, "The Shanghai Cooperation Organization, Trade and the Roles of Iran, India, and Pakistan, *Central Asian Survey,* Vol. 26, No. 3, September 2007, pp. 429-444; and Nicklas Norling and Nicklas Swanström, "The Virtues and Potential Gains of Continental Trade in Eurasia," *Asian Survey,* Vol. XKVII, No. 3, June 2007, pp. 351-373. On south Asia, see John W. Garver, *Protracted Contest: Sino-Indian Rivalry in the Twentieth Century,* Seattle: University of Washington Press, 2002; Swaran Singh, *China and South Asia: Issues, Equations and Policies,* New Delhi, India: Lancer Books, 2003; and Zhang Guihong, "Perceptions and Responses to the Rise of India: A View from China, *South Asian Studies in China,* 2003-14; October 9, 2008, *www.sasnet.cn/english/papers/papers.asp.* On the PLA, see Andrew Scobell, *China's Use of Military Force: Beyond the Great Wall and the Long March,* Cambridge: Cambridge University Press, 2003; Dennis Blasko, *The Chinese Army Today: Tradition and Transformation for the 21st Century,* New York: Routledge, 2006; and Xiaobing Li, *A History of the Modern Chinese Army,* Lexington: University of Kentucky Press, 2007.

2. These are two of the key missions set for the PLA in China's *2006 National Defense White Paper, www.china.org.cn/English/features/book/19485.htm.*

3. Liu Jingbo, ed., *21 Shiji Chu Zhongguo Guojia Anquan Zhanlue (Chinese National Security Strategy in the Early 21st Century),* Beijing, China: Shishi Chubanshe, 2006, pp. 200-202.

4. Ba Zhongtan, Fu Zhubian, Mi Zhenyu, and Wang Guozhong, *Zhongguo Guoji Anquan Zhanlue Wenti Yanjiu* (*Study of Issues on China's National Security Strategy*), Beijing, China: Junshi Kexue Chubanshe, 2003, pp. 143-146.

5. *Ibid.*, p. 150.

6. Daniel M. Hartnett, *Towards a Globally Focused Chinese Military: The 'Historic Missions' of the Chinese Armed Forces,"* CME D0018304.A1, Alexandria, VA: CNA Corporation, June 2008, p. 1. This was published as Open Source Center (hereafter OSC) CPP2008060632500, June 6, 2008.

7. "CMC's Guo Boxiong Urges Improving PLA Capabilities to "Fulfill Historic Missions," *Beijing Xinhua Domestic Service,* 1555GMT 27 Sep 05, in OSC CPP 20050927320021 (also cited in Hartnett, *Towards a Globally Focused Chinese Military,* p. 3).

8. Hartnett, *Towards a Globally Focused Chinese Military,* pp. 1, 10-12.

9. Wang Lidong, *Guojia Haishang Liyi Lun* (*A Discussion of China's National Maritime Interests*), Beijing, China: Guofang Daxue Chubanshe, 2007, p. 248. See also Ba *et. al, Zhongguo Guoji Anquan Zhanlue Wenti Yanjiu,* pp, 29-51, 128-161. Hang Wuchao makes essentially the same point in Han Wuchao, "Shixi Guojia Liyi yu Zhanlue Fangxiang" ("Analysis of National Interests and Strategic Orientation"), *Zhongguo Junshi Kexue* (*China Military Science*), Vol. 20, No. 1, 2007, pp. 84-90.

10. On the need to develop the capacity to secure China's interests abroad, see Jiang Yamin, *Yuan Zhan* (*Long Distance Operations*), Beijing, China: Academy of Military Science Press, 2007.

11. *Ibid.*, p. 231.

12. Han Wuchao, "Shixi Guojia Liyi yu Zhanlue Fangxiang," p. 90.

13. Yan Xuetong and Jin Deying, *Dongya Heping yu Anquan*

(*Peace and Security in East Asia*), Beijing, China: Shishi Chubanshe, 2005, pp. 117-126, 163-172; Zhu Tingzhang, *Zhongguo Zhoubian Anquan Huanjing yu Zhanlue* (*China's Peripheral Security Environment and Strategies*), Beijing, China: Shishi Chubanshe, 2002, 507-516; Guo Xuetang, "Zhong-Ou-Ya Diqu de Nengyuan yu Diyu Zhengzhi" ("Energy and Geopolitics in Central-Eurasia", *Zhongguo Junshi Kexue* (*China Military Science*), Vol. 19, No. 3, 2006, pp. 74-80.

14. Wang, *Guojia Haishang Liyi Lun*, p. 260.

15. *Ibid.*, p. 261.

16. Jiang Yamin, *Yuan Zhan* (*Long Distance Operations*), Beijing, China: Junshi Kexue Chubanshe, 2007, pp. 231-232.

17. John Wu and Andrei Chang, "PLA Navy's Future Aircraft Carriers," *Kanwa Intelligence Review*, August 21, 2008, accessed through *Nexis, www.kanwa.com/defr/*. The Kanwa authors believe that the PLA Navy has ordered four sets of arresting hooks for aircraft carrier operations from Russia. Also see Manu Pubby, "China Works on Matching India's Naval Fleet; China to have First Aircraft Carriers for Training by 2012," *Indian Express Online*, August 27, 2008, OSC FEA20080827760397. It is not clear if the Indian article is based on Kanwa's publication and is "circular reporting," but both predict that the *Varyag will* be the refitted training carrier for the PLA Navy.

18. Li Jie, "China to Build Aircraft Carrier in Light of Own Strategic Needs," *People's Daily Online*, April 25, 2007, in OSC CPP20070425701008.

19. Wang, *Guojia Haishang Liyi Lun*, p. 248; see also Yang Mingshu, *Haishang Tongdao Anquan yu Guoji Hezuo* (*Sea Land Security and International Cooperation*), Beijing, China: Shishi Chunbanshe, 2005, pp. 5-7, 357-376; Zheng Shenxia, "*Zhongguo Heping Fazhen yu Yatai Diqu Anquan*" ("Peace and Development in China and Asia-Pacific Security"), *Zhongguo Junshi Kexue* (*China Military Science*), Vol. 20, No. 1, 2007, pp. 1-4.

20. Zheng Shenxia, "*Zhongguo Heping Fazhen yu Yatai Diqu Anquan*" ("Peace and Development in China and Asia-Pacific Security"), *Zhongguo Junshi Kexue* (*China Military Science*), Vol. 20,

No. 1, 2007, pp. 1-4.

21. Discussion between the author and PLA officers in May 2004 and August 2005 in Beijing, China.

22. Discussion with Zheng Bijian on August 23, 2005, in Beijing, China.

23. Larry Wortzel, "China's Peaceful Rise," *The Asian Wall Street Journal,* September 5, 2005, p. A9.

24. "Afghanistan: China's Winning Bid for Copper Rights," *Radio Free Europe,* November 24, 0227, accessed through *Nexis;* Thomas Fuller, "Asia Builds New Road to Prosperity," *International Herald Tribune,* March 31, 2008, p. 1; "Construction of GMS Sectional Highway Begins in Myanmar," *Xinhua News Service,* April 1, 2008, *Nexis;* "Burmese Writer Says China's Procurement of Shwe Gas Part of Wider Scheme," *BBC,* January 17, 2008, accessed through *Nexis;* " Work on Missing Link Between Poipet and Sisophon to Start in 1st Quarter," *Malaysia Economic News,* January 17, 2008, accessed through *Nexis; Joshua Kucera, "Central Asia: A Vision for a Regional Transport Network Takes Shape," Eurasianet,* January 14, 2008, accessed through *Nexis;* "China Plans Rail Link to Central Asia," *The Times of Central Asia,* February 1, 2008, *Nexis;* ""Gwadar Deep Sea Port Operations," *Riyadh SPA,* March 15, 2008, *www.spa .gov.sa;* "Pakistan Moves to Finalize Rail Link with China, *The Press Trust of India,* April 22, 2008, *Nexis;* "CNPC Secures PetroKazakhstan Bid," *BBC News,* October 26, 2005, *news.bbc.co.uk/2/hi/business/437829.stm,* accessed April 27, 2008; "Oil Development Deal Struck with North Korea," *Los Angeles Times,* December 25, 2005, *Nexis;* "A Ravenous Dragon, Special Report on China's Quest for Resources," *The Economist,"* March 15, 2008, pp. 1-22; *China's Foreign Policy and "Soft Power" in South American, Asia, and Africa,* S. PRT. 110-46, A Study Prepared for the Committee on Foreign Relations of the U.S. Senate, Washington, DC:U.S. Government Printing Office, April 2008.

25. Stockholm International Peace Research Institute (SIPRI), SIPRI Arms Transfers Database, China Arms Transfers 2006-2007, *www.armstrade.sipri.org.*

26. Ba *et. al, Zhongguo Guoji Anquan Zhanlue Wenti Yanjiu,* pp.

137-138.

27. Ding Hao and Han Wei, "Cong Zhimindi Zouxiang Daguo de Jueqi Zhi Lu: Indu Guojia Anquan Zhanlue Xuanze" ("Road from a Former Colony to the Rise of a World Power: Strategic Choices of Indian National Security"), *Zhongguo Junshi Kexue* (*China Military Science*), Vol. 20, No. 3, pp. 82-83.

28. "*Nanfang Zhoumo* Cites PRC Experts on Prospects in Sino-India Relations," OSC, CPP20080118530006 in Guangzhou *Nanfang Zhoumo* (Internet Version-WWW) in Chinese, January 17, 2008.

29. Pravin Sawhney, "On the China Front; Only the Indian Air Force Can Provide Dissuasive Deterrence," *Force,* October 13, 2008, *www.forceindia.net/cover1.asp*; Gurmeet Kanwal, "India-China Territorial Dispute: More Heat than Light," *Vayu Aerospace and Defense Review,* May 1-June 30, 2008, p. 76, in OSC SAP20080715524008; see also "Fly Navy – The Chinese Way," *Vayu Aerospace and Defense Review,* May 1–June 30, 2008, pp. 68-70, in OSC SAP20080715524006; Andrei Chang, "India's Build-up of Air Power in the East," *UPI Asia Online, www.upiasiaonline.com/ Security/2008/08/20/indias_build-up_of_air_power_in_the_east/8060/*.

30. *Kanwa Intelligence Review,* "Kanwa: China Reinforces Nuclear, Conventional Deterrence Against India," OSC CPP20080623715012.

31. The author is grateful to Dennis Blasko for this insight.

32. Sudha Ramachandran, "India Takes the High Ground Against China," *The Asia Times,* June 14, 2008, *www.atimes.com/ atimes/South_Asia/JF14Df02.html*.

33. Gavin Rabinowitz, "India, China Jostle for Influence in Indian Ocean," *The Associated Press,* June 8, 2008, *Lexis.*

34. *Ibid.*

35. "India to Get Network Centric Warfare Capability by 2010-11, Saws Defense Chief," *Doordarshan News Online,* August 17, 2008, *www.ddines.gov.in*, in OSC SAP 200817384009.

36. "India's Eastward Movements and its Impact on China's Defense Strategy on the Western Front," *Kanwa Asian Defense Review,* July 8, 2008, accessed by *Nexis.*

37. Li Donghang and Jiang Xinghua, "Expert Comments on Sino-Indian Joint Anti-Terrorism Exercise," *Jiefangjun Bao,* in OSC CPP20071226704001, December 26, 2007, p. 6.

38. Yu Li, "A Partnership Between the Dragon and the Elephant that Transcends the Himalayas," *Nanfang Zhoumo, ,* OSC CPP 20080118530006 January 17, 2008. See also Chen Ruisheng, Zheng Ruixiang, and Ma Jiali, "The Sino-Indian Border Issue Has Seen Progress But no Breakthroughs—Experts Analyze the Significance of Singh's Visit to China and the Hot Issues in Sino-Indian Relations," *Nanfang Zhoumo,* January 19, 2008, in OSC CPP200801222530005. The Chen, Zheng, and Ma piece says that "it must be said that the likelihood of conflict erupting is minimal."

39. One observer opined that this silence is a result of a policy decision by the CCP Propaganda Department, putting negative articles on Sino-Indian relations off limits for Chinese commentators. There has been no independent confirmation of such a policy. However, the CCP Propaganda Department has shown that it will black out topics, as it did with the journal article on North Korea. See Wang Zhongwen, "Yi Xin Shijiao Shenshi Chaoxian Wenti Yu Dongbeiya Xingshi" ("Examining the DPRK Issue and Northeast Asian Situation from a New Viewpoint"), Beijing, China, *Zhanlue Yu Guanli (Strategy and Management),* Issue 4, July-August 2004, pp. 92-94, which it removed from the web site of the journal (see the discussion later in this chapter).

40. Wang Wei, "The Trend of Development of All-Around Cooperation Between China and South Asia," *Wen Wei Pao,* OSC CPP20080423710012, April 23, 2008.

41. Harsh V. Pant, "China, India: Back to the Boundary," *ISN Security Watch,* June 16, 2008, *Lexis.*

42. "Afghanistan: China's Winning bid for Copper Includes Power Plant, Railroad," *Radio Free Asia,* November 24, 2007, *Nexis.* The author notes that Afghanistan is one of the countries

classified by the United Nations as part of "Southern Asia," and that one could call it southwest Asia or part of Central Asia. For the purposes of this chapter, suffice it to say this landlocked country is in a transition zone.

43. "Gwadar Deep Sea Port Operates, *Riyadh SPA*," March 15, 2008, *www.spa.sa*, *Nexis*.

44. "Pakistan Moves to Finalize Rail Link with China," *The Press Trusts of India*, April 22, 2007, *Nexis*.

45. "Pakistan Signs Contract with Chinese Firm for Power Project," *The Economic Times*, April 1, 2008, *economictimes. indiatimes.com/news/News_by_industry/energy/pak_signs_contract_ with_Chines_firm_fror_power_ Project/articlesshow/2917816.cms*. "Pakistan, China Discussing 2nd Nuclear Power Plant," *Kyodo News International*, August 12, 2002, *findarticles.com/p/articles/ mim0WDQ/is_2002_August_12/ai_90297109*.

46. See *economictimes.indiatimes.com/News.News_by-industry/ Energy/Pak_signes_contract-with_Chinese_firm_for_power_project/ articleshow/2917816.cms*, accessed April 1, 2008.

47. See *www.bangladeshenergy.com*, April 4, 2008.

48. *Ibid.*

49. Thomas Fuller, "Asia Builds New Road to Prosperity," *The International Herald Tribune*, March 31, 2008, *Nexis*.

50. "China Signs Exploration Deals with Myanmar," *UPI Energy*, January 15, 2008, *Nexis*; "China-Myanmar Pipeline Still Under Discussion," *Xinhua News Agency*, March 10, 2008, *news. xinhuanet.com/english/2008-03/10/content_7756822.htm*, accessed March 12, 2008; "Burmese Writer Says China's Procurement of Shwe Gas Part of Wider Scheme," *BBC*, January 7, 2008, *Nexis*.

51. "China-Myanmar Oil Pipeline Construction to Begin this Year, Extends to Chongqing," *Xinhua Financial News*, March 26, 2007, *Nexis*; "Work on Missing Link Between Sisophon to Start in Q:1," *Malaysia Economic News*, January 17, 2008, *Nexis*.

52. "China and India Battle for Myanmar's Gas," *Petroleum Economist,* May 2006, *www.petroleumeconomist.com,* January 17, 2008.

53. Unless otherwise noted, all of the military sales and deliveries in this section are from SIPRI, SIPRI Arms Transfers Database, China Arms Transfers 2006-7, *www.armstrade.sipri.org.*

54. "Procurement Myanmar" and "Navy, Myanmar," *Jane's,* April 28, 2008, *www9.janes.com/search/documentView. do?docID+/content1/janesdata/sent/seasu/myans150.htm@ current&pageSelected+allJanes@keyword+myanmar&backPath+http:// search.janes.com/search.janes.com/search&prod_Name-SEAS&.*

55. Chang. See also Cheng Feng and Larry M. Wortzel, "PLA Operational Principles and Limited War: The Sino-Indian War of 1962," in Mark A. Ryan, David M. Finkelstein, and Michael A. McDevitt, eds., *Chinese Warfighting: The PLA Experience Since 1949,* Armonk, NY: M. E. Sharpe, 2002, pp. 173-197, especially the map on p. 175.

56. "Advantage China," *Force,* May 1, 2008, in OSC SAP20080513342005. This New Delhi journal gives no attribution for the article.

57. *Ibid.*

58. SIPRI Arms Transfers Database, China Arms transfers 2006-7, *armstrade.sipri.org.*

59. You Ji, "Dealing with the Malacca Dilemma: China's Effort to Protect its Energy Supply," *Strategic Analysis,* Vol. 31, No. 3, May 1-June 30, 2007, pp. 467-489, in OSC SAP20080506524003.

60. David Blair, "India Targeting China's Oil Supplies," *UK Telegraph,* September 15, 2008, *www.telegraph.co.uk/news/2957578/ India-targeting-Chinas-oil-supplies.html.*

61. *Ibid.*

62. You Ji, "Dealing with the Malacca Dilemma." You Ji

quotes from a text by Liu Yijian, *Zhihaiquan yu Haijun Zhanlue* (*The Control of the Sea and Maritime Strategy*), Beijing, China: Guofang Daxue Chubanshe, 2004, p. 233.

63. You.

64. See E-Kantipur (I/EK), *www.kantipuronline.com*, Nepal, August 23-24, 2008.

65. Stephen Blank, "The Strategic Importance of Central Asia: An American View," *Parameters,* Spring 2008, p. 75.

66. OSC, *Central Eurasia Daily Report,* CEP-99, January 2, 2004.

67. OSC, *Central Eurasia Daily Report,* CEP-950492, February 6, 2008; Elena Sadovskaya, "Chinese Migration to Kazakhstan," *China and Eurasia Forum Quarterly,* Vol. 5, No. 4, Winter 2007, pp. 147-170.

68. *Ibid.,* p. 78.

69. See the SCO website, *www.sectsco.org/html/00088.html.*

70. "Russia: Air Force CiC [Aleksandr] Zelin Discusses Current Air Force, Joint Air Defense Issues," *Voyenno-Promyshlennyy Kuryer,* in OSC CEP20080818548010, August 13, 2008.

71. *Ibid.*

72. "A Thin Bowl of Alphabet Soup," *The Economist,* August 9, 2008, pp. 55-56.

73. See James Bellacqua, *Terrorism in China: Perceptions of Vulnerability, Countermeasures,* Alexandria, VA: The CNA Corporation, July 2008, in OSC FEA 20080807746951, August 7, 2008, *https://www.opensource.gov/portal/server. pt/gateway/PTARGS_0_0_200_240_1019_43/http%3B/apps. opensource.gov%3B7011/opensource.gov/content/Display/9477907/ CPP20080807507001001.pdf.*

74. "China, Russia: Wrangling Over the Future of the Shanghai Cooperation Organization," *Stratfor Today,* July 25, 2008, accessed through *Nexis.*

75. Wei Wei, "PRC officer Interviewed on 'Peace Mission 2007'; Explains 'Four Key Words'," *Jiefangjun Bao* in OSC CPP20070719710014, July 19, 2007, p. 5.

76. "PRC FM Relevant Responsible Person Briefs Press on Hu Jintao's Three-Nation Trip," *Xinhua Domestic Service,* in OSC CPP20080820172010, 1302 GMT, August 20, 2008.

77. Kou Zhong, "Zhongya Yunqi Guandao Jianshe de Beijing ji Yiyi" ("Background and Perspectives on the Construction of Gas Pipelines in Central Asia"), *Guoji Shiyou Jingji (International Petroleum Economics),* Vol. 16, No. 2, 2008, *www.cnki.net,* June 20, 2008.

78. Pu Xiaogang and Li Xiaoman, "Zhongya Nengyuan zhi Zheng yu Wo Guo Nengyuan Anquan Wenti *Fenxi*" ("On the Central Asia Energy Struggle and China's Energy Security"), *Wulumuqi Zhiye Daxue Xuebao (Journal of the Urumqi Vocational College),* No. 4, 2007, pp. 17-20, accessed through *www.cnki.net,* June 20, 2008.

79. Russel Ong, "China's Security Interests in Central Asia," *Central Asian Survey,* Vol. 24, No. 4, December 2005, pp. 425-439.

80. Guo Xuetang, "The Energy Security in Central Eurasia: the Geopolitical Implications to China's Energy Strategy," *China and Eurasia Forum Quarterly,* Vol. 4, No. 4, 2006, pp. 117-137. The quotes are from page 135.

81. *Ibid.,* p. 135.

82. Joshua Kucera, "Central Asia: A Vision for a Regional Transport Network Takes Shape," *Eurasianet,* January 14, 2008, accessed through *Nexis.*

83. "China Plans Rail Link to Central Asia," *The Times of Central Asia,* February 1, 2008, *Nexis.*

84. *Ibid.*

85. "Kyrgyzstan to Join Transcontinental Transport Corridors," *The Times of Central Asia,* January 19, 2008, *Nexis.*

86. China Secures PetroKazakhstan Bid," *BBC News,* October 26, 2008, *news.bbc.co.uk/2/hi/asia-pacific/6935292.htm,* and "China to Build Second Oil Pipeline in Kazakhstan," *Comtex News Network, Inc.,* August 23, 2007, *Nexis.*

87. "China Prepared to Invest in Kyrgyzstan's Power Sector," *RIA Novosti,* August 2, 2006, *Nexis.*

88. "China Signs Agreement to Buy Turkmenistan Gas, Build Pipeline," *AP Financial Wire,* April 3, 2006, *Nexis.*

89. "China's CNPC Unit in 210 Million Dollar Uzbekistan Oil and Gas Deal," *Agence France Press,* June 15, 2006, *Nexis.* "Uzbekistan, China Sign Major Gas Pipeline Deal," *China Business News,* Hong Kong Trade and Development Council, May 2, 2007, *sme.tdctrade.com/content.aspx?data+emergingMkt_content_en&contentid+867436&src+BNT_OtherEastEur&w_sid+194&w_cid+867435&w_idt+1900-01-01&w_oid+343&w_jid=.*

90. Zhang Yingxiang, "Choppers Acquire Transport and Attack Capabilities," *Jiefangjun Bao Online*, OSC CPP20080812702008, August 11, 2008.

91. Willy Lam, "Harsh Chinese Crackdown Coming in Xinjiang," *The Asia Sentinel,* August 22, 2008, accessed through *Nexis;* Antoaneta Bezlova, "China's Tough Xinjiang Policy Backfires," *The Asia Times,* August 15, 2008, *www.atimes.com/atimes/China/JH15Ad01.html.*

92. Western Returned Scholars Association (WRSA), *The Unforgotten Korean War – Chinese Perspective and Appraisals,* Beijing, China: Unpublished Manuscript, WRSA, August 15, 2007, p. 7.

93. *Ibid.,* p. 31.

94. Jayshreee Bajoria, "The China-North Korea Border Relationship," *Council on Foreign Relations Backgrounder,* June 18,

2008, *www://cfr.org/publication.11097/chinanorth_korea_relatoinship. html*.

95. *Ibid*. Shen Dingli made similar statements to this author in an interview in June 2006 in Shanghai, China.

96. Shen, June 2006.

97. Roundtable at Fudan University between U.S. congressional advisers and faculty of Fudan University on June 24, 2006.

98. International Crisis Group (ICG), *China and North Korea: Comrades Forever?* Asia Report No. 112, February 1, 2006, pp. I, 6-9, *www.crisisgroup.org/home/index.cfm?id=3920*.

99. Fudan University, June 24, 2006.

100. Meetings with staff from the Academy of Military Science, China Institute of International Studies and China Institute of Contemporary International Relations, 2007 and 2008, in Beijing, China.

101. Cheng Shaohai, "Chaoxian Bandao He Wenti yu Dongbei Ya Anquan" ("The North Korean Nuclear Question and Northeast Asian Security"), *Heping yu Fazhan* (*Peace and Development*), No. 2, 2004, p. 23.

102. ICG, "China and North Korea."

103. "North Korea to Head Agenda at China-South Korea Summit," *Agence France Press,* August 21, 2008, in *www.spacewar. com/2006/080821063615.jp8ho6kf.html*, August 22, 2008.

104. *Ibid*.

105. Jayshee Bajoria, "The China-North Korea Relationship," *Council on Foreign Relations Backgrounder,* July 2, 2008 (updated July 18, 2008), *www.cfr.org/publication/11097/chinanorth_korea_ relationship.html*.

106. Zhang Wenling, "Constructing China's New Relations with Neighboring Countries," *Dangdai Yatai,* November 1, 2007,

pp. 3-11, in OSC "PRC Scholar Discusses Issues in China's Relations with Neighboring Countries," OSC CPP20080201590002.

107. *Ibid.*

108. Yoichi Funabashi, *The Peninsula Question: A Chronicle of the Second Korea Nuclear Crisis,* Washington, DC: The Brookings Institution Press, 2007, pp. 295-296, 323-324.

109. Charles L. Pritchard, *Failed Diplomacy: The Tragic Story of How North Korea Got the Bomb,* Washington, DC: The Brookings Institution, 2007, pp. 112-113.

110. Park Hee Kwon, *The Law of the Sea and Northeast Asia: A Challenge for Cooperation,* New York and Dordrecht: Kleuwer Law International, 2000, pp. 84-89. Also see Choe Sang-Hun, "Desolate Dots in the Sea stir Deep Emotions as South Korea Resists a Japanese Claim," *The New York Times,* August 31, 2008, *www.nytimes.com/2008/08/31/world/asia/31islands.html?th&emc=th.*

111. Interview with Member of the National Assembly of Korea, July 2, 2008, Washington, DC.

112. See *www.mofa.go.jp/region/asia-paci/takeshima/position.html.*

113. "Oil Development Deal Struck with North Korea," *Los Angeles Times,* December 25, 2005, *Nexis,* July 17, 2008.

114. See for example See Liu Jingbo, *21 Shijichu Zhongguo Guojia Anquan Zhanlue,* Zheng Shenxia and Liu Yuan, eds., *Guofang he Jundui Jianshe Guanshe Luoshi Kexue Fazhan Guan Xuexi Tiyao.*

115. Yang Yi, Liu Jianyong, Ma Junwci, and Wu Baiyi, "Shei Zai Weishe Dong Bei Ya Anquan?" ("Who is threatening Northeast Asia Security?"), *Guoji Zhishi (International Knowledge),* No. 4, 2004, p. 21. See also Yu Yingli, "Chao He Wenti yu dong Bei Ya Anquan Hezuo" ("The North Korea Problem and Northeast Asian Security"), *Guoji Guancha (International Review),* No. 6, 2004, pp. 34-39.

116. *China's National Defense in 2006,* Information Office of the State Council White Paper, December 29, 2006, Section I.

117. Meetings in Beijing, China, June 18-20, 2006.

118. Meetings between the author and Chinese scholars at the Shanghai Institute for International Studies in Shanghai, China, June 23, 2006.

119. Meetings in Beijing, China, April 22-23, 2007.

120. Meeting in Virginia, August 25, 2007.

121. Wang Zhongwen, "Yi Xin Shijiao Shenshi Chaoxian Wenti Yu Dongbeiya Xingshi" ("Examining the DPRK Issue and Northeast Asian Situation from a New Viewpoint"), *Zhanlue Yu Guanli* (*Strategy and Management*), Issue Four, July-August, 2004, pp. 92-94. The author thanks John Tkacik of The Heritage Foundation, for help in locating a copy of the article.

122. Xue Li, "A Comprehensive Strategic Framework for China's Response to the DPRK Issue," *Zhongguo Pinglun* (*China Critique*), No. 1, in OSC CPP20070201329001, February 2007.

123. Larry M. Wortzel, "PLA Command, Control, and Targeting Architectures: Theory, Doctrine, and Warfighting Applications," in Roy Kamphausen and Andrew Scobell, *Right-Sizing the People's Liberation Army: Exploring the Contours of China's Military,* Carlisle, PA: Strategic Studies Institute, U.S. Army War College, 2007, pp. 191-234. This entire book covers facets of the issue.

124. Dennis J. Blasko, *The Chinese Army Today: Tradition and Transformation for the 21st Century,* New York: Routledge, Taylor and Francis, pp. 146-151.

125. Wortzel.

126. See David M. Finkelstein, "China's National Military Strategy: An Overview of the 'Military Strategic Guidelines'," in Kamphausen and Scobell, eds., *Right-Sizing the People's Liberation Army,* pp. 69-140.

127. *Ibid.*, p. 131.

128. Zhang Yining *et al.*, eds., *Zhongguo Xiandai Junshi Sixiang Yanjiu (Research on Contemporary Chinese Military Thought)*, Beijing, China, Guofang Daxue Chubanshe, 2006. Also see Jun Li, "Dang de Junshi Zhidao Lilun de Xin Fazhan" ("New Development in the Party's Military Guidance Theory — A Study of Jiang Zemin's National Defense and Army Building Theory"), *Zhongguo Junshi Kexue (China Military Science)*, Vol. 16, No. 1, January 2003, pp. 42-49.

129. *Ibid.*, pp. 575-576. See also, Pan Shouyong, "Tuijin Xunlian Zhuanbian yu Jinjin Niu Zhu Lianhe Xunlian" ("Promoting Training Transformation by Intensively Tackling Joint Training"), *Jiefang Jun Bao,* April 15, 2006, p. 6, in OSC *CPP20080506436003001. pdf.* Pan makes it clear that he also sees Kosovo, Afghanistan, and Iraq as models for joint contingency operations.

130. Zhang Yining takes some of this from Jiang Zemin, *Jiang Zemin Wenxuan (Selected Works of Jiang Zemin)*, Beijing, China: Renmin Chubanshe, 2006, pp. 162, 563. See Zhang *et al.*, *Zhongguo Xiandai Junshi Sixiang Yanjiu*, p. 580.

131. Zhang *et al.*, *Zhongguo Xiandai Junshi Sixiang Yanjiu*, p. 581.

132. *Ibid.*, p. 581-582.

133. Hu Jintao, "Hold High the Great Banner of Socialism with Chinese Characteristics and Strive for New Victories in Building a Moderately Prosperous Society in all Respects," Report to the Seventeenth National Congress of the Communist Party of China, *Xinhua News Agency, news.xinhuanet.com/english/2007-10/24/ content_6938749.htm*, accessed August 3, 2008.

134. Chen Zhou, "Xin Shiqi de Jiji Fangyu Junshi Zhanlue A Strategy of Active Defense for the New Period," *Xuexi Shibao*, No. 1, August 18, 2008, *www.studytimes.com.cn*, in OSC *CPP20080818436001001.pdf.*

135. Jiang Yamin, 远战 (*Long-Distance Operations*), Beijing, China: Junshi Kexue Chubanshe, 2007, pp. i, iii.

136. *Ibid.*, p. ii.

137. This means to stop "the dagger-axe" [war] by being ready for war [building a strong military]. *Ibid.*, pp. i, iii.

138. Between August 26 and September 4, 1993, the U.S. Navy shadowed the Chinese Ship *Yin He* while U.S. intelligence insisted it was carrying banned chemical materials. Eventually the ship was searched in Saudi Arabia at U.S. insistence. See *Statement by the Ministry of Foreign Affairs of the People's Republic of China on the "Yin He" Incident,* September 4, 1993, *www.nti.org/db/china/engdocs/ynhe0993.htm,* September 12, 2008.

139. Wang Lidong, *Guojia Haishang Liyi Lun* (*On Maritime National Interest*), Beijing, China: Guofang Daxue Chubanshe, 2007, pp. 262-263.

140. *Statement by the PRC Ministry of Foreign Affairs,* September 4, 1993, p. 2.

141. It is important to remember that even in contingencies on land, the PLA Navy has been called upon to help with medical, logistics, and C4ISR assistance to the General Department of the PLA. This was the case even in the response to the earthquake in Mianyang, Chengdu Province, where, on the surface, it seems unlikely the Navy would be involved. See "PRC: Selected Articles from Navy Command Academy Seminar on Earthquake Relief," *Renmin Haijun* (*People's Navy*), July 21, 2008, p. 3, in OSC CPP20080826478007.

142. Note the coordination between Washington and Pyongyang in the wake of Kim Jong-Il's stroke. Phillip Sherwood and Stanislav Varivoda, "US and China in Secret Talks on N Korea Chaos Fears After Kim Jong-il Stroke," *UK Telegraph,* September 13, 2008, *www.telegraph.co.uk/news/worldnews/asia/northkorea/2909511,* accessed September 15, 2008.

APPENDIX I
CHINESE FOREIGN INFRASTRUCTURE
PROJECTS

Partnering Country	Type of Project	Details	Time Started/ Completed	Source
Afghanistan	Railroad	In 2007, China Metallurgical Group received rights to a large copper field south of Kabul in exchange for a large sum of investment including the construction of Afghanistan's first freight railroad. Total investment will amount to $2.8bn.	Completion expected in 2013, started in 2007.	Afghanistan: China's Winning Bid For Copper Rights Includes Power Plant, Railroad," *Radio Free Europe*, 24 November 2007, *Nexis*.
Burma	Road	Recently completed refurbishing Route 3, running from Kunming to Bangkok. Financed much of refurbishing in northern Burma, including Burma Road.	Completed March 2008.	Thomas Fuller, "Asia Builds New Road to Prosperity," *The International Herald Tribune*, 31 March 2008, p.1, *Nexis*.
Burma	Road	New section of the East-West Economic Corridor, which will stretch 22 km in Burma. The whole corridor will link South China Sea to Bay of Bengal, where China is attempting to build a port. It is also expected to link Europe to China through Central Asia. Part of Greater Mekong Subregion Economic Cooperation Program.	Entire project expected to be completed by 2010.	"Construction of GMS Sectional Highway begins in Myanmar," *Xinhua*, 1 April 2008, *opensource*.
Burma	Port	China is seeking to build a container port in Bhamo of Kachin State, which is Burma's nearest port to Yunnan province.	N/A.	Thet Khaing, "Burma Export Says China, India Keen to Invest to Develop Border Regions," *The Myanmar Times*, 9 April 2007, *Nexis*.
Burma	Port	Chinese media report on progress of port projects at Bay of Bengal in Mawlamyine as well as Andaman Sea, but witnesses say little progress has been made.	Unclear.	"Construction of GMS Sectional Highway begins in Myanmar," *Xinhua*, 1 April 2008, *open source*; also, "Burma Port Projects Said at Standstill," *BBC*, 9 August 2007, *Nexis*.
Burma	Port	Planning on creating a new port at Kyauk Phyu on Ramree Island, which would serve as a transfer point for oil and shift use away from the older Sittwe port, into which India has recently invested $100m.	Unclear.	Burmese Writer Says China's Procurement of Shwe Gas Part of Wider Scheme," *BBC*, January 7, 2008, *Nexis*.

Burma (and SE Asia)	Railroad	The Singapore-Kunming railroad will include 5,513 km of rail and will begin in Singapore and pass through Malaysia, Thailand, Cambodia, Burma, Laos, Vietnam, and end in Kunming in Yunnan province. It is part of the Trans-Asian railway to connect Asia with Europe. Total cost is expected to be $2bn.	First proposed at Bangkok ASEAN summit in 1995; expected completion by 2015.	"Work on Missing Link Between Poipet-Sisophon to Start in Q1:Chan," *Malaysia Economic News*, January 17, 2008, *Nexis*.
Central Asia (CAREC)	Transportation Corridors	In January 2008, CAREC, which China helps fund, announced a 10-year, $18.7 bn project to construct five new corridors, including connecting Kazakhstan to Xinjiang; an essential restoration of the silk road (Baku to Turkmenistan to Tajikistan to Kyrgyzstan to Xinjiang); Siberia into China through Mongolia; Siberia to Iran to eastern Kazakhstan, then splitting to Uzbekistan/ Turkmenistan and Kyrgyzstan/ Tajikistan/ Afghanistan; Pakistan to China through Afghanistan and Tajikistan.	10 year project to be completed in 2018.	Joshua Kucera, "Central Asia: A Vision for a Regional Transport Network Takes Shape," *Eurasianet*, January 14, 2008, *Nexis*.
Central Asia	Railroad	China-Kyrgyzstan-Uzbekistan railway which begins in Kashgar, Xinjiang.	Preparatory work began in 2008; completion in 2010.	"China Plans Rail Link to Central Asia," *The Times of Central Asia*, February 1, 2008, *Nexis*.
Kazakhstan	Railroad	Building a 6.2 billion yuan ($861m) railroad connecting Korgas (China-Kazakh border city) to inland Chinese railroads.	Expected to be completed in 2008.	"China Plans Rail Link to Central Asia," *The Times of Central Asia*, February 1, 2008, *Nexis*.
Kyrgyzstan	Road/Railroad	Through the Central Asian Regional Economic Cooperation (CAREC) program, China will assist 11 infrastructure projects in Kyrgyzstan, including a highway that connects Kyrgyzstan with China and Uzbekistan as well as Kyrgyzstan-Uzbekistan-China railroad. Total cost of the 11 projects is $1 6.	Began in 2008; Completion expected in 2018.	"Kyrgyzstan to Join Transcontinental Transport Corridors," *The Times of Central Asia*, January 19, 2008, *Nexis*.
Pakistan	Port	Deep sea port in the southern town of Gwadar, in Pakistan's Balochistan province. Cost $250 million, unclear how much paid for by China.	Became operational in March 2008.	Gwadar Deep Sea Port Operates, Riyadh SPA, March 15, 2008, *www.spa.gov. sa,opensource*.

380

Pakistan	Railroad	As of April 2007, China and Pakistan were in the final stages of planning rail linkages between Pakistan and Xinjiang in China's NW. No information was obtainable as to the results of those plans.	Unclear.	"Pakistan Moves to Finalize Rail Link with China," *The Press Trust of India*, April 22, 2007, *Nexis*.
Bangladesh	Coal Mine	In June 2005, the China National Machinery Import and Export Corporation joined forces with Xuzhou Coal Mining Group Company Ltd. and signed a contract to control the management and production of the Barapukuria mine in Bangladesh.	Unclear.	Found on main page of Bangladesh Energy website, www.bangladeshenergy.com, Accessed April 4, 2008.
Bangladesh	Nuclear Cooperation	In April 2005, an agreement was signed between China and Bangladesh on "nuclear cooperation." In this agreement, China will assist Bangladesh in exploration for nuclear material as well construction of a 600-MW nuclear power plant.	Unclear.	Found on main page of Bangladesh Energy website, *www.bangladeshenergy.com*, Accessed April 4, 2008.
Burma	Oil and Gas	Multiple oil and gas exploration deals were signed by China National Petroleum Corporation and Myanmar's Energy Ministry between October 2004 and January 2005. An additional deal was signed January 2008 related to three deep-sea blocks off the Rakhine coast.	Unclear.	China Signs Exploration Deals with Myanmar," *UPI Energy*, January 15, 2007, *Nexis*.
Burma	Oil Pipeline	In March 2007, Chinese and Burmese companies stated their intent to begin construction of the China-Myanmar oil pipeline later the same year. The city of Chongqing may be the destination for this pipeline and will build a crude refinery to process the oil imports.	Project is currently "under discussion." As of March 2008, construction has not yet been initiated.	"China-Myanmar Oil Pipeline Construction to Begin this Year, Extends to Chongqing," *Xinhua Financial News*, March 26, 2007, *Nexis*. Also see: "China-Myanmar Pipeline Still Under Discussion," Xinhua, March 10, 2008, *news.xinhuanet.com/ english/2008-03/10/content_7756822.htm*.
Kazakhstan	Acquisition of PetroKazakhstan	After approval by a Canadian court, China National Petroleum Corporation acquired PetroKazakhstan from a Canadian company.	Initial approval in October of 2005. Exact date of acquisition unclear.	"CNPC secures PetroKazakhstan Bid," BBC News, October 26, 2005, *news.bbc. co.uk/2/hi/business/4378298.stm*. Also see: "China's Increasing Hold over Kazakh Oil," BBC News, August 20, 2007, *news.bbc.co.uk/2/hi/asia-pacific/6935292. stm*.

Kazakhstan	Oil Pipeline	In 2006, China and Kazakhstan built an oil pipeline from central Kazakhstan to Xinjiang province of China. Additionally, a second pipeline is being constructed between China and Kazakhstan which will also provide oil and gas from Turkmenistan.	Unclear.	"China to Build Second Oil Pipeline in Kazakhstan," *Comtex News Network, Inc.*, August 23, 2007, *Nexis*.
Kyrgyzstan	Electricity/ Power Stations	Chinese electr c company representatives are considering constructing electric power stations in Kyrgyzstan. The Chinese also are interested in investing in existing power infrastructure such as the Sarydzhaz and Kambarat hydropower stations.	Unclear.	"China Prepared to Invest in Kyrgyzstan's Power Sector," *RIA Novosti*, August 2, 2006, *Nexis*.
North Korea	Oil	In December 2005 China and North Korea signed a deal to jointly develop offshore oil reserves. No specific information was provided on location of these offshore sites.	Unclear.	Oil Development Deal Struck with North Korea," *Los Angeles Times*, December 25, 2005, *Nexis*.
Pakistan	Electricity/ Power Station	In April 2008, China's Dongfang Electric Corporation and Pakistan's Government signed a deal to construct the Chichoki Malian Power Plant in Pakistan.	"Within a year" from April 2008. No specific month for target completion provided.	"Pakistan S gns Contract with Chinese Firm for Power Project," The Economic Times (India Times), April 1, 2008, *economictimes.indiatimes.com/News/ News_By_Industry/Energy/Pak_signs_ contract_with_Chinese_firm_for_power_ project/articleshow/2917816.cms*.
Pakistan	Electricity/ Power Stations	In April 2001, Pakistan announced that it would set up a 600-megawatt nuclear power plant at Chashma in the Mianwali district of Punjab with Chinese assistance. An additional 300-megawatt nuclear power plant was completed in Chashma with Chinese assistance in 2001.	600mw Chashma Plant: Unclear. 300mw Chashma Plant: Completed March 2001.	"Pakistan, China Discussing 2nd Nuclear Power Plant," Kyodo News International, August 12, 2002, f*indarticles.com/p/ articles/mi_m0WDQ/is_2002_August_12/ ai_90297109*.
Turkmenistan	Gas/Oil Pipeline	In April 2006, China and Turkmenistan signed an agreement to build a gas pipeline to Guangzhou, China.	Construction began February 22, 2008. Completion date unclear.	"China S gns Agreement to Buy Turkmenistan Gas, Build Pipeline," *AP Financial Wire*, April 3, 2006. *Nexis*. Also see: "China Approves Pipeline to Move Imported Turkmenistan Gas," *AP Financial Wire*, September 27, 2006. *Nexis*.

Uzbekistan	Oil and Gas	In June 2006, China National Petroleum Corporation announced its plans to invest $210 million into gas and oil exploration in Uzbekistan.	Unclear.	"China's CNPC Unit in 210 Million Dollar Uzbekistan Oil and Gas Deal," *Agence France Presse*, June 15, 2006, *Nexis*.
Uzbekistan	Gas Pipeline	In May 2007, Uzbekistan announced that it will build a gas pipeline to China with an annual throughput capacity of 30 billion cubic meters. No details have been provided on when the project will be completed or which companies will be involved.	Unclear.	"Uzbekistan, China S gn Major Gas Pipeline Deal," China Business News (Hong Kong Trade Development Council), May 2, 2007. *sme.tdctrade.com/content. aspx?data=EmergingMkt_content_ en&contentid=867435&src=BNT_ OtherEastEur&w_sid=194&w_ pid=1401&w_nid=13504&w_ cid=867435&w_idt=1900-01-01&w_ oid=343&w_jid=.*

ENDNOTES - APPENDIX I

1. According to Tang Hai, commercial counselor at the Chinese embassy in Burma, from 1992 to October 30, 2007, Burmese Investment Commission has approved 30 China-funded infrastructure projects totaling $638 million. ("Chinese Diplomat Interviewed on Economic Cooperation with Burma," *BBC*, December 10, 2007, *Nexis*.)

2. Difficult to find specifics on Sino-DPRK infrastructure projects, but Vice-Governor of Jilin province did announce that "[e]fforts will be made to improve the construction of the infrastructure facilities at the ports and roads to the DPRK." ("Northeast Chinese City to Boost N Korean Economic, Trade Ties — Vice-Governor, *Xinhua*, June 21, 2007, *Nexis*.)

3. China, Myanmar, and Bangladesh had been in discussions to develop a tri-state highway system, shortly after Bangladesh and Myanmar came to such an agreement in July 2007. These plans were put on hold in the second half of 2007, due to unrest in Burma, but Bangladesh resumed calls for talks on such a highway

in October-November 2007, hoping to accelerate the process. ("Bangladesh Signs Pact with Myanmar on Road Connectivity," *The Press Trust of India*, July 27, 2007, *Nexis*; also, "Bangladesh Proposes Meeting to Accelerate Dhaka-Kunming Road," *Asia Pulse*, November 23, 2007, *Nexis*; also, "Several Bilateral Deals Between Bangladesh, Burma on Hold Following Unrest, *The Daily Star*, October 11, 2007, *Nexis*.)

4. China has expressed its desire to join the Iran-Pakistan-India gas pipeline project. No statements have yet been made indicating official inclusion of China in the project. ("Iran Gas: China Waits as India Wavers," *Asia Times*, March 6, 2008, *www. atimes.com/atimes/South_Asia/JC06Df03.html*.)

5. In addition to the major energy deals listed above, many cases of smaller, less extensive Chinese energy investments have been discovered. These cases generally are of Chinese companies purchasing minority stakes in Central Asian energy companies. For example, in March 2003, British Gas International agreed to sell its 8 percent stake in Agip Kazakhstan North Caspian Operating Company (AgipKCO) to China's Sinopec International Petroleum and Production Corporation. ("Kazakhstan Economic Review," *Kazkommerts Securities,* January-March 2003, *www. kazakhstaninvestment.com/support-files/ker-mar2003.pdf.*)

APPENDIX II
CHINESE ARMS DEALS AND MILITARY
ASSISTANCE

Partnering Country	Type of Transfer	Details	Time Started/ Completed	Source
Bangladesh	Weapons Sale	China sold one Crotale class surface-to-air missile to Bangladesh; version FM-90, designed for DW-2000 frigate.	Ordered in 2004, delivered in 2007.	Stockholm International Peace Research Institute (SIPRI), SIPRI Arms Transfers Database, China Arms transfers 2006-07, *armstrade.sipri.org.*
Bangladesh	Weapons Sale	Sold Bangladesh an unknown number of PL-7 class air-to-air missiles, designed for F-7MG combat aircraft.	Ordered in 2004, all 69 delivered by 2006.	SIPRI, SIPRI Arms Transfers Database, China Arms transfers 2006-07, *armstrade.sipri.org.*
Bangladesh	Weapons Sale	Sold Bangladesh 69 QW-2 surface to air missiles.	Ordered in 2004, 100 delivered by 2007.	SIPRI, SIPRI Arms Transfers Database, China Arms transfers 2006-07, *armstrade.sipri.org.*
Bangladesh	Weapons Sale	Sold Bangladesh an unknown number of C-801/C-802 coast defense system missiles.	Sold in 2005, current status is unknown.	SIPRI, SIPRI Arms Transfers Database, China Arms transfers 2006-07, *armstrade.sipri.org.*
Bangladesh	Weapons Sale	Sold Bangladesh 56 type 96 D-30 122mm towed gun systems	Sold in 2005, 65 guns delivered in 2006.	SIPRI, SIPRI Arms Transfers Database, China Arms transfers 2006-07, *armstrade.sipri.org.*
Bangladesh	Weapons Sale	Sold Bangladesh an unknown number of PL-9 short-range air-to-air missiles, designed for F-7MG aircraft.	Ordered in 2005, 10 delivered by 2006.	SIPRI, SIPRI Arms Transfers Database, China Arms transfers 2006-07, *armstrade.sipri.org.*
Bangladesh	Weapons Sale	Sold Bangladesh 20 R-440 Crotale class surface-to-air missiles, designed for DW-2000 frigate.	Sold in 2005, 20 delivered by 2007.	SIPRI, SIPRI Arms Transfers Database, China Arms transfers 2006-07, *armstrade.sipri.org.*

Bangladesh	Weapons Sale	Sold Bangladesh 16 F-7MG fight aircrafts. Total cost estimated between $44m to $118m.	All 16 sold and delivered in 2006.	SIPRI, SIPRI Arms Transfers Database, China Arms transfers 2006-07, *armstrade. sipri.org.*
Pakistan	Weapons Sale	Sold Pakistan 20 C-802/ CSS-N-8/Saccade anti-ship missiles, for Jalalat missile boats.	Ordered in 2003, 20 delivered by 2006.	SIPRI, SIPRI Arms Transfers Database, China Arms transfers 2006-07, *armstrade. sipri.org.*
Pakistan	Weapons Sale	Sold Pakistan 2 Type-347G fire control radar systems designed for Jalalat missile boats.	Ordered in 2003, 2 delivered in 2006.	SIPRI, SIPRI Arms Transfers Database, China Arms transfers 2006-07, *armstrade. sipri.org.*
Pakistan	Weapons Sale	Sold Pakistan 10 YLC6 Air surveillance radar systems.	Sold in 2003, 10 deliverd by 2006.	SIPRI, SIPRI Arms Transfers Database, China Arms transfers 2006-07, *armstrade. sipri.org.*
Pakistan	Weapons Sale	Sold Pakistan 6 AS-565SA *Panther* Helicopters.	Sold in 2005, status currently uncertain.	SIPRI, SIPRI Arms Transfers Database, China Arms transfers 2006-07, *armstrade. sipri.org.*
Pakistan	Weapons Sale	Sold Pakistan 40 C-803 Anti-ship missiles, designed for *Jiangwei* (F-22P) frigates.	Sold in 2005, status currently uncertain.	SIPRI, SIPRI Arms Transfers Database, China Arms transfers 2006-07, *armstrade. sipri.org.*
Pakistan	Weapons Sale	Sold Pakistan an unknown number of *Red Arrow-8* anti-tank missiles.	Original sale in 1989, by 2007 had delivered 14,600 missiles.	SIPRI, SIPRI Arms Transfers Database, China Arms transfers 2006-07, *armstrade. sipri.org.*
Pakistan	Weapons Sale	Sold Pakistan an unknown number of QW-1 *Vanguard* portable surface-to-air missiles.	Original sale in 1993, by 2007 had delivered 1150 missiles.	SIPRI, SIPRI Arms Transfers Database, China Arms transfers 2006-07, *armstrade. sipri.org.*
Pakistan	Weapons Sale	Sold Pakistan 300 Type-90-2/ MBT-2000 tanks.	Original sale in 1997, by 2007 had delivered 55 tanks.	SIPRI, SIPRI Arms Transfers Database, China Arms transfers 2006-07, *armstrade. sipri.org.*

Pakistan	Weapons Sale	Sold Pakistan 150 JF-17 *Thunder*/FC-1 fighter aircraft, which was developed for Pakistan and included some production and assembly in Pakistan.	Original sale in 1999, had delivered 2 aircraft by 2007.	SIPRI, SIPRI Arms Transfers Database, China Arms transfers 2006-07, *armstrade. sipri.org.*
Pakistan	Weapons Sale	Sold Pakistan 4 *Jiangwei* F-22P frigates. Total value of the deal estimated to be between $500m and $750m. Ships included assembly and production in Pakistan.	Original sale in 2005, expected delivery between 2009-13.	SIPRI, SIPRI Arms Transfers Database, China Arms transfers 2006-07, *armstrade. sipri.org.*
Pakistan	Weapons Sale	Sold Pakistan 27 K-8 Karakorum-8 trainer/combat aircraft, which included some production and assembly in Pakistan.	Original sale in 2005, by 2007 12 planes had been delivered.	SIPRI, SIPRI Arms Transfers Database, China Arms transfers 2006-07, *armstrade. sipri.org.*

ENDNOTES - APPENDIX II

1. According to SIPRI Arms Transfers Database, Chinese Arms trade with Bangladesh in 2006 was $210m but dropped to just $17m in 2007 (2004 and 2005 levels were $6m and $1m respectively, so 2006 appears to be an anomaly). (Source: SIPRI, Arms Transfers Database, TIV of Arms Exports from China 2004-2007, *sipri.org/contents/armstrad/ooutput_types_TIV.html*.)

2. SIPRI has no data for arms transfers between China and Myanmar or North Korea in 2006 or 2007, but China did offer Myanmar $25m in arms in 2005. (Source: SIPRI, Arms Transfers Database, TIV of Arms Exports from China 2004-2007, *sipri.org/contents/armstrad/ooutput_types_TIV.html*.)

3. In 2006 and 2007, China transferred $107m worth of arms to Pakistan per year. This is an increase on 2004-5 levels, which were between $78m and $79m per year. (Source: SIPRI, Arms Transfers Database, TIV of Arms Exports from China 2004-2007, *sipri.org/contents/armstrad/ooutput_types_TIV.html*.)

4. China is expected to market its FC-1 aircraft, which it is developing in cooperation with Pakistan, as well as its KJ-200 AWACS aircraft and the J-10 fighter aircraft to SE Asia, in particular Myanmar (Burma). (Source: P. Parameswaran, "U.S., Russia, China Vying to Sell Fighters in Asia," Agence France-Presse, March 23, 2008, *defensenews.com*.)

5. China is modernizing at least six naval bases in Burma, according to Rahul Bedi, an Indian security analyst. (Source: Shaikh Azizur Rahman, "India Seen Arming Burma to Counter Chinese; Democracy Activists Fear Being Targeted," *The Washington Times*, March 24, 2007.)

6. According to the United Nations Register of Conventional Arms, which collects self-reported data on arms transfers (China resumed participation in the register in 2007, for data pertaining to 2006), in 2006 China a total of 10 battle tanks to Pakistan as well as 114 missiles/missile launchers and 16 combat aircraft to Bangladesh. (Source: UN Register of Conventional Arms, China: Exports 2006, *disarmament.un.org/UN_REGISTER.NSF*.)

7. China is reportedly Burma's largest arms provider and, as of July 2006, had been providing Burma with jet fighter aircraft to help develop its air force. However, Russia and India have also been providing Burma with aircraft and the quality of the Chinese aircraft has been questionable. (Source: Manjeet Kripalani, "India's Role in Burma's Crisis; New Delhi has sympathy for the troubled nation, but energy needs and relations with China are complicating the equation" *Business Week Online*, October 22, 2007, *Nexis*; also, "Burma reportedly Upgrading Air Force – Paper," *BBC Monitoring Asia Pacific – Political*, July 28, 2006, *Nexis*.)

8. According to Turkmenistan's defense minister, as of December 2007, China was set to loan Turkmenistan USD3 million for "army needs." (Source: "Russian Paper Says China Boosts Influence in Central Asia through Loans," *BBC Monitoring Central Asia Unit*, December 11, 2007, *Nexis*.)

9. China's recent military exchanges with the DPRK remain unclear, but as recent as April 22, 2008, China's Defense Minister met with senior DPRK military officials, including the Air

Force Commander, stressing military cooperation and air force exchanges. (Source: "Chinese Defense Minister Meets DPRK Air Force Commander ," *Xinhua*, April 22, 2008, *Nexis*.)

10. China has loaned Turkmenistan's Ministry of Defense USD3 million worth of military uniforms as well as computers. The loan is separate from the USD300 million loan granted to Turkmenistan by China for various economic projects. China is also allowing Turkmen soldiers to attend Chinese military academies without cost and offering other military financing to prepare the Turkmen army for joint training exercises. (Source: "China Gains Firm Foothold in Turkmenistan, USA Left on Sidelines – Paper," *BBC Monitoring Central Asia Unit*, January 13, 2008, *Nexis*.)

11. China has pledged further military cooperation with Uzbekistan (as it has with all of the Shanghai Cooperation Organization members) but as of yet, specifics are not available as to what China is actually providing Uzbekistan. Source: "China, Uzbekistan Vow to strengthen Cooperation in Defense, Security," *Xinhua*, June 28, 2007, *Nexis*.

ABOUT THE CONTRIBUTORS

DENNIS C. BLAIR, a retired U.S. Navy admiral, became the nation's third Director of National Intelligence on January 29, 2009. From September 2007 through January 2009 he held the John M. Shalikashvili (Shali) Chair in National Security Studies at the National Bureau of Asian Research (NBR), during which time he contributed the introduction to this volume. Prior to retiring from the Navy in 2002, Admiral Blair served as Commander in Chief, U.S. Pacific Command, the largest of the combatant commands. During his 34-year Navy career, he served on guided missile destroyers in both the Atlantic and Pacific fleets and commanded the Kitty Hawk Battle Group. Ashore, he served as Director of the Joint Staff and as the first Associate Director of Central Intelligence for Military Support at the CIA. He has also served in budget and policy positions on the National Security Council and several major Navy staffs and as a White House Fellow at the Department of Housing and Urban Development. From 2003 to 2006, Admiral Blair was President and CEO of the Institute for Defense Analyses--one of the nation's foremost national security analysis centers. Most recently, in addition to his capacity as the holder of The Shali Chair at NBR, he held the Omar Bradley Chair of Strategic Leadership at the U.S. Army War College and served as the Deputy Director of the Project on National Security Reform, an organization that analyzes the U.S. national security structure and develops recommendations to improve its effectiveness. Admiral Blair graduated from the U.S. Naval Academy and earned a master's degree in History and Languages from Oxford University as a Rhodes Scholar.

DEAN CHENG is a Senior Asia Analyst at CNA, a not-for-profit think-tank, where he specializes in Chinese military issues, with an emphasis on China's space program. He has spent over a decade studying Chinese and Asian security and economic issues. Dr. Cheng has written a number of papers and book chapters examining the military and technological implications of the Chinese space program, including its relationship with Chinese military doctrine.

MARK COZAD is the Defense Intelligence Officer for East Asia at the Defense Intelligence Agency (DIA). He is a career intelligence officer having served in both the U.S. Air Force and as a civilian analyst with DIA.

BATES GILL is Director of the Stockholm International Peace Research Institute (SIPRI), an independent think-tank focusing on bettering the conditions for a more stable and secure world through research and analysis on international and regional security issues. Before joining SIPRI, he held the Freeman Chair in China Studies at the Center for Strategic and International Studies from 2002 to 2007, and previously established and led centers of research on East Asian issues at the Brookings Institution and the Center for Nonproliferation Studies at the Monterey Institute. He serves on the Boards of the U.S.-China Policy Foundation, the Feris Foundation of America, the Geneva Centre for Security Policy, and the China-Merck AIDS Partnership. Dr. Gill is the author, co-author, or co-editor of six books, including the forthcoming *Asia's New Multilateralism* (Columbia University Press, 2009), *Rising Star: China's New Security Diplomacy* (Brookings, 2007), and *China: The Balance Sheet: What the World Needs to Know Now About the Emerging Superpower* (Public Affairs, 2006).

Dr. Gill received his Ph.D. in Foreign Affairs from the Woodrow Wilson Department of Government and Foreign Affairs, University of Virginia.

CHIN-HAO HUANG is a researcher with the Stockholm International Peace Research Institute (SIPRI), Stockholm, Sweden. Previously, he worked at the Freeman Chair in China Studies at the Center for Strategic and International Studies (CSIS), Washington, DC. Mr. Huang coordinated the CSIS China-Africa project, a multiyear initiative examining Chinese intentions, policies, and practices in Africa and implications for U.S. strategic interests. He has authored and co-authored several monographs and book chapters on China-Africa-U.S. relations. He has also published other works on Chinese foreign and security policy in *China Security*, *China and Eurasia Forum Quarterly*, *PacNet*, *South China Morning Post*, *Asia Times*, and *China Brief*. He is also a contributing co-author (with Robert Sutter) for the chapter on China-Southeast Asia relations for the Pacific Forum CSIS quarterly publication, *Comparative Connections*. Mr. Huang is a graduate of the Edmund A. Walsh School of Foreign Service, Georgetown University.

ROY D. KAMPHAUSEN is Vice President for Political and Security Affairs and Director, Washington, DC, The National Bureau of Asian Research. A retired U.S. Army China Foreign Area Officer, Mr. Kamphausen served as the China Country Director in the Office of the Secretary of Defense, China Branch Chief in the Directorate for Strategic Plans and Policy for the Joint Chiefs of Staff, and at the Defense Attaché Office of the U.S. Embassy in the People's Republic of China. He has served as a consultant for the Office of the

Secretary of Defense, Department of State and other U.S. government agencies. His areas of professional expertise include China's Peoples Liberation Army (PLA), U.S.-China defense relations, U.S. defense and security policy toward Asia, and East Asian security issues. Mr. Kamphausen co-authored the chapter, "Military Modernization in Taiwan," in *Strategic Asia 2005-06: Military Modernization in an Era of Uncertainty*, with Michael Swaine; wrote the chapter, "PLA Power Projection: Current Realities and Emerging Trends," in *Assessing the Threat: The Chinese Military and Taiwan's Security* (2007) with Justin Liang; edited the volume, *Right-Sizing the People's Liberation Army: Exploring the Contours of China's Military* (2007), with Andrew Scobell; and edited the volume, *The "People" in the PLA: Recruitment, Training, and Education in China's Military* (2008), with Andrew Scobell and Travis Tanner.

DAVID LAI has recently joined the Strategic Studies Institute (SSI) as Research Professor of Asian Security Studies. Before assuming this new position, he was on the faculty of the International Security Studies Department at the U.S. Air War College. He taught the National Strategy and Decision Making and Global Security core courses and engaged students and faculty on pressing issues in U.S.-China and U.S.-Asia relations. In addition, Dr. Lai also taught the Air War College Regional and Cultural Studies (RCS) program and made many field-study trips to Asian nations such as Japan, South Korea, Taiwan, Vietnam, Cambodia, Thailand, and Malaysia. Dr. Lai holds a bachelor's degree from China and a Master's degree and Ph.D. in political science from the University of Colorado.

MARC MILLER is a Research Assistant with The National Bureau of Asian Research, where he works on a variety of NBR initiatives and publications. He completed a Master of Science in Foreign Service at Georgetown University, with a concentration in Conflict Management and a focus on China and East Asia. Mr. Miller will soon begin a career as a Foreign Service Officer with the U.S. Department of State.

ROBERT O. MODARELLI III is currently Policy Director for the U.S. National Center for Asia-Pacific Economic Cooperation (APEC) in Seattle, Washington. His responsibilities include development and oversight of strategic planning for the National Center's activities in support of U.S. private sector interests in the APEC process, as well directing the Center's coordination with U.S. Government agencies in the APEC policy process. His current work in Asia-Pacific policy is focused on regional economic integration, multilateral trade and economic policy dynamics, and regional security as relates to the regional economic environment. Prior to joining the National Center Mr. Modarelli completed a 20-year career in the U.S. Army as an armor officer, Foreign Area Officer, and Asia-Pacific policy specialist. His assignments included 4 years as Chief of the Asia-Pacific Branch in Army International Affairs at Headquarters, Department of the Army; 3 years as U.S. Army Attaché at the U.S. Consulate-General in Hong Kong; and 18 months in training at the Defense Attaché office, U.S. Embassy, Beijing, China. Mr. Modarelli holds a Masters Degree in East Asian Regional Studies from Harvard University and is fluent in Mandarin Chinese.

JAMES MULVENON is Vice-President of Defense Group, Inc.'s (DGI) Intelligence Division and Director of DGI's Center for Intelligence Research and Analysis where he has recruited and trained a team of more than 15 Chinese, Arabic, Farsi, Pashto, Urdu, Russian, and Korean linguist-analysts performing cutting-edge contract research for the U.S. intelligence community. He is chairman of the board of the Cyber Conflict Studies Association, and a member of the National Committee for U.S.-China Relations and International Institute for Strategic Studies. A specialist on the Chinese military, Dr. Mulvenon's research focuses on Chinese command, control, communications, computers, intelligence, and reconnaissance (C4ISR), defense research/development/acquisition organizations and policy, strategic weapons programs (computer network attack and nuclear warfare), cryptography, and the military and civilian implications of the information revolution in China. Dr. Mulvenon's book, *Soldiers of Fortune* (Armonk, NY: M. E. Sharpe, 2001), details the rise and fall of the Chinese military's multibillion dollar international business empire. He is the author of numerous chapters, articles, and monographs on the Chinese military. Dr. Mulvenon holds a Ph.D. in political science from the University of California, Los Angeles, and attended Fudan University in Shanghai from 1991-92.

BRAD ROBERTS is a member of the research staff at the Institute for Defense Analyses (IDA) in Alexandria, Virginia. IDA provides analytical support to the Office of the Secretary of Defense and other U.S. Government agencies. Dr. Roberts is also an adjunct professor at George Washington University and vice chairman of the United States Committee of the Council for Security

Cooperation in the Asia Pacific (CSCAP). He also serves as a member of the Defense Department's Threat Reduction Advisory Committee, special advisor to the U.S. STRATCOM Strategic Advisory Group, and is a member and former chairman of the Threat Reduction Program Review Committee at Los Alamos National Laboratory. His work on China nuclear issues at IDA has been sponsored by the Defense Threat Reduction Agency, the Defense Intelligence Agency, and other government sponsors in partnership with PACOM, STRATCOM, and OSD Forces Policy. Dr. Roberts holds a BA from Stanford University, an MSc from the London School of Economics and Political Science, and a doctorate from Erasmus University, Rotterdam.

ANDREW SCOBELL is Associate Professor of International Affairs at the Bush School of Government and Public Service at Texas A&M University located in College Station, Texas. From August 1999 until August 2007, he was Associate Research Professor in the Strategic Studies Institute at the U.S. Army War College and Adjunct Professor of Political Science at Dickinson College, both located in Carlisle, Pennsylvania. He is the author of *China's Use of Military Force: Beyond the Great Wall and the Long March* (Cambridge University Press, 2003) and other publications. Dr. Scobell holds a Ph.D. in political science from Columbia University.

MURRAY SCOT TANNER joined CNA's China Team as a China Security Analyst in 2008. He has published extensively on China, in particular its internal security, policing and intelligence systems, trends in social order, challenges of reforming the legal system and strengthening human rights, as well as China-North Korea relations and China-Taiwan economic relations.

Prior to joining CNA, Dr. Tanner worked for the U.S. Senate, the RAND Corporation, and as a professor of political science at Western Michigan University. Among his publications are "Principals and Secret Agents: Central vs. Local Control of Policing in China," *The China Quarterly*, September 2007; "China Rethinks Unrest," *The Washington Quarterly*, Summer 2004; and *Chinese Economic Coercion Against Taiwan: A Tricky Weapon to Use* (RAND, 2007). Dr. Tanner holds a Ph.D. in Political Science from the University of Michigan.

LARRY M. WORTZEL is a retired U.S. Army colonel who spent 12 of his 32-year military career in the Asia-Pacific region, including two tours of duty as a military attaché at the American Embassy in China, 1988-90 and 1995-97. He served as professor of Asian Studies and director of the Strategic Studies Institute at the U.S. Army War College from 1997-99, and Asian studies director and then vice president for foreign policy and defense studies at The Heritage Foundation. During 2008, Dr. Wortzel was one of 12 commissioners appointed by the leadership of Congress to the U.S.-China Economic and Security Review Commission. He was appointed to the Commission in 2001. He served as chairman of the Commission for the 2006 and 2008 reporting years. Dr. Wortzel has written or edited 10 books about China as well as numerous policy papers and journal articles. Dr. Wortzel is a graduate of the Armed Forces Staff College, the U.S. Army War College, and the Infantry Officer Candidate School, as well as both Airborne and Ranger schools. Dr. Wortzel holds a B.A. from Columbus College, Georgia, and an M.A. and Ph.D. from the University of Hawaii.

www.ingramcontent.com/pod-product-compliance
Lightning Source LLC
Chambersburg PA
CBHW080401270326
41927CB00015B/3310